FROM SAUL
to
PAUL

WILLIAM VICTOR BLACOE

FROM SAUL PAUL

THE ROAD TO APOSTLESHIP

CFI
An Imprint of Cedar Fort, Inc.
Springville, Utah

ISBN 13: 978-1-4621-1468-9

Published by CFI, an imprint of Cedar Fort, Inc.
2373 W. 700 S., Springville, UT 84663
Distributed by Cedar Fort, Inc., www.cedarfort.com

LIBRARY OF CONGRESS CATALOGING-IN-PUBLICATION DATA

Blacoe, William Victor, 1954- author.
From Saul to Paul / William Victor Blacoe.
    pages cm
Includes bibliographical references.
ISBN 978-1-4621-1468-9
1. Paul, the Apostle, Saint. I. Title.

BS2506.3.B585 2014
225.9'2--dc23
[B]

                    2014026542

Cover design by Shawnda T. Craig
Cover design © 2014 Lyle Mortimer
Edited and typeset by Kevin Haws

Printed in the United States of America

10 9 8 7 6 5 4 3 2 1

Printed on acid-free paper

Dedication

To all who study the holy scriptures
and desire further understanding.

Contents

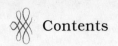

Contents

Acknowledgments

Special gratitude and appreciation to my wife, Reingard, for her enduring sacrifice and support during the research of this project. I also offer my appreciation to the translators and scholars in past centuries who provided insightful understanding. This work is perhaps a dedication to so many whose efforts in a bygone era have dwindled into obscurity on the shelves of libraries across the Christian world. In this new era, we also owe acknowledgment to those dedicated to providing gospel resources on the Internet. Their accessible resources turn every home into a living university.

Introduction

In 1895, George Findlay wrote in the preface to his book *The Epistles of Paul the Apostle*, "Why another book about St. Paul? We have Commentaries, Lives, and Introductions to the great Apostle in abundance."[1] A valid question; however, we soon realize that the study of the life and letters of St. Paul has not yet arrived at its conclusion. Until such time as we possess all the answers to all the questions, we will continue to produce books about him.

This present work about the Apostle Paul is not an exhaustive work, but is based upon the resources available at the time of writing. No attempt has been made to answer every question, but possibly to provoke more. "There is too much tendency to demand from the first century writers an answer to all the questions we should like to put."[2]

To gain an understanding of the Apostle Paul, we must not only analyze what he said and wrote, but also come to knowledge of the circumstances that prompted his reactions. The circumstances and environment in which he lived went into the development of his thoughts; only a part is given to us in the epistles preserved to our day, and the commentary provided by Luke in his Acts of the Apostles is brief, though descriptive and revealing. The contribution that Paul makes to our Christian life today is poignantly declared in these words: "It is almost impossible to overstate what Paul meant to Christianity."[3]

If after reading this book, Saul of Tarsus, Saul the Pharisee, Saul the convert, Paul the Apostle, and Paul the missionary come to life, his heart beating across the centuries, then this work has achieved its purpose. It has brought Paul to life for you.

To my family I leave this challenge: read all of this book at least once for yourself and for me. You may learn more about William Victor Blacoe than you learn about the Apostle Paul. If I am still alive to discuss with you what you have read, then perhaps we will both get to know each other just a little better also.

William V. Blacoe
Rodenbach, Germany
17 March 2014

1: Gods and Emperors Many

The Mediterranean World

The life of the Apostle Paul is not just the story of one man, but also a history of the Christian church in its beginnings. The story of Paul was shared with Luke, Barnabas, Silas, Mark, Timothy, Titus, Philemon, Onesimus, and others of the original Twelve Apostles like Peter, James (Jacob), and John. We will read the letters he wrote and follow him in the historical journal (the Book of Acts) written by Luke that primarily tells us about Paul.

Paul's mortal years were all during the reign of the Julio-Claudian emperors. Paul was born in Tarsus during the reign of the first Julio-Claudian emperor and was executed during the reign of the fifth (and last). In addition to the military power of its legions, the Roman Empire was under the heritage of their legal system, which for good and bad provided an operating infrastructure that maintained the existence of the Empire.

Augustus

During the reign of Emperor Augustus, Saul of Tarsus (later known as Paul) was born. By the time Christ and Saul were born, a consolidated empire existed, and there was a temporary peace in the Mediterranean world. There was never a more fitting time frame in which this labor of eternal importance could be performed. During his administration, Augustus established an efficient civil service and government. At the battle of Actium in 31 BC, the army consisted of sixty-six legions. Thereafter, Augustus systematically reduced the size of the army, so that at his death in AD 14 there were only twenty-eight legions, totalling between 250,000–300,000 soldiers.[4] New highways were constructed across the Roman Empire, increasing the flow of commerce. A regular policing of the trade routes almost completely eliminated road robberies by bandits.

The Emperor Augustus
Emperor 27 BC–AD 14 • Gaius
Julius Caesar Octavianus

Augustus's strength stemmed from his knowledge of human psychology. Religion had always been a rather integral part of the conscience of mankind. Augustus recognized this and secured the ecclesiastical position of High Pontiff (*Pontifex Maximus*) of the College of Pontifs (*Collegium Pontificum*) of the priesthood of Jupiter (Zeus) in 13 BC. Little did Augustus or anyone else foresee that centuries later, this very title would be ascribed to the Pontiff (Latin *Pontifex*) of the Roman Catholic religion. Following the death of Augustus, the Senate of Rome declared him divine and erected temples to their new god.

Tiberius

Tiberius was the adopted son of Augustus, born to his wife Livia by her first husband. His statues portrayed him as extremely handsome by leaving out his defects. In his later years, Tiberius moved away from Rome and became a recluse on the island of Capri. We shall not elucidate the immoral obscenities he indulged while on his island sanctuary. To catalogue the degenerate barbarities of Tiberius would be repugnant.

The Emperor Tiberius
Emperor AD 14–37 • Tiberius
Claudius Nero

Caligula

Gaius (or Caius) was a grandnephew of Tiberius and nephew of Claudius. As a child when his father, Germanicus, was commander of the legions on the Rhine in Germany, he wore a miniature Roman soldier's uniform. This led to the soldiers dubbing him Caligula, meaning "little boots."[5] After reigning for a few months, Gaius suffered an illness that apparently altered his character. When he recovered, Gaius displayed a rather contorted personality, described as "a megalomaniac and tyrant" and "a fidgety neurotic."[6] One pertinent outcome was what

The Emperor Caligula
Emperor AD 37–41 • Gaius Caesar

Caligula termed a metamorphosis. He declared himself to be no longer mortal but now a god and therefore in need of his own temple so that he could be worshipped. Executions, inquisitions, new taxes, and bold extravagance replaced the previous austerity. "He could not control his natural brutality and viciousness."[7] The rich treasury accumulated by Tiberius was squandered. Finally in AD 41, a tribune of the Praetorian Guard, Cassius Chaerea, and others assassinated him.

Claudius

Claudius, the uncle of Gaius (Caligula), was proclaimed emperor by the Praetorian Guard, contrary to his own wishes. And though

Caligula disposed of many of the family contenders for the throne, Claudius evaded the assassins, mostly due to his insignificance. During his years of obscurity, he devoted himself to much study,

The Emperor Claudius
Emperor AD 41–54 • Tiberius Claudius Nero Germanicus

writing over eighty volumes of history and autobiography. Claudius expanded the frontiers of the Empire by invading Britain. In old age, Claudius became absentminded, and palace servants became the most influential people in Rome. The Roman historian Tacitus recorded in his *Annals* that Agrippina the Younger, the second wife of Claudius (and the mother of Nero), poisoned him. Following his death in AD 54, he—like Augustus—was declared a god by the Roman Senate.

Nero

Nero, the grandnephew of Claudius, was born at Antium in AD 37. Claudius adopted him and appointed Senator Seneca as his tutor.[8] Nero was only seventeen when he became emperor. He introduced festivals with contests in chariot racing, music, and dancing. The gladiatorial games gained prominence under the sponsorship of the emperor, even establishing a ministry of amusement. His extravagant manner depleted the treasury that Claudius had established, unleashing a new terror on the Empire in the

The Emperor Nero (adapted from Coneybeare and Howson, *The Life and Epistles of St. Paul*, v. 2. New York: Charles Scribner, Sons, 442.)
Emperor AD 54–68 • Nero Claudius Caesar

form of confiscation. The degradation and debauchery to which Nero descended was excessive. Above all else, we remember Nero for his infamous persecution of the Christian community, especially in Rome. In AD 68, Nero had Apostles Peter and Paul executed. Eventually the army and Senate dethroned him. Following protracted hesitation, his secretary Epaphroditus assisted Nero in committing suicide.

Religious Beliefs in Roman Times

We now take a brief look into the various religious persuasions prevalent in the lands at the time that warrant our attention. During the ministry of Paul, he encountered each of these belief systems, to a greater or a lesser degree. It has been said, "The Jew, the Greek, and the Roman appear to divide the World between them."[9]

Judaism

Judaism was a general term, just as Christianity is a generic expression today for a multitude of denominations. In particular, Judaism had six major denominations:

Samaritans were considered by the Romans to be a sect of the Palestinian believers of Jehovah, but to their Jewish neighbors in Galilee and Judea, the Samaritans were not Jewish at all. According to the Jews, the Samaritans were composed of Assyrian and Babylonian colonialists along with resident Jews who were not taken into Babylonian captivity and thereafter intermarried, which gave the Samaritan people their Jewish semblance (see 2 Kings 17:24; Ezra 4:2, 10). The Jews of Galilee, who pilgrimaged to Jerusalem for the feast occasions, usually circumvented Samaria by crossing over and traveling down the east side of the Jordan River, and then entering Judea by recrossing again at Jericho.

Pharisees were the strictest sect of Judaism, the Calvinists of their era. At the time of Christ, there were about 6,000 members.[10] They held a belief in the reality of the resurrection and the ministration of angels (Acts 23:8). By their zeal for observance of all aspects of the Mosaic law, they reduced the law to pitfalls of complexity, through a multiplicity of rules, rites, and ritualistic observance. "The Pharisees elaborated the Law until the people became its slaves."[11] Jesus rebuked them for their nitpicking approach (Luke 11:37–43).

Sadducees formed the echelons of Judaic society: the aristocratic, old priestly families of the Maccabean era. They tenaciously rejected the Pharisaic doctrines concerning immortality of the soul, resurrection, and the oral tradition. Instead, they adhered to the cannon of the Mosaic law vigorously. They read only the five books of Moses as scripture and used their temple privileges to become rich and politically powerful.

Herodians were of the opinion that they as the Herodian family were the Maccabean kings of the Jews. To maintain their power, they politically associated with the Romans to preserve their leadership.

Essenes lived a communal ascetic (and sometimes celibate) life in secluded locations. Scholars believe that the communities that lived in the mountain settlements of the Dead Sea area were of this denomination. The 1946 rediscovered Dead Sea Scrolls are the primary Essene legacy we possess today.

Zealots are the classification for the more militant parties among the Jews. This group amounted to about 4,000 followers.[12] They sought to overthrow Roman occupation and reestablish a Jewish nation state. Romans considered them terrorists. The Apostle Simon was given the appendage of *Zelotes* (Zealot), indicating that he may have converted from one of these sects (Luke 6:15). The Zealot sect was the primary instigator of the AD 66 Jewish Revolt, remnants of which were extinguished by the Roman army at Masada.

Though we may consider these sects individually, they are all grouped together under one belief: the existence of one God, the Father of all humanity. By His will, no statues of God or unauthorized images existed in His temples, in Jerusalem or on Mount Gerzim (Exodus 20:3–5).

Gentiles, Pagans, and Barbarians

The Greco-Roman Deities: In contrast to monotheism, the Greek and Roman world accepted a pantheon of deities, a god for every occasion. All the traditional gods of the Greco-Roman world have names that are still familiar to us today: Zeus (or Jupiter), Minerva, Apollo, Mars, Saturn, Pluto, Venus, Hermes (or Mercury), Neptune, and Artemis (or Diana). Each one had temples, rites, and philosophies. The Homeric gods of *The Iliad* and *The Odyssey* were the traditional gods of the Hellenistic world. As Alexander of Macedonia extended his

The Greco-Roman God Zeus (or Jupiter)

conquests to the east, a multitude of oriental deities were annexed to the pantheon of Olympian gods. "There never was an age in which religious toleration was practiced with such liberality."[13] Also add the family gods, street gods, guild and trade gods, and town and city gods! Priests and priestesses abounded in all their varieties before these temples, acting as intermediaries between the populace and the respective god. Athens was particularly known for its temples and images, even to the Unknown God (*Agnosto Theô* in Acts 17:23). It was Paul who declared to the assembly at Athens, "Whom therefore ye ignorantly worship, him declare I unto you" (Acts 17:23).

Emperor Worship

In Rome, a profusion of temples abounded. Religion became an appendage of the monarchy with the appointment of Augustus as High Pontiff (*Pontifex Maximus*) of Jupiter, meaning he presided over the priesthood that officiated in the primary temples. Following his death, the Senate voted Augustus a god. Temples honoring his divinity were erected throughout the Empire. AS mentioned before, even Emperor Gaius (Caligula) proclaimed himself divine, and in the winter of AD 39–40 he attempted to put his statue in the Temple of Jehovah in Jerusalem. This was, however, opposed by the Jews and retracted with his assas-

A divine Augustus radiating with stars

sination. On another occasion, an offer by the Romans to erect a statue to Jehovah in Rome, the city of all gods, evoked similar opposition from the Jews.

Other secular monarchs added themselves to the pantheon of gods whenever the radiance of their egos was sufficient to entertain the illusion. Appropriately, they gave themselves new names: Antiochus Epaphines, Ptolemaios Euergetes, Ptolemaios Soter, Nikator, and so on. In any community a man might select from a menu of gods to worship. The proselyte souls weighed the extravagant promises—relative to the present mortality and the hereafter—of each, comparing and contrasting them. The more mystic and cosmic the knowledge (*gnôsis* γνῶσις) offered, the more it subjugated the mortal mind of devotees.[14]

Philosophies

Platonism was a philosophy founded by Socrates (469–399 BC) of Athens, but it attained its development under his pupil Plato (429–347 BC). Many today consider Socrates to be the founder of ethics.

Plato   Socrates

He believed in the immortality of the soul and in upholding human virtue. His philosophy was not centered around the mythological gods of the ancients, but rather on his code of ethics.

Aristotelian was named after Aristotle (384–322 BC), who was admired as the father of science—as much as we honor Hippocrates as

the father of medicine. Aristotle's works form an encyclopedia of philosophy. He wrote books on many principles: logic, thought and reasoning, persuasion and versatility of the mind, physics, biology, psychology, drama and the arts, ethics, politics, and sociology.

Aristotle

Epicureanism, named after Epicurus (341–270 BC), was a theology which espoused the notion that the world was created by chance phenomenon and that God—if He existed at all—was indifferent to the affairs of the universe. It was therefore up to the individual to provide the greatest degree of personal pleasure for himself, for God laid no bounds to man's action. For some this meant "that pleasure is the supreme good and the basis of morality; devoted to pleasure, especially the more refined varieties of

Epicurius

sensuous enjoyment."[15] We can call Epicureanism the theology of pleasure. They espoused chance origination of atoms sticking to each other and forming all organized matter. They further believed that at death we disintegrate and cease to exist.[16] Epicureanism is very much alive today (though rebranded) as a free-thinking culture without ethical or religious boundaries or personal responsibilities.

Zeno

Stoicism was set forth by Zeno (336–264 BC), who established a school of theology at Athens circa 308 BC. Zeno taught that there was a Divine Mind that did not create but only organized and maintained order in the universe. Man was relegated to accept things as they are, which placed him at odds with nature as to who was made for what. He taught "that virtue is the highest good, and that the passions and appetites should be rigidly subdued."[17] And so "they laid down the rule that if we cannot get what we want we must train ourselves to want what we can get."[18] At death, they believed that the soul of man was absorbed into the Divine Mind.

Mysteries

Beyond the traditional religions and philosophies were the occult mysteries. They had secret initiation rites, vows, and oaths. They asserted

that they could, through their rites and mysticism, provide the individual with access to the gods and thereby gain a salvation status that was not available to the

Eleusinian Mysteries (Thomas Taylor, *The Eleusinian & Bacchic Mysteries*. New York: 8. J. W. Boston.)

general populous. The primary examples of this form of worship are the cults of Eleusis, Dionysus, Mithras, Osiris, Attis, and several others. As a sample of this form of religion, one author gives the following short on the cult of Dionysus:

With the advent of the Orphic Mysteries in the sixth century BC, a new conception of soul and immortality was spread abroad. The cult of Dionysus had existed in Greece for some time, but it received a new impulse when the Thracian rites were blended with it in the sixth century. The result was a widespread religious revival. The new doctrine was that the soul was no mere shade, but a divine, immortal creation which had greater liberty outside of the body than within it. The background to the Orphic faith was the myth of Zagreus or Dionysus. This god was, as a child, torn to pieces and devoured by Titans so that particles of the divine flesh entered each Titan body. Athena saved the child's heart and, from it, Zeus created a new Dionysus. The Titans were destroyed for their impiety and, from their ashes, the human race was created. Man, therefore, inherits partly the nature of the Titans, and partly the nature of the god, Dionysus. The godlike element is the human soul.[19]

Mystery religions "combined ideas from eastern religions, such as Zoroastrianism or Judaism, with ideas from the religious traditions of Egypt, Greece, and Rome. . . . One of these religions later came to be closely associated with Christianity. It was given the name 'Gnosticism,' because it claimed to show the way to a secret 'knowledge' (*gnôsis*), the possession of which was a man's only hope of salvation."[20]

Greeks and Romans Lost Faith in Their Gods

Humanity had offered their devotion to the gods of the centuries. But the Greek philosophers questioned the motivation to worship. The tales of the gods began to drift into the realm of superstition. Inanimate philosophy supplanted the traditional gods of Mount Olympus. This religious vacuum was inevitably filled with cultic exuberance by the new mystery religions. The populace clamored to obtain knowledge that would provide emotional satisfaction, and by so doing, they abandoned the traditional gods. Religion began to offer salvation to the human soul by means of initiation rites and complex rituals.[21]

The Roman god of time and the beginnings of things, Janus. Our month January is named for this god. He is "two-faced," looking to the past and future. (Adapted from Gnecchi, Cav. Francesco, *Roman Coins*, 2nd edition, 49. London Numismatic Society, London.)

The ethnic mixture of the Roman Empire did not have the unifying system of belief that the Church of Christ provides. The people sought for the kingdom of the true God but found only the kingdoms of the underworld. Amidst this religious array, the seekers of divine truth were overwhelmed with a plethora of Satan-inspired nonsense, of irreligious espionage. The truth was sought by many, but the quest had failed. A theological Messiah was needed by all.

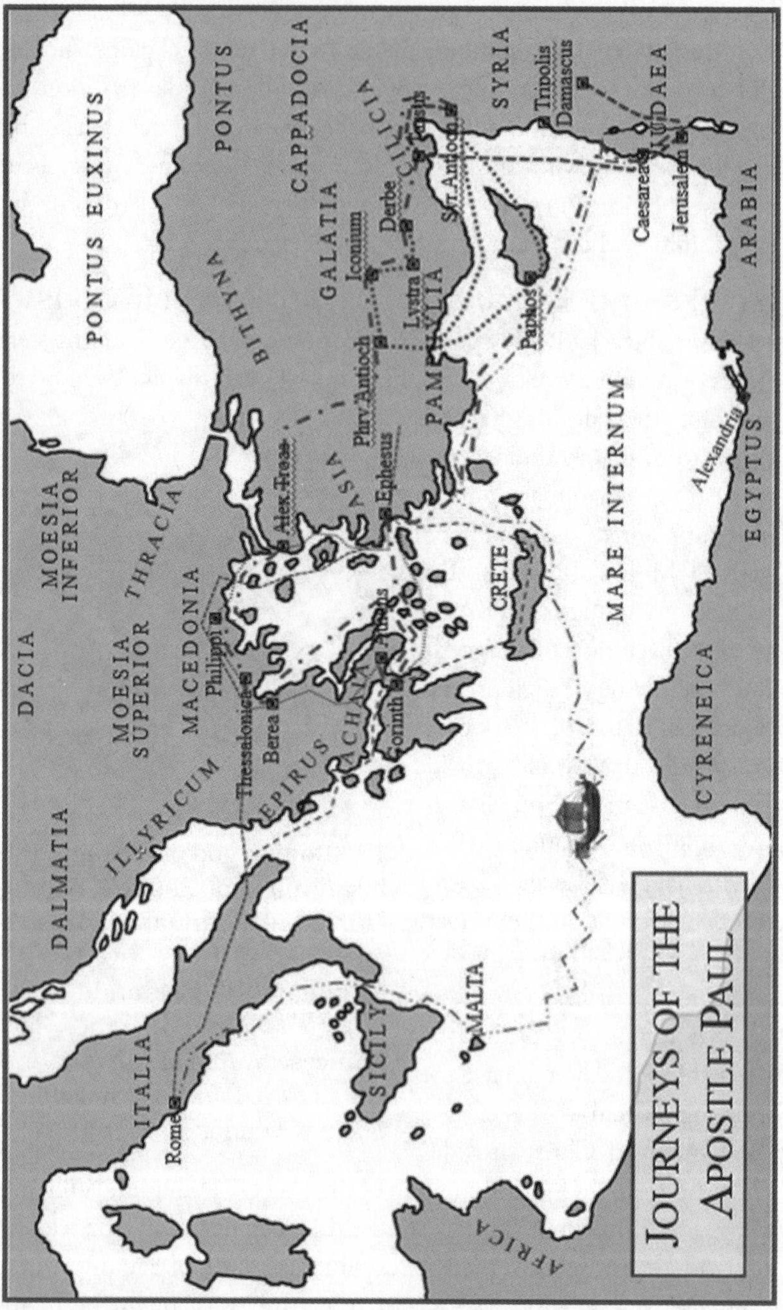
JOURNEYS OF THE APOSTLE PAUL
PONTUS EUXINUS
PONTUS
CAPPADOCIA
GALATIA
BITHYNIA
CILICIA
SYRIA
JUDAEA
ARABIA
EGYPTUS
CYRENEICA
AFRICA
MARE INTERNUM
CRETE
ASIA
PAMPHYLIA
THRACIA
MACEDONIA
MOESIA INFERIOR
MOESIA SUPERIOR
DACIA
DALMATIA
ILLYRICUM
EPIRUS
ACHAIA
ITALIA
SICILY
MALTA
Rome
Thessalonica
Berea
Philippi
Corinth
Athens
Alex. Troas
Ephesus
Phry. Antioch
Iconium
Lystra
Derbe
Tarsus
Syr. Antioch
Paphos
Tripolis
Damascus
Caesarea
Jerusalem
Alexandria

2: Born at Tarsus

The Birth of Saul

Saul was born in approximately AD 6. The Roman Empire ruled the known world under Emperor Augustus (Octavian, 31 BC–AD 14). This is the emperor who decreed "that all the world should be taxed" (Luke 2:1), which brought Joseph and pregnant Mary to Bethlehem, where Jesus the Messiah was born (Matthew 1:25; Luke 2:7). Time passed and the kings from the East came and then returned to their homes (Matthew 2:12). The holy family departed for Egypt to avoid Herod's wrath (Matthew 2:13–15) and then settled back in Nazareth of Galilee (Matthew 2:19–23; Luke 2:39–40).

Tarsus

In 170 BC, the citizens of the city Tarsus asked Seleucid King Antiochus IV if they could govern themselves independently. Antiochus granted Tarsus the status of a Greek city-state. Later in 64 BC, Pompeius Magnus defeated the Seleucid dynasty and Tarsus was reconfirmed with city-state status and was made the capital of the Roman province of Cilica.

Tarsus received the status first of *urbs libera* during the years of Mark Anthony's residency. The Senate of Rome granted Tarsus the status of a duty-free city (*civitas libera et immunis*). There were citizens who had Roman citizenship in Tarsus granted by either General Pompey (*Pompeius Magnus*), General Julius Caesar, General Mark Antony (*Marcus Antonius*), General Octavianus Caesar (*Augustus* in Luke 2:1), or General Quirinius (*Publius Sulpicius Quirinius* in Luke 2:2). The population of

Tarsus at the time was over 250,000 inhabitants. The largest sources of income for the city were mineral deposits and lumber supplies from the Tarsus Mountains north of the city.[22]

Hebrew, Pharisee, and Roman Citizen (Acts 16:36–39; 21:29; 22:25–29; 23:27; Philippians 3:5)

Here, under these circumstances at Tarsus, begins the life of Saul (Acts 9:11; 21:39; 23:34). "Circumcised the eighth day, of the stock of Israel, of the tribe of Benjamin, an Hebrew of the Hebrews;[23] as touching the law, a Pharisee" (Philippians 3:5; see also Romans 11:1). The members of this Hebrew family were citizens of Rome. Paul later declared, he was free-born and "not purchased with money" (Acts 16:36–39; 22:25–29; 23:27).

Roman generals, by virtue of the powers invested in them by the Senate, held *imperium* (authority) in their respective provinces and had the power to grant Roman citizenship within their provinces to people deemed worthy to receive it. In the first century, when the citizenship was still jealously guarded, the *civitas* may be taken as proof that his family was one of distinction and at least moderate wealth.

Being a Roman, Saul had a nomen and praenomen, probably taken from the Roman officer who gave his family *civitas*. Though named *Saulus* in Hebrew, his cognomen was *Paulus* in Roman Latin. Tradition suggests that his nomen was *Aemilius*. Saul's ancestry must have been several generations in Tarsus to have *civitas*, as otherwise they would have been merely *incolae* residents. It can be concluded that the family had been planted in Tarsus with full rights as part of a colony settled there during the Greek Seleucid dynasty. For whatever reason, Roman *civitas* was conferred on his forefathers prior to Saul's birth (Acts 22:28).

Society in the Roman Empire was structured into three socio-political classes of citizens called *ordines*: peasants (*populus*), including freed slaves (*libertine*); equestrian middle class (*ordo equestris*) with a capital worth of 400,000 sesterces or rank loss; and senatorial order aristocrats (*ordo senatorius*), composed of only 500–600 nobility. Beyond this, Roman social hierarchy were non-citizens, meaning disenfranchised citizens, foreigners, and slaves. Citizenship had two statuses: political and civil. Political rights included the rights to vote (*ius suffragii*) and hold office (*ius honorum*). Civil rights included the right of appeal (*ius provocationis*) and exemption from the arbitrary power of magistrates, commercial trade (*commercii*), intermarriage (*connubii*), and leaving a will (*testamenti*).[24]

Sauls of the Tribe of Benjamin

Saul was apparently named after King Saul of the same tribe of Benjamin. He had a great stature to measure up to (1 Samuel 9:1–2). Saul of Tarsus was "a choice young man" of goodly characteristics, though only "about five feet high" (152 centimeters).[25] And though referred to as Saul and then later Paul, neither is correct. The name Saul that we use in our English translations is the transliterated form of the Hebrew *Shauwl*—meaning "asked for" or "prayed for"—through Greek *Saulos*, *Saul*, and *Paulos*.

Family and Home Life (Acts 23:16; Romans 16:7, 11, 21; Ephesians 6:4; Colossians 3:21)

What is actually known of Paul's extended family? We know of a sister, as Luke made mention of "Paul's sister's son"—a nephew—living at Jerusalem (Acts 23:16). There is also a reference by Paul to some cousins: "Andronicus and Junia, my kinsmen" (Romans 16:7); "Herodion my kinsman" (Romans 16:11); and "Lucius, and Jason, and Sosipater, my kinsmen" (Romans 16:21).[26] He also indicated that Andronicus and Junia "were in Christ before me" (Romans 16:16), or became Christian converts prior to Paul at Damascus.

Envision the boy Saul playing in the streets of Tarsus. The Greek boys of Tarsus played soldiers in the fashion of the Greeks, like Ulysses and Jason acting out the stories of Troy and of Marathon, or the conquests of Alexander the Great. The Roman boys emulated Julius Caesar, Mark Anthony, and Octavian. Correspondingly, Saul was moved by the stories of Adam, of the great patriarch Enoch and his city of righteousness, of Noah and the ark of animals. Saul also learned of Abraham and his devotion to God, the virtues of Joseph when in Egypt, Moses and the burning bush, and the triumphs of the army of Joshua in the Caanan conquest. So when the Gentile children of Tarsus were taught of Jupiter, Mercury, Venus, and Diana, Saul was schooled in the knowledge of the Almighty Jehovah.[27] While Saul played on the streets of Tarsus, Jesus, being six years older, was in Nazareth experiencing "the lilies of the field" (Matthew 6:28).

Elementary Education (Acts 18:23)

The vocational skill Saul received was that of a tentmaker, as it was customary for all Jewish boys to learn a trade (Acts 18:3). Apparently the family was financially capable of funding the education of their son Saul as a student in the rabbinic school of Gamaliel (a member of the Sanhedrin and an astute doctor of the law) at Jerusalem. "His mastery of the Greek literary technique of the diatribe and his occasional citation of Greek authors are considered by some as evidence that he frequented the Hellenistic schools of rhetoric."[28] The education of a first-century Jew occurred mostly at home.

No doubt Saul received instruction in the school attached to the local synagogue, where he would have learned to read and write through studying the holy scriptures and the oral law. Beginning at the age of five, he started reading the law contained in the five books of Moses. At age ten, the oral traditions were added to the studies. At thirteen years, he participated in the religious life of the community at the synagogue. His coming of age would have been marked with his *Bar Mitzvah*, when he had become a son of the law.

"At this age he was so far emancipated from parental authority that his parents could no longer sell him as a slave. At this age he became a *ben hat-tôrah*, or son of the Torah. Up to this age he was called *katón*, or little; henceforth he was *gadôl*, or grown up, and was treated more as a man; henceforth, too, he began to wear the *tephillín* [*tefillin*], or phylacteries, and was presented by his father in the synagogue on the Sabbath, which was called from this circumstance the *Shabbath tepillín*."[29] He would also be called upon in the synagogue to read from the law scroll or, on the Sabbath, from one of the scrolls of the prophets. Members of the extended family would have gathered to the synagogue for the momentous occasion and the celebration that would most certainly have followed in the Jewish community.

Linguistics (Acts 21:37–40)

Being of the Hebrews, Paul no doubt spoke the Hebrew of the scriptures together with the public conversational Aramaic. However, being a Jew of the Diaspora, he would normally have spoken Greek outside of the home. Paul wrote fluently in Koine Greek, a dialect commonly spoken in his native city of Tarsus. He also quoted Classical Greek, which indicated that he had been exposed to Greek learning at the university level (Acts 21:37–40).[30] Paul usually quoted from the Greek Septuagint, the Greek translation of the Old Testament.

Saul Studies at Jerusalem (AD 21)

"Every Israelite was required to pay the sacred tribute of half a shekel [*Machatzit Hashekel*, Exodus 30:13] each year, as atonement for his soul—and applied to the expenses of the Tabernacle service."[31] Did Saul, in his youth, go to Jerusalem with his parents to participate in the Feast of the Passover, Purim, Pentecost, or Tabernacles, as did Jesus when He was twelve years old (Luke 2:40–42)?

To have become a student of a member of the Sanhedrin, Saul's abilities must have been known to the influential ears and eyes of Jerusalem. It is likely that at fifteen (AD 21) he went to Jerusalem to begin his higher studies at the Hillel Rabbinical School under the tutelage of Rabban Gamaliel I. Most likely, he was accompanied by his parents or some other relative (Romans 16:7, 11, 21),[32] bringing the teenager to the temple city. This journey may have been arranged to coincide with the Passover or Pentecost, to mention just a couple of possibilities. There would have been great joy and excitement in sending off their son, an example for all others. They would have taken passage on a ship south to the port of Caesarea Maritima or Joppa.

During this time, the population of Jerusalem was estimated at 55,000 inhabitants:[33] a city of sanctity mixed with apostasy and degradation. Here, the imported cultures of the Romans and the Greeks flourished. The Palestine that Saul entered as a teenager had been ruled by the Greeks from 333 BC until the Romans took over in 63 BC. A forceful attempt was made by the Seleucid Greeks in the period 198–168 BC to hellenize this land and the Jewish people. Such attempts led to revolt under the Maccabees, which were generally successful except for the continued use of the Greek language among the educated. "Greek terms were used to designate such essentially Jewish institutions as the Sanhedrin, and it has been claimed that more than 1,100 Greek terms are used in the Talmud."[34]

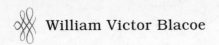

Rabban Gamaliel, Doctor of the Law
(Acts 5:25–40; 22:3)

There were two eminent traditional rabbinical schools of thought in Jerusalem at this time: the rabbinical schools of Rabbi Shammai and Rabbi Hillel the Elder. Saul enrolled himself in the Hillel Rabbinical School under the tutelage of Rabban Gamaliel I, Nasi (אִישׂ) prince of the Sanhedrin[35] and grandson of Hillel. "Gamaliel, a doctor of the law, [was] had in [good] reputation among all the [Jewish] people" (Acts 5:34). He had come into contact with the Church following the Ascension of Jesus, demonstrated by him speaking respectfully of the ministry of Peter and John (Acts 5:25–40).

If Gamaliel followed in the teachings of his grandfather, Hillel, then Saul was taught that the Gentiles needed evangelization. This principle is what Hillel taught while Rabbi Shammai, his contemporary, saw no place for the Gentiles in the sphere of Judaism.[36] Jesus spoke of the proselyting efforts of the liberals: "Woe unto you, scribes and Pharisees, hypocrites! For ye compass sea and land to make one proselyte" (Matthew 23:15). While studying "at the feet of Gamaliel" (Acts 22:3), Saul would have listened to various interpretations of the law and the prophets. Little did he realize the future that lay before him. Because of the manner in which Stephen addressed the Sanhedrin (Acts 7), it is assumed that he also was a rabbinical student. Judging by the ages of Stephen and Saul, we may postulate that they were acquainted with each other through theological studies.

Saul Returns to Tarsus (Acts 18:3; 1 Corinthians
11:11; 2 Corinthians 5:16; Hebrews 13:4)

Many scholars assume, prior to the active ministry of Jesus (AD 30–33), Saul returned to Tarsus, or at least was nowhere within the region of Palestine during the ministry of Jesus. Saul probably returned to Tarsus about the age of twenty-four (AD 29). If so, he would have taken a wife, for custom would have necessitated him doing so—and since he was a Hebrew in the strictest sense, he would have fulfilled this most important of all commandments. "Neither is the man without the woman, neither the woman without the man, in the Lord" (1 Corinthians 11:11). Paul also advised, "Marriage is honourable in all" (Hebrews 13:4).

Following the Resurrection of Jesus (AD 36)

After the Crucifixion of Jesus (AD 33), those who plotted His death felt certain that Christianity was at an end. As we know, the reverse happened: the conversion rate exploded out of all proportions (120 members by Acts 1:15, an additional 3,000 in Acts 2:41, and increasing to 5,000 in Acts 4:4). There was division among the Sanhedrin members themselves, and fear for what Christianity was doing to their power and authority. An inquisition had to take place and an army of loyal zealots versed in the teachings of the traditional order had to be recruited. No doubt Saul of Tarsus was one of the appointed inquisitors (AD 35).

The Stoning of Stephen
(Acts 6:5; 8:1; 22:20 • AD 36)

We first meet Saul in connection with the stoning of Stephen (AD 36). The scriptures record, "Stephen, a man full of faith and of the Holy Ghost . . . did great wonders and miracles among the people" (Acts 6:5, 8). "Then there arose certain of the synagogue, which is called the synagogue of the Libertines,[37] and Cyrenians,[38] and Alexandrians, and of them of Cilicia and of Asia [Minor], disputing with Stephen" (Acts 6:9). These synagogues[39] covered quite a wide selection of Mediterranean provinces, including Cilicia, the homeland of Saul, possibly even a synagogue he frequented. The account continues: "And they were not able to resist the wisdom and the spirit by which he [Stephen] spake. Then they suborned [bribed] men . . . and they stirred up the people, and the elders, and the scribes, and came upon him, and caught him, and brought him to the Council" (Acts 6:10–12).

Stephen said, "Ye stiffnecked and uncircumcised in heart and ears [see Deuteronomy 10:16], ye do always resist the Holy Ghost: as your fathers did, so do ye. Which of the prophets have not your fathers persecuted? . . . Then they cried out with a loud voice, and stopped their ears, and ran upon him with one accord" (Acts 7:51–52, 57). Mob injustice "cast him out of the city, and stoned him: and the witnesses laid down their clothes at a young man's feet, whose name was Saul [who was consenting unto his death; see Acts 8:1]. And they stoned Stephen" (Acts 7:58–59). If Saul did hear the trial of Stephen, then he also heard the testimony he bore of the divinity of Jesus. Such a testimony we feel was a revelation to prepare the mind of Saul for the events that would soon befall him.

Persecuting the Gospel with the Mosaic Law (Acts 8:3; 22:45, 19; 26:911; 1 Corinthians 15:9; 1 Timothy 1:13, 15 • AD 36)

"As for Saul, he made havoc[40] of the church, entering into every house, and haling men and women committed them to prison" (Acts 8:3; 22:19). Saul says of himself: "I verily thought with myself, that I ought to do many things contrary to the name of Jesus of Nazareth. Which thing I also did in Jerusalem: and many of the saints did I shut up in prison, having received authority from the chief priests; and when they were put to death, I gave my voice against them" (Acts 26:9–10; 22:4). "Also the high priest doth bear me witness, and all the estate of the elders" (Acts 22:5) that indeed "I persecuted the church of God" (1 Corinthians 15:9).

"And at that time there was a great persecution against the Church which was at Jerusalem; and they were all scattered abroad throughout the regions of Judea and Samaria, except the apostles" (Acts 8:1). Even though the Saints suffered persecution by Saul, and we are quite sure by others also, insomuch that they departed from the capital to the relative calm of the countryside, Saul was not deterred. He says further: "And I punished [persecuted] them [the Christians] oft in every synagogue, and compelled [coerced] them to blaspheme [Christian testimony]; and being exceedingly mad [vengeful] against them, I persecuted them unto strange [foreign] cities" (Acts 26:11).

As a Sanhedrin inquisitor, Saul compares well with the Dominican monk Tómas de Torquemada (AD 1420–1498), who instigated the Spanish Inquisition of the Jews. The difference is Saul later repented of his ways. Thirty-one years later, he wrote to Timothy, saying he "was before [Christian conversion] a blasphemer, and a persecutor, and injurious: but I obtained mercy, because I did it ignorantly in unbelief. This is a faithful saying, and worthy of all acceptation, that Christ Jesus came into the world to save sinners; of whom I am chief" (1 Timothy 1:13, 15).

3: The First Vision of Saul

Threatenings and Slaughter (Acts 9:12; 22:5; 26:12 • AD 36)

Now Saul was becoming so successful in his vendetta that every Saint would have known of his methods and been afraid. The role of persecutor was not enough for Saul; he was on a cleansing crusade, unknowingly fulfilling the prophetic words of the Master: "The time cometh, that whosoever killeth you will think that he doeth God [a] service" (John 16:2). "And Saul, yet breathing out threatenings and slaughter against the disciples of the Lord, went unto the high priest, and desired of him letters to Damascus to the synagogues, that if he found any of this way [Christian], whether they were men or women, he [Saul] might bring them bound unto Jerusalem" (Acts 9:1–2).

Once he received the necessary letters (Acts 22:5), Saul said, "I went to Damascus with authority [legal power] and commission [appointment] from the chief priests" (Acts 26:12).[41] "The Greek word for an envoy is *apostolos* (ἀπόστολος). An *apostolos* was anyone sent out with a delegated authority from some higher owner; and, of course, *apostolos* is the Greek origin of the English word *apostle*. When Paul set out to Damascus, he was the apostle of the Sanhedrin."[42]

Since Saul possessed letters, authority, commission, and the consenting vote, he must have held a judiciary post on some sub-committee of inquisition appendaged to the Sanhedrin Council of the Elders.

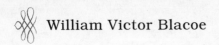

William Victor Blacoe

Was Saul Married? (Acts 8:1; 1 Corinthians 9:5; Philippians 4:3)

Being zealous for "the weightier matters of the law" (Matthew 23:23), surely he had obeyed the command that "therefore shall a man leave his father and his mother, and shall cleave unto his wife: and they shall be one flesh" (Genesis 2:24; Ephesians 5:31). There are other good reasons to believe that Saul was married. We read that "Saul was consenting unto his [Stephen's] death" (Acts 8:1; 22:20).

Consenting is the Greek word *suneudokeo* (συνευδοκέω) and means "casting a vote." For Saul to have this authority required him to be a husband, and generally also a father. This requirement was necessary as the Jews considered he should be more likely to lean toward mercy[43] when casting his vote in judicial matters. From other sources, we learn that "Peter and Philip had families, and Philip gave his daughters in marriage, while Paul himself does not hesitate in one of his epistles to address his yoke-fellow, whom he did not take round with him for fear of hindering his ministry."[44] The verse reads: "And I entreat thee also, true yokefellow, help those women which laboured with me in the gospel, with Clement also, and with other my fellowlabourers, whose names are in the book of life" (Philippians 4:3). *Yokefellow* in Greek *syzygos* (σύζυγος) would naturally mean "wife" or "companion." Paul further declared, "Have we not power to lead about a sister, a wife, as well as other apostles, and as the brethren of the Lord, and Cephas [Peter]?" (1 Corinthians 9:5).

The Road to Conversion (Acts 7; 22:9 • AD 36)

In the year AD 36, Saul was about thirty years old and journeying to Damascus with his letters of authority and commission, and certain men accompanied him (Acts 22:9). Since his intent was to bring Christians back to Jerusalem for trial, we may assume his companions were hired strong men to secure the prisoners.

Surrounded by likely unschooled men, Saul had almost a week to ponder and meditate. With "slaughter and threatenings" foremost in his thoughts as he left Jerusalem, perhaps he followed the road over the Mount of Olives, passing the olive tree withered by Jesus (Mark 11:12–14, 20–21), then through Bethany, where Jesus had spent His last days of mortal comfort. From there, down the mountain pass to

Jericho, crossing the Jordan River at the Bethabara fords where the children of Israel, under the direction of Joshua, had crossed into the promised land (Joshua 3; 4), and where John had baptized Jesus six years earlier (Matthew 3:1–6; Mark 1:5; 1 Nephi 10:9).

Saul's company crossed the River Jordan, thereafter going north and following the footsteps of the prophet Elijah when the ancient prophet followed the command of Jehovah: "Go, return on thy way to the wilderness of Damascus" (1 Kings 19:15). They would have passed through several towns in the region of Perea and Decapolis.

Considering all the history, what did Saul think about that week? The testimonial of Stephen before the Sanhedrin, with his countenance serene and calm and even forgiving his persecutors. Was Moses a prototype of the Messiah? Is there an apostasy in Israel (Acts 7)? The words shouted by Stephen before his death would have seemed strange, "Lord, lay not this sin to their charge" (Acts 7:60). How does a man feeling the pain of a stoning focus his thoughts on the welfare of those who condemn him to death?

Saul's First Vision of the Resurrected Messiah (Acts 9:35; 22:68; 26:13–15 • AD 36)

It happened on the last day of the journey. As Paul journeyed, he came "nigh unto Damascus, about noon" (Acts 22:6; 26:13). In the heat of the Arabian noonday sun, all travel was suspended. Saul and his guards must have rested in whatever shade the land could provide. The fowls of the air would have likely gone to rest, silence pervading. Saul's companions were possibly asleep, but he meditated upon his errand with the city of Damascus.

"Suddenly there shone from heaven a great light round about" (Acts 22:6; 9:3) that was "above the brightness of the sun, shining round about me [Saul] and they which journeyed with him" (Acts 26:13). They "all fell to the earth" (Acts 26:14; 9:4; 22:7), lying in the dust by the Damascus road as fear of the unknown gripped their hearts. Saul later declared, "I heard a voice speaking unto me, and saying in the Hebrew tongue, Saul, Saul, why persecutest thou me?" (Acts 26:14; 9:4; 22:7). Confused, Saul asked, "Who art thou, Lord?" (Acts 9:5; 22:8; 26:15). It was normal practice for Jews—out of reverence for God—not to utter the name Jehovah. The Lord had said *persecute*, so Saul was perplexed.

His confusion increased by the answer that he next received: "I am Jesus of Nazareth, whom thou persecutest" (Acts 22:8; 9:5; 26:15).

Saul heard the words with horrendous realization, the blood of the "persecuted but not forsaken" (2 Corinthians 4:9) martyred Saints crying from the ground. While Saul contemplated the eternal consequences of his persecutions, the Lord Jesus Christ continued, "It is hard for thee to kick against the pricks" (Acts 9:5; 26:14). The phrase *kick against the goads* was a Greek proverb for "useless resistance."

The Response (Acts 9:6–8; 17:28; 22:10–11; 26:16–18 • AD 36)

"And he trembling and astonished said, Lord, what wilt thou have me to do?" (Acts 9:6; 22:10). The devastated Saul received unexpected grace of a loving God:

> But rise, and stand upon thy feet [see Ezekiel 2:1]: for I have appeared unto thee for this purpose, to make thee a minister and a witness both of these things which thou hast seen, and of those things in the which I will appear [show] unto thee; delivering thee from the people, and from the Gentiles, unto whom now I send thee, to open their eyes, and to turn them from darkness to light, and from the power of Satan unto God, that they may receive forgiveness of sins, and inheritance among them which are sanctified by faith that is in me [quoting Isaiah 42:7]. Arise, and go into Damascus; and there it shall be told thee of all things which are appointed for thee to do. (Acts 9:6; 22:10; 26:16–18)

With Saul caught up in the vision, the accompanying men would have heard his words, "Who art thou, Lord?" They also would have heard his other question: "Lord, what wilt thou have me to do?" It is written, "And they who were journeying with him saw indeed the light, [which at noonday was outshining the sun in its glory], and were afraid; but they heard not the voice of him [Jesus] who spake to him [Saul]" (JSIV Acts 9:7; AKJV Acts 22:9). It should be observed that Acts 9:7 says that "the men which journeyed with him stood speechless, hearing a voice, but seeing no man." It *should* read, "hearing no voice, and seeing no man." The Joseph Smith Inspired Version corrects this error, as quoted above. And then in Acts 22:9, "And they that were with me saw indeed the light, and were afraid; but they heard not the voice of him that spake to me." Their eavesdropping on the conversation—from one side only—would have evidenced to them that a celestial vision was open to Saul and that a divine personage therein presented Himself to Saul's eyes.

Then this first vision ended. "And Saul arose [was raised][45] from the earth; and when his eyes were opened, he saw no man[46] for the glory of that light" (Acts 9:8; 22:11). His traveling companions, once assured that he was coherent, would have asked some pointed questions: What name did the personage give when Saul asked, "Who art thou, Lord?" Did Saul tell them the answer that he received? Or, What did the personage say that Saul was to do when he asked, "Lord, what wilt thou have me to do?" To this last question, Saul at least told them of the command to "go into Damascus; and there it shall be told [me] of all things which are appointed for [me] to do."

Led by the Hand (Acts 9:89, 11; 22:10; 1 Corinthians 2:5; 7:10 • AD 36)

"But they led him by the hand, and brought him into Damascus" (Acts 9:8; 22:10). Sapped of all his physical strength, Saul required the assistance of his companions to reach the city. It is safe to suppose that the incident occurred quite close to the city limits, for the account says "into Damascus" whereas, if they had been farther afield, it would have been more appropriate to say "on to" or "toward Damascus."

They led Saul through the west gate and brought him to the home of one

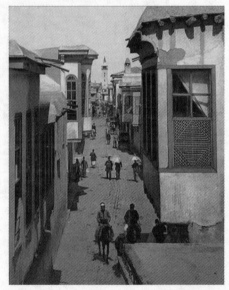

Straight Street, Damascus known as *Via Recta* in Roman times. (The Prints and Photographs Division, Library of Congress).

Judas (Judah) on the street called Straight (Acts 9:8, 11). Straight Street (Latin *Via Recta*) was, and still is, the main thoroughfare in the

Christian quarter of Damascus.[47] Today, the street is called *Souk el Tawil* which means "Long Bazaar." Obtaining accommodation on the main market street would seem to imply that Saul was lodged at an inn. We can presume that, being physically weak, he soon passed into deep sleep.

Three Days of Fasting and Prayer (Acts 9:9 • AD 36)

"And he was three days without sight, and neither did eat nor drink" (Acts 9:9). Three days in which Saul was left to meditate, to ponder, and to fast and pray about the sudden change in his life. Saul was harrowed up by a consciousness of his guilt. Outside on Straight Street, the hum of humanity could have been heard each day as a

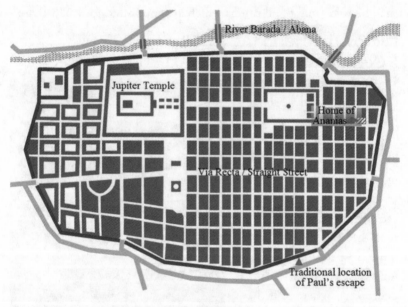

Map of Damascus

metamorphosis took place within the room of a common Damascus inn. Because of his Pharisaic training in the law, we wonder if Saul recalled the words of Moses: "If thou wilt not hearken unto the voice of the Lord thy God, to observe to do all his commandments and his statutes which I command thee this day; that all these curses shall come upon thee, and overtake thee. . . . The Lord shall smite thee with madness, and blindness, and astonishment of heart: and thou shalt grope at noonday, as the blind gropeth in darkness, and thou shalt not prosper in thy ways: and thou shalt be only oppressed and spoiled evermore, and no man shall save thee" (Deuteronomy 28:15, 28–29).

Ananias Is Called to Minister to Saul
(Acts 9:10–16; 22:12 • AD 36)

While Saul was in his darkened state, a few streets away to the northeast, a disciple of Christ—and likely bishop of the Damascus Christian congregation—Ananias, "a devout man according to the law, having a good report of all the Jews" in Damascus (Acts 22:12), received divine instruction. Whether he was asleep or in prayer is not clear.

> To him said the Lord in a vision, Ananias. And he said, Behold, I am here, Lord.
>
> And the Lord said unto him, Arise, and go into the street which is called Straight, and inquire in the house of Judas for one called Saul, of Tarsus: for, behold, he prayeth,
>
> And hath seen in a vision a man named Ananias coming in, and putting his hand[s] on him, that he might receive his sight. (Acts 9:10–12)

Ananias (Hebrew *Hananiah*, meaning "the Lord is gracious"), likely confused, thought it his duty to remind the Lord who Saul of Tarsus was, just in case He might not recollect.

> Then Ananias answered, Lord, I have heard by many of this man, how much evil he hath done to thy saints at Jerusalem:
>
> And here he hath authority from the chief priests to bind all that call on thy name.
>
> But the Lord said unto him, Go thy way: for he is a chosen vessel unto me, to bear my name before the Gentiles, and kings, and the children of Israel:
>
> For I will shew him how great things he must suffer for my name's sake. (Acts 9:13–16)

The Priesthood Ministration of Ananias
(Acts 9:17–18; 22:13–16 • AD 36)

Obedient to the Lord's will, "Ananias went his way," going to Straight Street, "and entered into the house [of Judas on the south-side]; and putting his hands on him said, Brother Saul, the Lord, even Jesus, that appeared unto thee in the way as thou camest, hath sent me, that thou mightest receive thy sight, and be filled with the Holy Ghost" (Acts 9:17). "Brother Saul, receive thy sight" (Acts 22:13). "And immediately there fell from his eyes as it had been scales: and he received sight forthwith" (Acts 9:18).

Ananias had been told by the Lord that Saul "is a chosen vessel." Immediately upon meeting Saul, Ananias called him *Brother* Saul. There is a lesson to be learned from Ananias's reaction. He was aware of Saul's persecuting background, yet the word of the Lord made it explicitly clear that Saul was chosen to become a Christian convert. That Ananias knew about the vision would have been a confirmation to Saul that Ananias was commissioned with authority from the God he had seen.

After the blessing, Saul tells us, "And the same hour I looked up upon him [Ananias]. And he [Ananias] said, The God of our fathers hath chosen thee [Saul], that thou shouldest know his will, and see that Just One, and shouldest hear the voice of his mouth. For thou shalt be his witness unto all men of what thou hast seen and heard. And now why tarriest thou? Arise, and be baptized, and wash away thy sins, calling on the name of the Lord" (Acts 22:13–16). Whereupon hearing, Saul forthwith "arose, and was baptized" (Acts 9:18). The word *arose* in verse 8 implies that he had some physical strength returning, and it should be remembered that for three days he did neither eat nor drink (Acts 9:9).

Hereafter, we learn that following his baptism, "when he had received meat, he was strengthened" (Acts 9:19).

The Baptism & Confirmation of Saul (Acts 8:17; 9:6, 9, 19; 19:2 • AD 36)

Though Saul had beheld a vision of the risen Lord, this did not of itself admit him as a member of the Church of God on earth. "Except a man be [is] born of water and of the Spirit, he cannot enter into the kingdom of God" (John 3:5). Paul became a member of the Church of Jesus Christ by the ordinance of baptism and confirmation (Acts 9:6). Before eating, Saul was baptized by the hands of Ananias, possibly in the River Barada[48] just outside the north wall of the city. For Saul, the "River of Damascus" became what the "River of Judah" never was, for he was baptized and washed in it and was made clean (2 Kings 5:12).

Following the baptism, they most likely did not return to his inn accommodation, but rather went to the home of Ananias. Together with another elder, Ananias would have confirmed Saul a member of the Church and bestowed the gift of the Holy Ghost (between Acts 9:18–19). No doubt this elder and the congregation must have been similarly shocked at the prospect of ministering to Saul, the former Jewish inquisitor. In years to come, Saul would ask certain Ephesian disciples, "Have ye received the Holy Ghost since ye believed?" (Acts 19:2).

After three days of darkness and dread, how welcome would it have been for the Spirit, that intelligence and understanding, to flow in abundance. This experience presents itself to all who embrace the gospel, but more so to those who are prepared. In the case of Saul, three days of prayer and fasting subjugated the carnal man to spiritual alertness. "And when he received meat, he was strengthened. Then was Saul certain days with the disciples which were at Damascus" (Acts 9:19).

The chapel in the home of Ananias at Damascus, Hananiah Street (*Aj-Jourah*), Damascus, Syria

A Suitable Time Frame (Acts 9:20 • AD 36)

If Saul had left Jerusalem after the previous Sabbath and Damascus was a five- or six-day journey, he would have taken from Sunday until Thursday or Friday (afternoon), spent three days with blindness, meaning from Friday until Sunday, when he was baptized. Then passed "certain days" until the next Sabbath (Saturday), whereupon we are told that "straightaway he preached Christ [Jesus] in the synagogues, that He [Jesus] is the Son of God" (Acts 9:20).[49] As long as they were allowed, Jewish converts to Christianity attended the synagogue on Saturday and held a Christian sacrament service on Sunday, as it was the Lord's Day (Acts 20:7; 1 Corinthians 10:2).

Saul Preaches in the Synagogue at Damascus (Acts 9:1, 21–22; 26:12, 19–20 • AD 36)

Normal proceedings in a synagogue called for the minister (rabbai) to read a passage of scripture—from either the five books of Moses or the writings of the prophets—then sit on a chair that was set to the side of the podium (table) and discourse upon the passage he just read. But when there was a visiting dignitary, such as Saul possessing authority and commission from the chief priests in Jerusalem, in which case the dignitary was given the privilege of doing the reading and giving the discourse. Jesus did this Himself in Nazareth, and at that time He read Isaiah 61:1. And to the congregation, whose eyes "were fastened on him . . . he began to say unto them, This day is this scripture fulfilled in your ears" (see Luke 4:16, 32), which caused nothing short of an uproar in the synagogue.

Paul later said, "I was not disobedient unto the heavenly vision: But shewed first unto them of Damascus . . . that they should repent and turn to God, and do works meet for repentance" (Acts 26:19–20). So Saul entered into the synagogue—the Saints were aware of his conversion in the previous days—but the opposing element in the congregation were of a mind that Saul had come with "authority and commission," and "yet breathing out threatenings and slaughter against the disciples of the Lord" (Acts 26:12; 9:1).

No doubt he introduced himself to the leaders and graciously accepted their offer of being the guest speaker. As to which passage he read as the basis for his comments we know not. What we know is that "all that heard him were amazed, and said; Is not this he that destroyed[50] them which called on this name in Jerusalem, and came hither for that intent, that he might bring them bound unto the chief priests?" (Acts 9:21).

They were likely thinking, *Are we hearing clearly? This is Saul of Tarsus, authorized by the Sanhedrin?* "But Saul increased the more in strength, and confounded the Jews which dwelt at Damascus, proving [from the holy scriptures] that this [Jesus of Nazareth] is [the] very Christ" (Acts 9:22). He also called upon those present "that they should repent and turn to God, and do works meet for repentance" (Acts 26:20).

Paul's Solitude in the Arabian Desert (Galatians 1:15–17 • AD 36–39)

Conversion can be a painful process that takes much time and effort. Saul had to change his way of thinking. He apparently considered it most inopportune at the present time to return to Jerusalem or Tarsus and therefore decided upon the solitude of the Arabian Desert to make peace with God (Galatians 1:17).

Saul spent three or so years (AD 36–39) in the desert before returning to Jerusalem. Following this period of reconciliation, he says, "But when it pleased God, who separated me from my mother's womb, and called me by his grace, to reveal his Son in me, that I might preach Him among the heathen; immediately I conferred not with flesh and blood" (Galatians 1:15–16). When the time ended, Saul "returned again unto Damascus" (Galatians 1:17).

4: A Christian Convert

Unwelcome Return (Acts 8:1; 9:1, 20, 23–24; 2 Corinthians 11:32–33; Galatians 1:18 • AD 39)

Times were changing: The emperor Tiberius died in AD 37 and Gaius (Caligula) was the emperor of Rome. Sheik Aretas IV Philopatris (his daughter, Phasaelis, married Herod Antipas the Tetrarch) ruled at Damascus. No doubt Saul's newfound friends in the gospel greeted him with open arms and hospitality. The Jews of Damascus were plotting to destroy Saul. His "authority" and "commission" were now a liability.

"And after that many days were fulfilled, the Jews took counsel to kill him: But their laying await [in wait] was known of Saul. And they watched the gates day and night to kill him" (Acts 9:23–24). "The governor under Aretas, the king [sheik], kept the city ... with a garrison, desirous to apprehend me: And through a window [of a dwelling built at the city wall] in a basket was I let down by the wall by night, and escaped his hands" (2 Corinthians 11:32–33; Acts 9:25).[51]

Sheik Aretas IV Philopatris (9 BC–AD 40)
(Thomas Lewin, *The Life and Epistles of St. Paul*. New York: Scribner-Welford-Armstrong, 67.)

The phrase *many days* is also used in the Old Testament to mean a period of three years: "And Shimei dwelt in Jerusalem many days. And it came to pass at the end of three years" (1 Kings 2:38–39). Never again would Saul visit the city of his conversion; Damascus was his day of preparation. The road to Damascus then became the road to Jerusalem. "Then after three years I went up to Jerusalem to see Peter" (Galatians 1:18).

Fleeing from Damascus with some provision for the journey, Saul headed off into the night. We know not what motivated or inspired him to journey back to Jerusalem. Perhaps he passed the place on the Damascus road where Jesus had appeared and paused to reflect. Then he departed for that long journey southeast to Judaea. Approaching the city, did he visit that spot where three years earlier he "was consenting unto his [Stephen's] death" (Acts 8:1)?

What did Saul (Paul) Look Like?

Describing the physical features of someone is generally not an easy task. This becomes more complex when writing about the entire lifespan of a person. Particular traits and physical features are prevalent in various periods of life. The photographs of my grandfather from childhood to old age make it evident that one physical description will not suffice for a lifetime.

Over the centuries, artists have presented Paul in a multitude of mosaics, statues, frescoes, icons, and paintings. Some are appealing to the eye and inspire a perception of how he might have looked in that era of his life. In addition to the artist, there are a few written descriptions of what the man may have looked like, physically and characteristically, with the understanding that the descriptions represent a snapshot out of a lifetime.

Living in a time when we are nigh two millennia removed from the mortal exploits of Paul, a formidable imagination is required to put reality to his personality without knowing what he looked like. In part, we gain a view of his personality from the Epistles that he penned, but how should we ascertain his temperament? What was his physical appearance? He quoted a view that others saw of him: "For his letters, say they, are weighty and powerful; but his bodily presence is weak, and his

Istanbul, Turkey

Ravena, Italy

Barcelona, Spain

Berea, Greece

speech contemptible" (2 Corinthians 10:10). In response, he said: "But though I be [am] rude in speech, yet not in knowledge; but we have been thoroughly made manifest among you in all things" (2 Corinthians 11:6).

In a New Testament apocryphal writing, Paul is described as being "a man small of stature, with a bald head and crooked legs, in a good state of body, with eyebrows meeting and nose somewhat hooked, full of friendliness; for now he appeared like a man, and now he had the face of an angel."[52]

Paul was small in size, and his personal appearance did not correspond with the greatness of his soul. He was ugly, stout, short, and stooping, and his broad shoulders awkwardly sustained a little bald head. His sallow countenance was half hidden in a thick beard; his nose was aquiline, his eyes piercing; and his eyebrows heavy and jointed across his forehead. Nor was there anything imposing in his speech, for his timid and embarrassed air gave but a poor idea of his eloquence.[53]

Paul was a man of small and meager stature, with an aquiline nose, and sparkling eyes: in the Greek type the face is long and oval, the forehead high and bald; the hair brown, the beard long and flowing, and pointed. . . . We find them most strictly followed in the old Greek mosaics, in the early Christian sculpture, and the early pictures, in all which the sturdy dignity and broad rustic features of Saint Peter, and the elegant contemplative head of Saint Paul, who looks like a Greek philosopher, form a most interesting and suggestive contrast.[54]

Paul is set before us as having the strongly marked and prominent features of a Jew, yet not without some of the finer lines indicative of Greek thought. His stature was dim intuitive, and his body disfigured by some lameness or distortion, which may have provoked the contemptuous expressions of his enemies. His beard was long and thin. His head was bald. The characteristics of his face were, a transparent complexion, which visibly betrayed the quick changes of his feelings, a bright gray eye under thickly overhanging united eyebrows, a cheerful and winning expression of countenance, which invited the approach and inspired the confidence of strangers. It would be natural to infer from his continual journeys and manual labor, that he was possessed of great strength of constitution. But men of delicate health have often gone through the greatest exertions: and his own words on more than one occasion show that he suffered much from bodily infirmity.[55]

On Tuesday, 5 January 1841, Joseph Smith described Saul: "He is about five feet [1.52 meters] high [tall]; very dark hair; dark complexion; dark skin; large Roman nose; sharp face; small black eyes, penetrating as eternity; round shoulders; a whining voice, except when elevated, and then it almost resembled the roaring of a lion. He was a good orator, active and diligent, always employing himself in doing good to his fellow men."[56]

Another description in a different account reads that "Paul was a small man physically, a giant spiritually. In outward appearance he had little to recommend him; his features and physique probably repelled rather than attracted others. But because of his inward grace and goodness, and as a result of his overpowering zeal for Christ, he radiated an influence that led thousands to forsake all in the Master's Cause."[57]

Jerusalem, the First Time As a Christian (Acts 6:9; 9:2, 26; 22:5; 26:12 • AD 39)

This little man arrived in Jerusalem, not bearing Christian men and women in manacles for trial, but as one who had embraced the Christian belief. Though three years had passed since Saul was last in the city, his reputation among the Christian community had in no way diminished over the passage of time: "And when Saul was come to Jerusalem, he assayed to join himself to the disciples: but they were all afraid of him, and believed not that he was a disciple" (Acts 9:26).

When he went to Damascus, Saul carried with him letters from the chief priests (Acts 9:2; 22:5; 26:12). So then did he bring with him letters from the priesthood leaders of Damascus to certify his baptism and confirmation into the Church of Jesus Christ for the brethren in Jerusalem? Disparagingly, the brethren likely considered the persecutor to be seeking, by cunning methods, to destroy the disciples through intrigue. Who among the disciples had not lost a relative, or a dear friend, in the previous years to the vengeful Saul of Tarsus? The doors and hearts of the faithful closed on him throughout the city. None would give credence to his testimony and none would linger long enough to hear his words.

The Fellowship of Barnabas, Peter, and James (Acts 1:4–11, 23; 4:36; 8:3; 9:27; Galatians 1:18–19 • AD 39)

Destitute of a friend in the gospel in Jerusalem, Saul finally found a listening ear. Barnabas was a Levite (Acts 4:36), which would have placed him in the priestly caste. He was one of the two brethren considered to fill the vacancy in the Quorum of the Twelve Apostles following the suicide of Judas Iscariot (Acts 1:23). Joseph Barnabas—known as "the son of consolation" (Acts 4:36)—listened to the story of Saul's conversion, and then "took him, and brought him to the apostles, and declared unto them how he had seen the Lord in the way, and that he had spoken to him, and how he had preached boldly at Damascus in the name of Jesus" (Acts 9:27). As for meeting the Apostles, it is likely that some, if not most, of them would not be in Jerusalem, but rather spreading the gospel through proselyting efforts. It therefore seems understandable to read that Saul met "Peter . . . but other of the apostles saw I none, save James, the Lord's brother" (Galatians 1:18–19).

Saul would have related his remorse over his wickedness and the persecution that he suffered the Saints to endure. Here, we can envision Saul questioning Peter and James about many things concerning the mortal sojourn of Jesus Christ, as they knew Jesus during His years in mortality. That Saul knew much concerning the events of Jesus's ministry is evident from his Epistles. Saul would have asked Peter to tell him of Jesus, of all that he knew about His ministry. James, the brother of Jesus (James 1:19; Matthew 13:55; Mark 6:3), would have related concerning the younger years of Jesus and their home years in Nazareth; the obedient nature of Jesus to His parents Joseph and Mary, how Jesus "was subject unto them"; and also how "Jesus increased in wisdom and stature, and in favour with God and man" (Luke 2:51–52). Peter would have likely related the call that his brother Andrew and he received from Jesus, when they were "casting a net into the sea [of Galilee]: for they were fishers. And he saith unto them, Follow me, and I will make you fishers of men" (Matthew 4:18–19).

Perhaps they then took Saul out to Bethany, where Lazarus and his sisters, Mary and Martha, lived, to see the tomb from which Lazarus was raised from the dead with Christ's powerful words, "Lazarus, come forth" (John 11:43). At Bethany they would have shown Saul from whence Jesus ascended into heaven. In Bethphage, Saul would have been shown where the barren fig tree had stood that Christ by command had withered.

Perhaps he visited the Garden on the Mount of Olives, and Peter and James showed Saul the site of the Atonement, where Jesus, "being in an agony he prayed more earnestly: and his sweat was as it were great drops of blood falling down to the ground" (Luke 22:44). Saul might have seen the place where Jesus, as a divine being, was sacrificed upon an altar of olive wood, an olive press wherewith His blood was pressed out for the salvation of humanity. To walk on the holy ground where the life-giving blood of Jesus soaked the soil. Were it permitted, the soil would have cried its testimonial of that solemn event.

Perhaps they took him over to Golgotha to behold the ground of the Crucifixion to feel the ground where the atoning cross stood. They related to Saul, "And when the sixth hour was come, there was darkness over the whole land until the ninth hour. And at the ninth hour Jesus cried with a loud voice, saying, *Eloi, Eloi, lama sabach-thani.* . . . And Jesus cried with a loud voice, and gave up the ghost" (Mark 15:33–34, 37).

They then would have taken Saul to see the garden tomb made available by Joseph of Arimathaea, where the body of Jesus the Christ was laid to rest. The angelic voices still echoed forth from the tomb: "Why seek ye the living among the dead? He is not here, but is risen!" (Luke 24:5–6).

Perhaps they showed him the upper room in the house where that memorable last supper, the Passover meal, the first sacrament of the new covenant was partaken (Matthew 26:20–32; Mark 14:17–27; Luke 22:13–38; John 13:1; 17:26). It is also possible that this was the room where the resurrected Lord appeared to the disciples (Mark 16:14; Luke 24:36–39; John 20:19–23). Would Saul have declared how he had rejected the Light of the World for so long, how "he made havoc of the Church" (Acts 8:3)? If so, Peter would have told of his denying Christ three times before the cock crowed (Matthew 26:69–75; Mark 14:66–72; Luke 22:55–62; John 18:15–18, 25–27). He also would have told how at Gethsemane, when Judas and the soldiers came, "they all [as disciples] forsook him [Jesus], and fled" (Mark 14:50).

Saul Preaches in Jerusalem (Acts 9:28–29; 22:17–21; 2 Corinthians 10:10; 11:6; Galatians 4:16; Ephesians 6:19 • AD 39)

Saul took up his missionary zeal in the Jewish capital and its surroundings, "and he was with them coming in and going out at Jerusalem. And he spake boldly in the name of the Lord Jesus, and disputed against the Grecians [Hellenist Jews]: but they went about to slay him" (Acts 9:28–29). Rather than saying Saul "disputed," it would be more correct to say he was spoke too bluntly—a trait he never lost. He once said of himself: "Though I be [am] rude [abrupt] in speech, yet not in knowledge" (2 Corinthians 11:6).

He quoted others as saying about him: "His letters . . . are weighty and powerful; but his bodily presence is weak, and his speech contemptible" (2 Corinthians 10:10). Such words as, "Am I therefore become your enemy, because I tell you the [gospel] truth" (Galatians 4:16)? Or, "that utterance may be given unto me, that I may open my mouth boldly" (Ephesians 6:19). He most likely visited those synagogues where Stephen preached before his martyrdom, endeavoring to undo the damage that he inflicted on these congregations in times past.

> And it came to pass, that when I was come again to Jerusalem, even while I prayed in the temple, I was in a trance [vision];
>
> And saw him [Jesus] saying unto me, Make haste, and get thee quickly out of Jerusalem: for they will not receive thy testimony concerning me.
>
> I said, Lord, they know that I imprisoned and beat in every synagogue them that believed on thee:
>
> And when the blood of thy martyr Stephen was shed, I also was standing by, and consenting unto his death, and kept the raiment of them that slew him.
>
> And he said unto me, Depart: for I will send thee far hence unto the Gentiles. (Acts 22:17–21)

The Second Assassination Plot against Saul (Acts 9:30–31; Galatians 1:18, 21–24 • AD 39)

Saul "abode with Peter for fifteen days" (Galatians 1:18). And "when the brethren knew [concerning the assassination threat upon Saul], they brought him down to Caesarea [Maritima], and sent him forth to Tarsus. Then had the churches [congregations] rest throughout all Judea and Galilee and Samaria, and were edified; and walking in the fear of the Lord, and in the comfort of the Holy Ghost, were multiplied" (Acts 9:30–31). We can believe that his departure from Jerusalem was covert. To leave the city by night was not possible, as the city gates were locked and guarded by the Romans. Clandestine withdrawals were normally achieved by passing out of the gate minutes before they were closed for the night, thereby forestalling others from organizing a pursuit until morning. An established Christian community already existed in Antioch, and Saul possibly spent some time there before going to Tarsus.

We must accept that the major portion of his energies was expended in Tarsus, for we have just read the words of Luke, that the brethren "sent him forth to Tarsus." In leaving Jerusalem, he left his reputation, old and new. "And [I, Saul,] was unknown by face unto the churches [congregations] of Judea which were in Christ: But they had heard only, That he which persecuted us in times past now preacheth the faith which once he destroyed. And they glorified God in me" (Galatians 1:22–24).

The Years at Home in Tarsus (Acts 23:16; 26:16–18; Romans 16:7, 11, 21; 1 Corinthians 2:14; Galatians 1:21 • AD 39–43)

The time had come for Saul to be a missionary to his own home country. He says, "Afterwards I came into the regions of Syria and Cilicia" (Galatians 1:21). He remained in his Tarsus for the next four years (AD 39–43). Saul had it revealed to him that he would be a missionary to the Gentiles (Acts 26:16–18), but the way was not open for Gentile proselyting—their time had not yet come. Saul had to await the call.

Can anyone envisage Paul keeping the knowledge of the reality of the Messiah's ministry to himself after he was converted? No! His family and friends in Tarsus and the citizens throughout the region would have been informed of the glorious message of the gospel, heralded by the spiritual giant in his uncomely frame.

Was it during this time that his kinsmen Andronicus, Junia, Herodion, Lucius, Jason, and Sosipater, and also his sister and brother-in-law and their son accepted the gospel? These are among the relatives of Saul mentioned in the scriptures (Romans 16:7, 11, 21; Acts 23:16). "And I, brethren, when I came to you, came not with excellency [superiority] of speech or of wisdom, declaring unto you the testimony of God. For I determined not to know any thing among you, save Jesus Christ, and him crucified. And I was with you in weakness [frailty], and in fear, and in much trembling. And my speech and my preaching was not with enticing words of man's wisdom, but in demonstration of the Spirit and of power" (1 Corinthians 2:1–4).

As Saul brought the gospel message to his homeland, in all probability he was the founder of a Christian congregation at Tarsus. It is therefore also possible that he served in the capacity of a bishop in Tarsus for some of the years he was here.

It must also be assumed that, being a Roman citizen enrolled in Tarsus and now of adult age, he was called upon to serve in public office. Roman *civitas* required participation in the public service, either as a magistrate or some other public function, even if only being in charge of coordinating annual festivities or public games.

The Unclean Are Made Clean
(Acts 10:9–48; 11:1–18 • AD 42–43)

For a time, the missionary endeavors of Saul remained among the Jews alone. Peter, the living prophet of the day, had to proclaim the acceptable day of the Lord. Peter departed from Jerusalem and descended the Judean hills to Joppa on the coast. Luke records that, while in residence there,

> Peter went up upon the housetop [roof terrace] to pray about the sixth hour [see Psalms 55:17]:
>
> And he became very hungry, and would have eaten [wished to eat]: but while they made ready [the meal], he fell into a trance [vision],
>
> And saw heaven opened, and a certain vessel descending unto him, as it had been a great sheet knit [bound] at the four corners, and let down to the earth:
>
> Wherein were all manner of fourfooted beasts of the earth, and wild beasts, and creeping things [like quadrupeds and reptiles], and fowls of the air.
>
> And there came a voice unto him, Rise, Peter; kill, and eat.
>
> But Peter said, Not so, Lord; for I have never eaten anything that is common or unclean [Leviticus 11; see also Leviticus 7:22–27, Ezekiel 4:14; Exodus 22:31].
>
> And the voice spake unto him again the second time, What God hath cleansed, that call not thou common.
>
> This was done thrice: and the vessel [sheet] was received up again into heaven. (Acts 10:9–16)

"Now while Peter doubted in himself what this vision which he had seen should mean, behold, the men which were sent from

Cornelius had made inquiry for Simon's house, and stood before the gate, and called, and asked whether Simon which is surnamed Peter, were lodged there. While Peter thought on the vision, the Spirit said unto him, Behold, three men seek thee. Arise therefore, and get thee down, and go with them, doubting nothing: for I have sent them" (Acts 10:17–20). Peter then accompanied the three men to Caesarea Maritima and to the house of the Roman Centurion Cornelius, a Gentile, where he learned that the Lord had revealed to Cornelius to send for Peter. Cornelius says, "Now therefore are we all here present before God, to hear all things that are commanded thee of God. Then Peter opened his mouth, and said, Of a truth I perceive that God is no respecter of persons: But in every nation he that feareth him, and worketh righteousness, is accepted with him" (Acts 10:33–35).

Peter preached the gospel of Jesus Christ unto this Gentile and his household:

> While Peter yet spake these words, the Holy Ghost fell on all them which heard the word.
>
> And they of the circumcision which believed [Jewish Christians] were astonished, as many as came with Peter, because that on the Gentiles also was poured out the gift of the Holy Ghost.
>
> For they heard them speak with tongues, and magnify God. Then answered Peter,
>
> Can any man forbid water, that these should not be baptized, which have received the Holy Ghost as well as we?
>
> And he [Peter] commanded them to be baptized in the name of the Lord. (Acts 10:44–48)

The Gentiles had been deemed by the Lord clean for admission into the fold of Christ. The household of Cornelius had set a pattern for other nations.

All was not so readily accepted by other Christians. Upon the return of Peter to Jerusalem, he encountered rebuke and opposition to Gentile baptisms. Here, Peter rehearsed the happenings of the event without interpretation—the plain truth seldom, if ever, requires it. He concluded his explanation of their actions with, "And as I began to speak, the Holy Ghost fell on them, as on us at the beginning. Then remembered I the word of the Lord, how that he said, John indeed baptized with water; but ye shall be baptized with the Holy Ghost. Forasmuch then as God gave them the like [same] gift as he did unto us, who believed on the Lord Jesus Christ; what was I, that I could withstand God? When they heard these things, they held their peace, and glorified God, saying, Then hath God also to the Gentiles granted repentance unto [eternal] life" (Acts 11:15–18; see also 1–18).

The Church had become more than a Jewish denomination. Peter was prophet and the Church accepted his authority. The day had come when every faithful, worthy soul in the world could receive baptism and enjoy with his loved ones every blessing that flows from the ordinance. Accordingly, all should receive baptism.

The Gentile Explosion (Acts 9:26–27; 11:19–21, 23–24 • AD 43)

"Now they which were scattered abroad upon the persecution that arose about Stephen [when he was stoned to death in AD 36] travelled as far as Phenice [Lebanon], and Cyprus, and Antioch[-on-the-Orontes], preaching the word to none but unto the Jews only. And some of them were men of Cyprus and Cyrene [Libya], which, when they were come to Antioch[-on-the-Orontes], spake unto the Grecians [Hellenists], preaching the Lord Jesus" (Acts 11:19–20).

As it is now, so was it then: when the Church membership increased in certain areas, leadership required training from Church authorities. Antioch-on-the-Orontes, "which is the metropolis of Syria, and without dispute, deserves the place of the third city in the habitable earth that is under the Roman empire, both in magnitude and other marks of prosperity,"[58] had quite recently attained to a large membership, and "then tidings of these things came unto the ears of the church which was in Jerusalem: and they [the Apostles] sent forth Barnabas, that he should go as far as Antioch" (Acts 11:22).

Barnabas was the one who introduced Saul to the brethren when he had come from Damascus to Jerusalem (Acts 9:26–27). Barnabas, "who, when he came, and had seen the grace of God, was glad, and exhorted them all, that with purpose of heart they would cleave unto the Lord. For he [Barnabas] was a good man, and full of the Holy Ghost and of faith: and much people was added unto the Lord" (Acts 11:23–24).

"The harvest truly is plenteous, but the laborers are few" (Matthew 9:37). Barnabas was faced with a "harvest" greater that he had the ability to officiate. Help was needed, and from the actions of Barnabas, it appeared most likely he had been counseled previously by the brethren as to where to turn to for assistance, when he would have needed it.

Saul Is Endowed from on High (2 Corinthians 12:26 • circa AD 43)

Many years later (AD 57), in writing to the Corinthians, Saul said, "I knew a man in Christ above fourteen years ago [AD 42 or 43], (whether in the body, I cannot tell; or whether out of the body, I cannot tell: God knoweth;) such an one caught up to the third [or celestial] heaven. And I knew such a man . . . how that he was caught up into paradise, and heard unspeakable words, which it is not lawful [permitted] for a man to utter" (2 Corinthians 12:2–4). We believe the "unspeakable words" were the endowment. There must have been Endowment Houses; this would be where Paul obtained knowledge unspeakable before the coarse ear.

Barnabas Comes to Tarsus (Acts 11:25–26 • circa AD 43)

We pick up the footsteps of Saul in these words: "Then departed Barnabas to Tarsus, for to seek Saul: and when he had found him, he brought him unto Antioch" (Acts 11:25–26). Barnabas located Saul, and he extended a call to him to assist in the work of spreading the gospel and organizing the Church on a larger scale than just one congregation.

The City of Antioch-on-the-Orontes (in Syria)

We attach *on-the-Orontes* to this Antioch to distinguish it from the Antiochia in the district of Phrygia in the province of Galatia, which, because of the neighboring Pisidan District, is sometimes deceptively called Pisidan-Antioch. For clarity in this work, we shall refer to that other Antioch by its proper geographic appendage: Antiochia-in-Phrygia.

During this time, the population of Antioch was not much smaller than Alexandria in Egypt; this would give it a population of about 300,000 free-born inhabitants.[59] The Jewish proportion of the population was estimated at 15–20 percent.

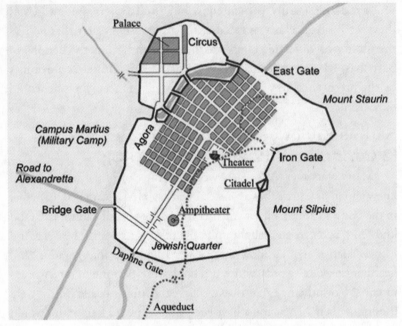

Antioch-on-the-Orontes, Syria

Much of the city was new, or newly renovated during the early years of the reign of Tiberius.[60] However, an earthquake devastated the city on 9 April, AD 37, only a few weeks after Caligula had been proclaimed emperor (18 March, AD 37). Then, in AD 40, civil strife developed during an event in the local circus. A riot ensued, the Gentiles attacked the Jews, and several inhabitants were killed. Historians have indicated there were retaliatory measures made by the Jews upon the other inhabitants.[61]

The first year Saul was in Antioch, the emperor Claudius established the Olympic Games in the city (AD 43–44).[62] It is possible that Saul and Barnabas attended the first of these games that year. These games, or more correctly festivals, consisted of athletic and horse-racing events and theatrical contests. The games were held every fifth year and lasted for thirty days, commencing with the new moon in the month of *Hyperberetaios* (October).[63] Thousands of people would have poured into Antioch for the festival games, creating a proselyting opportunity. This singular event may actually have been the reason for Barnabas to call Saul to serve at Antioch. The festival games were frequented by a diverse Gentile population from many places in the east Mediterranean lands.

The Saints Meet in Singon Street

A tradition, which has been preserved by the historian John Malalas (circa AD 491–578),[64] records that Barnabas and Saul did their preaching in a house, "in an alley [or street] called Singon or Siagon near the Pantheon."[65]

There also exists a tradition that one Theophilus—the friend to whom Luke wrote his Gospel account and the Acts of the Apostles—made available his luxurious house for use as a church at Antioch.[66] The Jew and the Gentile converts most likely gathered for worship in separate congregations, as we read in the writings of Luke. It would be appropriate to consider that the Jewish congregations met somewhere in the Jewish sector, while the Gentile congregations met elsewhere. No doubt each would have been presided over by a bishopric of like origins as the congregation.

A tradition is preserved that Evodius[67] was a bishop in Antioch for twenty-nine years, between AD 44–73. Another bishop in Antioch was Ignatius,[68] author of seven Epistles in the New Testament Apocrypha. Because of the large numbers of Gentiles that were embracing the gospel fold, the Church had begun to lose its Jewish exclusiveness, gradually becoming less a recognizable sect of Judaism in Antioch, and more a new religion with Judaic origins.

The Disciples Are Called Christians in Antioch (Acts 11:26 • AD 43–44)

"And it came to pass, that a whole year they [Joseph Barnabas and Saul] assembled themselves with the church, and taught much people. And the disciples were called Christians first in Antioch[-on-the-Orontes]" (Acts 11:26).

We conclude that the title of *Christians* was given in ridicule, not in honor. The two instances of the term's use were from Gentile sources. Among themselves, they addressed each other by the designations *brethren*, *disciples*, *believers*, or *saints*. The Jews, on the other hand, referred to the Christian community as being merely a sect of the Nazarines, for they considered that nothing good could ever come out of Nazareth.

To this, we add that the word *Christos* is the Greek for "anointed" (*Meshiach* in Hebrew). The Jews would never have used such a reverend address to what they considered to be a Nazarite sect.[69] Christians were followers of Christ, and as the designation intimates, anointed in Christian ordinances.

Prophets Come from Jerusalem (Acts 11:27–30; 13:1 • Autumn AD 43–early AD 44)

Membership increased so quickly at Antioch-on-the-Orontes that further assistance was called for from Jerusalem. "And in these days came prophets from Jerusalem unto Antioch" (Acts 11:27). It is possible that these "prophets" included Simeon Niger, Lucius of Cyrene, and Manaen (Acts 13:1).

One author raises the question if this Simeon with the dark skin is the same Simeon of Cyrene who helped Jesus carry His cross (Matthew 27:32; Mark 15:21; Luke 23:26). Or was this Lucius of Cyrene the one of dark skin? It is also asserted that this Manaen is "the foster-brother of Herod the Tetrarch,"[70] who had John the Baptist beheaded. Another one of these was Agabus, who in the winter of AD 43–44 "signified by the Spirit that there should be great dearth [famine] throughout all the world: which came to pass in the days of Claudius Caesar" (Acts 11:28). Members of the Christian Church considered this a prophetic pronouncement since the famine had not yet started. Had there been a famine in progress, it could hardly have been "signified by the Spirit" and considered a prophecy.

An account of a famine and some aspects of humanitarian relief, recorded by the historian Flavius Josephus, appears to correspond to the famine prophesied by Agabus. We are told that "the disciples, every man according to his ability, determined to send relief unto the brethren which dwelt in Judea: Which also they [in Syrian-Antioch] did, and sent it to the elders by the hands of Barnabas and Saul" (Acts 11:29–30). Seeing as the passage makes no mention of bringing food supplies, only financial contributions, we can therefore conclude that food was available for purchase at Jerusalem. The local leaders probably purchased food for the welfare needs of the Saints, just as they do today.

Let us not forget that Jerusalem was the only large city with Jews in the majority and Gentiles in the minority. With justification, we conclude that many a Christian proselyte in Jerusalem lost their employment, and possibly their homes, because of their conversion. The united order (a welfare system) of the Church no doubt was able to provide for the destitute members, who would have lost the compassion and generosity of the Jewish Levitical priesthood at the Jerusalem temple, where poor Jews could obtain alms. The famine in question seems to have been intended as a judgment upon a wicked people whose lack of love for their fellow men was worthy of the judgment of God.

The Persecutions of Herod Agrippa I (Acts 12:1–24; Colossians 4:10 • Autumn AD 44)

Now about that time Herod [Agrippa I] the king stretched forth his hands to vex certain of the church.

And he killed James [Jacob] the brother of John [the Beloved] with the sword.

And because he saw it pleased the Jews, he proceeded further to take Peter also. (Then were the days of unleavened bread.)

And when he had apprehended him, he put him in prison, and delivered him to four quaternions [squads] of soldiers to keep him; intending after Easter [Passover] to bring him forth to the people.

Peter therefore was kept in prison: but prayer was made without ceasing of the church unto God for him.

And when Herod would have brought him forth, the same night Peter was sleeping between two soldiers, bound with two chains: and the keepers [sentries] before the door kept the prison.

And, behold, the angel of the Lord came upon him, and a light shined in the prison: and he smote [knocked] Peter on the side, and raised him up, saying, Arise up quickly. And his chains fell off from his hands.

And the angel said unto him, Gird thyself, and bind on thy sandals. And so he did. And he saith unto him, Cast [Wrap] thy garment [cloak] about thee, and follow me.

And he went out, and followed him; and wist not that it was true which was done by the angel; but thought he saw a vision.

When they were past the first and the second ward, they came unto the iron gate that leadeth unto the city; which opened to them of his [its] own accord: and they went out, and passed on through one street; and forthwith the angel departed from him.[71]

And when Peter was come to himself, he said, Now I know of a surety, that the Lord hath sent his angel, and hath delivered me out of the hand of Herod, and from all the expectation of the people of the Jews.

And when he had considered the thing, he came to the house of Mary the mother of John, whose surname was Mark; where many were gathered together praying.

And as Peter knocked at the door of the gate, a damsel came to hearken, named Rhoda.

And when she knew Peter's voice, she opened not the gate for gladness, but ran in, and told how Peter stood before the gate.

And they said unto her, Thou art mad. But she constantly affirmed that it was even so. Then said they, It is his angel.

But Peter continued knocking: and when they had opened the door, and saw him, they were astonished.

But he, beckoning unto them with the hand to hold their peace, declared unto them how the Lord had brought him out of the prison. And he said, Go shew these things unto James, and to the brethren. And he departed, and went into another place.

Now as soon as it was day, there was no small stir among the soldiers, what was become of Peter.

And when Herod had sought for him, and found him not, he examined the keepers, and commanded that they should be put to death. And he went down from Judea to Caesarea, and there abode. (Acts 12:1–19)

With Jerusalem in such a clamor over their Christian citizens, there was danger of arrest or execution. Barnabas and Saul probably concealed their presence in the city, if indeed they entered the city at all. How they traveled, where they stayed, we do not know. With pirates by sea and highwaymen on the roads, any travel with a bag of gold and silver was dangerous. To whom "of the elders" they handed over the contributions they brought, we are not aware; for in all probability Peter was in prison or in hiding (Acts 12:1–19), as were all other Apostles if they were in Jerusalem.

Another historic event occurred in the year AD 44. "And Herod was highly displeased with them of Tyre and Sidon: but they came with one accord to him, and, having made Blastus the king's chamberlain their friend, desired peace; because their country was nourished by the king's country. And upon a set day Herod, arrayed in royal apparel, sat upon his throne, and made an oration unto them. And the people gave a shout, saying, It is the voice of a god, and not of a man. And immediately the angel of the Lord smote him, because he gave not God the glory: and he was eaten of worms, and gave up the ghost." (Acts 12:20–23)[72]

The last of the Herodeans then ascended to the position of king: Agrippa II, son of Agrippa I. He received only a portion of his father's kingdom and continued to harass the Judean Church. "But the word of God grew and multiplied" (Acts 12:24) in spite of the harassment.

Having delivered the alms to Jerusalem, Barnabas and Saul returned again to Antioch-on-the-Orontes, bringing with them John Mark, nephew (or cousin) of Joseph Barnabas (Acts 12:25; Colossians 4:10) and later the author of the Gospel bearing his name (Mark).

5: The First Mission Tour (I)

The Call to the Quorum of the Twelve Apostles (Acts 9:1–22; 13:13, 47; Galatians 1:17 • February–March AD 45)

Antioch now contained numerous "prophets," possibly even several of the Quorum of the Twelve Apostles. "As they ministered to the [Church of the] Lord, and fasted, [the Lord, by] the Holy Ghost said, Separate me Barnabas and Saul for the work whereunto I have called them. And when they had fasted and prayed, and laid their hands on them [to set them apart to the work], they [the brethren] sent them [Barnabas and Saul] away [on a mission]" (Acts 13:2–3).

The phrase *sent them away* used in verse 3 has been incorrectly translated. The Greek word *apélusan* (ἀπέλυσαν) means "to free fully, relieve, release, set at liberty."[73] Luke indicates that Barnabas and Saul were released from their call of service to the Church in Antioch to take up a new assignment. A further comment is made by Paul later in his preaching that "the Lord commanded us, saying, I have set thee to be a light of the Gentiles, that thou shouldst be for salvation unto the ends of the earth" (Acts 13:47). The singularity of the wording of this blessing indicates that Saul specifically received a commission to the Gentiles.

Also, observe that it was declared in this blessing that the ministry of Saul was to "be for salvation unto the ends of the earth." For the people of the Roman world, the ends of the earth meant the limits of the Roman Empire, including all lands surrounding the Mediterranean

Sea. We might also consider that this blessing was to carry—since God knows no bounds—beyond the mortal sojourn of Saul, into the centuries ahead of him, in the form of the New Testament Epistles.

This revelation, to call Saul and Barnabas to the work, may have been the occasion in which they were called to fill vacancies in the Quorum of the Twelve Apostles. Saul made this remark years later: "Neither went I up to Jerusalem to them which were apostles before me" (Galatians 1:17). If indeed they were called to the Quorum of the Twelve, then we must conclude that there were at least two vacancies in the Quorum to be filled; the leader of the Church, Simon Peter, must have been at Antioch-on-the-Orontes (as well as others of the living Apostles with the priesthood keys to ordain); and because Barnabas and Saul were released from their present assignments, others must have been called and set apart to preside over the congregations of Antioch (Acts 9:5; see also 1–22). "Paul was both an Apostle and a prophet."[74]

Barnabas: A Companion to Saul (Acts 4:36–37 • February–March AD 45)

Luke identified Barnabas as the senior companion to Saul. This was by no means strange, in that Joseph Barnabas was actively engaged in Church service for some time prior to his introducing Saul to the brethren (AD 39). Joseph Barnabas was introduced by two descriptive verses that tell much about him. "And Joses [Joseph] who by the apostles was surnamed Barnabas, (which is, being interpreted, the Son of Consolation,) a Levite, and of the country [the island] of Cyprus, having land, sold it, and brought the money, and laid it at the apostles feet" (Acts 4:36–37).

Coming from Cyprus, he undoubtedly spoke Greek, therefore an obvious candidate for this missionary venture. Additionally, young John Mark accompanied Saul and Barnabas, as mentioned a few verses later.

Proselyting on Cyprus Island (Acts 13:46 • March–Summer AD 45)

"So they [Barnabas, Saul, and John Mark], being sent forth by the Holy Ghost, departed unto Selucia[-Pieria]" in the spring of AD 45 (Acts 13:4).

From Antioch to the port of Selucia by road is one day journey, and they had traveled this road many times. "And from thence they sailed to Cyprus" (Acts 13:5). The missionaries were specifically heading for Salamis, the hometown of Barnabas. "And when they were at Salamis, they preached the word of God in the synagogues of the Jews: and they had also John [Mark] to their minister" (Acts 13:5). There must have been a significant Jewish population living at Salamis, for there were *synagogues* (Acts 13:5), meaning more than one. As to how well they were received in Salamis, nothing is recorded by Luke. Leaving Salamis, they traversed "through the isle unto Paphos" (Acts 13:6).

From Saul to Paul (Acts 13:6–12 • July–August AD 45)

They arrived in Paphos, which was then the capital city of the Senatorial Province of Cyprus with the proconsul Lucius Sergius Paulus in residence. Just a few years earlier, Paphos had been destroyed by an earthquake.

Here at Paphos, Saul changed his name from the Hebrew *Saul* to the Latin *Paulus* (English *Paul*). This change occurred during their visit with the proconsul Sergius Paulus. Perhaps Saul, wishing to be on familiar ground with the proconsul, introduced himself as *Paulus*. Until now, we have kept the name *Saul* in accordance with the records of Luke; since Luke now changes all reference into the Greco-Roman form, we will do likewise. (The name change is part of the character and personality of Paul.)

Upon arrival, "they found a certain sorcerer, a false prophet, a Jew, whose name was Bar-jesus [son-of-Jesus]: Which was with the deputy of the country, Sergius Paulus, a prudent [circumspect] man, who called for Barnabas and Saul, and desired to hear the word of God" (Acts 13:6–7). What his primary motives were in desiring audience of Barnabas and Saul is unknown. This man *bar-Iesos* also known as "Elymas [*Elumas*] the sorcerer (for so is his name by interpretation) withstood them, seeking to turn away the deputy [Sergius Paulus] from the faith" (Acts 13:8).

This apostate Jew kept himself well employed by his divination services to the proconsul. We must consider this sorcerer as being a member of the governor's court. No doubt the knowledge that this sorcerer was a Jew infuriated Paul, if not by his Christian conversion, certainly by his strict Pharisaic background.

Apparently sorcery was not uncommon among the Jews in the first century AD. It is most likely that the Jews began their sorcery practice in the time of the Babylonian captivity, wherein some less faithful individuals delved into the mysteries of Oriental magic. "Elymais is the Hellenic version of the Arabian *Ulema* [singular *Alim*], i.e., wise man. An Elymas was not an ignorant and uneducated magician or medicine man; such a man would never have had access to the court of Sergius [Paulus]. But he was generally an educated theosophist who had studied the secret teachings of Egypt, Babylonia, and Persia."[75]

Unquestionably, the Elymais was functioning in a some religious capacity to the proconsul; otherwise he would have felt no threat to his position. Seemingly, this man persistently interrupted Paul teaching the gospel to Governor Sergius Paulus. Eventually, Paul had enough, and "filled with the Holy Ghost, set his eyes on him, and said, O full of all] subtlety [deceit] and of all mischief [trickery], thou child [son] of the devil, thou enemy of all righteousness, wilt thou not cease to pervert the right ways of the Lord? And now, behold, the hand of the Lord is upon thee, and thou shalt be blind, not seeing the sun for a season [time]. And immediately there fell on him a mist and a darkness; and he went [groped] about seeking some to lead him by the hand" (Acts 13:9–11).

Since Paul was before the proconsul, a high ranking dignitary, it was therefore by his will that his astrologer was permitted to accost Paul's preaching. It would appear that Paul continued his discourse under this interruption, patiently awaiting the rebuke of the proconsul to silence this disturbance. But no such action was forthcoming. We get the notion that the proconsul was not intent upon hearing the doctrine expounded by Paul as he was about enjoying the theatrical value of the moment. So the rebuke expressed by Paul may have been meant not only for the disturber, but also for the arrogance of the proconsul.

"Then the deputy, when he saw what was done, believed, being astonished at the doctrine of the Lord" (Acts 13:12). Elymais was a proclaimed seer. Therefore, when Paul cursed Elymais with blindness, he could no longer see, physically or by divination. It is interesting to notice the wording of rebuke that is used by Paul. The wizard was named *bar-Iesous*, which literally means "son of Jesus" (or correctly *bar-Jeshua*) in Aramaic. In his rebuke, Paul made a pun on his name by calling him *yie-Diabóloy*, which literally means "son of the devil" in Greek.

It is traditionally accepted that Sergius Paulus was baptized into the Church. This would be an obvious interpretation of the statement that the consul believed. With the baptism of Sergius Paulus, the Province of Cyprus and Cilicia would have gained the notable distinction of being the first land in the Roman Empire to be governed by a Christian leader. Possibly some time was spent in Paphos preaching: no doubt, word of the veil of darkness brought upon the wizard and the subsequent conversion of the governor was capitalized upon by our missionary trio to great effect.

Paul Receives His Thorn in the Flesh (Acts 13:13; 2 Corinthians 12:7–10; Galatians 4:13–15 • August–September AD 45)

Barnabas, Paul, and Mark departed from the island of Cyprus, taking passage to the mainland port of Attalia, then across the open sea to the Pamphylian port of Attaleia; from there, inland to the city of Perga the main city of Pamphylia in southern Galatia.

Something happened now that would, in a future encounter, separate Barnabas and Paul. "They came to Perga in Pamphylia: and John [Mark] departing from them returned to Jerusalem" (Acts 13:13) by ship from the port. John, whose surname was Mark, terminated his mission and returned home. He was one of the two early returned missionaries in the New Testament.

The convert governor of Cyprus, Sergius Paulus, had estates at Colonia Caesarea Antiochia in Phrygia. Assuredly, Paul and Barnabas possessed a letter of introduction from Sergius Paulus to his family there. While near Perge, Paul likely contracted malaria, which "illness" impinged upon his missionary service while he was "preaching to the Galatians."[76] A further reference was given by Paul himself twelve years later when, writing to the Corinthians (2 Corinthians 13:1), he said,

And lest I should be exalted above measure through the abundance of the revelations, there was given to me a thorn in the flesh, the messenger of Satan to buffet me, lest I should be exalted above measure.

For this thing I besought the Lord thrice, that it might depart from me.

And he said unto me, My grace is sufficient for thee: for my strength is made perfect in weakness. Most gladly therefore will I rather glory in my infirmities, that the power of Christ may rest upon me.

Therefore I take pleasure in infirmities, in reproaches, in necessities, in persecutions, in distresses for Christ's sake: for when I am weak, then am I strong. (2 Corinthians 12:7–10)

The Pamphylian port of Attaleia was on the Cestrus River. According to the geographer Strabo, malaria was and is a continual harassment in this coastal pocket of Pamphylia (2 Corinthians 12:7).[77] "It is a probable and generally accepted view that the physical weakness . . . was the same malady which tormented him at frequent intervals. . . . This malady was a species of chronic malaria fever."[78] For some, "malaria fever tends to recur in very distressing and prostrating paroxysms. . . . The sufferer can only lie [down] and feel himself a shaking and helpless weakling."[79]

The difficulties experienced by Paul are further understood when considering ancient times and people's lacking understanding. The general belief was that malaria was the result of demonic possession, inflicted by the gods upon those who defiled a holy place or in some other way mocked the gods.

To add further insult to the dilemma, superstition motivated the inhabitants of Asia Minor to spit at the sight of an unfortunate victim of malarial fever.[80]

Later in AD 57–58, to the Galatians, Paul said, "Ye know how through infirmity of the flesh I preached the gospel unto you at the first. And my temptation which was in my flesh ye despised not, nor rejected; but received me as an angel of God, even as Christ Jesus. . . . If it had been possible, ye would have plucked out your own eyes, and have given them to me" (Galatians 4:13–15). We therefore have sufficient evidence to establish that when he arrived in Galatia the first time, he had "a physical ailment" (RSV Galatians 4:13) that was considered by many to be a "disease" (Jerusalem Bible, Galatians 4:14).

Engraved stone at Colonia Caesarea Antiochia from the estate of Sergius Paulus

Colonia Caesarea Antiochia, Galatia (Acts 13:14; 2 Corinthians 11:26 • September AD 45)

"But when they departed from Perga, they came to Antioch[ia]" (Acts 13:14). In this journey inland, Paul may have experienced some of those occasions wherein he declared that he was "in perils of waters [from river floods], in perils of robbers, . . . [and] in perils in the wilderness" (2 Corinthians 11:26). It was a common practice in former days to travel in a caravan or, if the opportunity presented itself, in company with a detachment of soldiers. The city of Antiochia was the major city in the Phrygian District, refounded as a Roman colony of army veterans from the fifth and seventh legions in 25 BC. This city possessed a Roman garrison, their main task being to police the Roman highway that passed through the region. The extent of the estate of Sergius Paulus was indicated by the engraved stone bearing his name that was discovered at Antiochia.

The Synagogue of Antiochia (Acts 13:14–16)

As they entered the city, they passed the arched columns carrying the Roman aqueduct, which supplied the city with water from

William Victor Blacoe

the nearby mountains that overshadowed the city.[81] The scriptural account continues with their arrival in the city: They "went into the synagogue on the sabbath day, and sat down. And after the reading [see 2 Corinthians 3:14; 1 Timothy 4:13] of the law and the prophets the rulers[82] of the synagogue sent unto them, saying, Ye man and brethren, if ye have any word of exhortation for the people, say on" (Acts 13:14–15).

We might wonder why it was that the rabbi should offer Paul—a stranger in their midst—the opportunity to speak. "It was customary to invite visitors to address the synagogues of the Dispersion; it may already have been customary for emissaries to be sent from Palestine to visit those synagogues and to encourage them to persevere in their faith."[83] As speaker in a Jewish synagogue, "Paul stood up" and read the scriptural passage of the day and discoursed to the congregation (Acts 13:16).

Paul addressed two groups, first the "men of Israel," and second "ye that fear God." Some understanding of a synagogue is necessary: Women were separated from the men usually by a screen or partition of lattice-work. In some cases, they were up in a gallery or in a separate room. In addition to this division, there were often proselyte Gentiles in attendance who had come to accept the God of Israel, but were not willing to become a full Jew of the circumcision. In most instances, they were seated separately at the rear. The focal point of the room was the table or pulpit, where the scroll of the law was opened to be read (Nehemiah 8:1–8). Next to this podium were the chief seats (Matthew 23:6), where the leaders of the synagogue sat facing the people.

Paul delivered a powerful testimony of the divinity of Jesus Christ, from Moses to the Resurrection. Following the opening prayer, two segments of scripture were read. The first reading was taken from the single scroll containing the five books of Moses, the Torah Law called *parashah*. The second reading was taken from a prophet scroll (Joshua through to Malachi) called *haphtarah*. These scriptural passages were read by a competent man in the congregation or a visiting dignitary who received permission from the *rôsh hak-kenéssth*. Following the respective reading, the speaker had the liberty to discourse his own *Midrash* commentary.[84]

Paul Discourses (Acts 13:17–43 • September AD 45)

The God of this people of Israel chose our fathers, and exalted the people when they dwelt as strangers in the land of Egypt, and with an high arm brought he them out of it.

And about the time of forty years suffered he their manners in the wilderness [of Sinai].

And when he had destroyed seven nations in the land of Channan [Canaan or Palestine], he divided their land to them by lot.

And after that he gave unto them judges about the space of four hundred and fifty years,[85] until Samuel the prophet.

And [then] afterward they desired a king: and God gave unto them Saul the son of Cis [Kish], a man of the tribe of Benjamin, by the space of forty years.

And when he had removed him [Saul], he raised up unto them David to be their king; to whom also he gave testimony, and said, I have found David the son of Jesse [quoting 1 Samuel 13:14], a man after mine own heart, which shall fulfill all my will [quoting Psalm 89:20].

Of this man's seed hath God according to his promise raised unto Israel a Savior, Jesus:

When John had first preached before his coming the baptism of repentance to all the people of Israel.

And as John fulfilled his course, he said, Whom think ye that I am? I am not he [the Messiah]. But, behold, there cometh one after me, whose shoes of his feet I am not worthy to loose.

Men and brethren, children of the stock [descendents] of Abraham, and whosoever among you [Gentiles who] feareth God, to you is the word of this salvation sent.

For they that dwell at Jerusalem, and their rulers, because they knew him not, nor yet the voices of the prophets which are read every sabbath day, they have fulfilled them in condemning him.

And though they found no cause in him, yet desired they Pilate that he should be slain.

And when they had fulfilled all that was written [see Isaiah 53:1–12] of him, they took him down from the tree, and laid him in a sepulchre.

But God raised him from the dead:

And he was seen many days of them which came up with him from Galilee to Jerusalem, who [now] are his witnesses unto the [Jewish] people.

And we declare unto you glad tidings, how that the promise which was made unto the [our] fathers,

God hath fulfilled the same unto us their children, in that he hath raised up Jesus again; as it is also written in the second psalm, Thou art my Son, this day have I begotten thee [quoting Psalm 2:7].

And as concerning that he raised him up from the dead, now no more to return to corruption, he said on this wise, I will give you the sure mercies of David [quoting 2 Samuel 7:12–17, or Isaiah 55:3].

Wherefore he saith also in another psalm, Thou shalt not suffer thine Holy One to see corruption [quoting Psalm 16:10].

For David, after he had served his own generation by the will of God, fell [died] on sleep, and was laid [buried with] unto his [fore-]fathers, and saw corruption [decomposition]:

But he, whom God raised again, saw no corruption [decomposition (through resurrection)].

Be it known unto you therefore, men and brethren, that through this man [Jesus Christ] is preached unto you the forgiveness of sins:

And by him all that believe are justified from all things, from which ye could not be justified by the law of Moses.

Beware therefore, lest that come upon you, which is spoken of in the prophets;

Behold, ye despisers, and wonder, and perish: for I work a work in your days, a work which ye shall in no wise believe [quoting Habakkuk 1:5], though a man declare it unto you.

And when the Jews were gone out of the synagogue, the Gentiles besought that these words might be preached to them the next sabbath.

Now when the congregation was broken up [dismissed], many of the Jews and religious proselytes followed Paul and Barnabas: who, speaking to them, persuaded [urged] them to continue in the grace of God. (Acts 13:17–43)

In *Saint Paul the Traveler and the Roman Citizen*, Ramsay says,

Paul's address to the assembled Jews and proselytes was doubtless suggested by the passages; one from the Law, one from the Prophets, which were read before he was called to speak. It has been conjectured that these passages were Deuteronomy 1 and Isaiah 1, which in the Septuagint Version contain two marked words employed by Paul: the Scriptures were probably read in Greek in this synagogue of Grecised [Greek] Jews. Deuteronomy 1 naturally suggests the historical retrospect with which Paul begins; and the promise of remission of sins rises naturally out of Isaiah 1:18. Dean Farrar mentions that "in the present list of Jewish lessons, Deuteronomy 13:22 and Isaiah 1:1–22 stand forty-fourth in order." That list is of decidedly later origin; but probably it was often determined by older custom and traditional ideas of suitable accompaniment.[86]

The rabbi who gave Paul the privilege of addressing the congregation must have all too suddenly recognized he had started something that was beyond his control to halt. A comfortable priestcraft was ready to be toppled from its podium. For Antiochia, the separation of the wheat from the tares had begun. Many of the congregation followed Paul and Barnabas, wanting to know more.

Something else happened here for which we have no explanation. From the time of their call, Barnabas was mentioned before Paul, but from then on Paul was given the senior reference. The first inclination was given with reference to their departure from Cyprus: "Paul and his company" (Acts 13:13). This same verse talks of John Mark departing for Jerusalem.

The Next Sabbath Day (Acts 13:44–50 • September AD 45)

"And the next sabbath day came almost the whole city together to hear the word of God" (Acts 13:44). Since reference was given to only one synagogue in this city, it can be assumed that the Hebrew congregation was not in the majority and that "almost the whole city" had reference to a predominance of Gentiles being in attendance to hear Paul and Barnabas. "But when the Jews saw the multitudes, they were filled with envy, and spake against those things which were spoken by Paul, contradicting [his teachings] and blaspheming [considering his doctrine blasphemous]" (Acts 13:45).

Is it therefore any wonder that Luke says, "Then Paul and Barnabas waxed bold, and said, It was necessary that the word of God should have been spoken to you: but seeing ye put it from you, and judge yourselves unworthy of everlasting life, lo, we turn to the Gentiles. For so hath the Lord commanded us, saying, I have set thee to be a light of the Gentiles, that thou shouldst be for salvation unto the ends of the earth [quoting Isaiah 49:5; see also Isaiah 42:6]. And when the Gentiles heard this, they were glad, and glorified the word of the Lord: and as many as believed were ordained unto eternal life" (Acts 13:46–48; JSIV Acts 13:48).

By this we may conclude that these believing individuals were baptized and confirmed into the Church of Jesus Christ. The proud spiritual bigotry of the Jews was roused. They would not entertain the prospect of having their religious privilege being offered freely to the Gentiles. That the Messiah should come to the Hebrew nation was an expected reality, but the concept of a Messiah who should come to spiritually emancipate the Gentiles also could not be reconciled with their Jewish theology. The word of God had come to this city and a branch—predominantly Gentile in its membership—was established.

"And the word of the Lord was published throughout all the region [of Phrygia]" (Acts 13:49). As the farmers came to sell their produce in the city, they learned of the new doctrine being taught. Returning to the countryside, they expounded the news of the city, thus assisting in the spread of the doctrine of Christ.

"But the Jews stirred up the devout and honourable women, and the chief men of the city, and raised persecution against Paul and Barnabas, and expelled them out of their coasts" (Acts 13:50). In that the support of the Gentile "honourable women" could be solicited leads us to surmise that these women were among those "that fear God" and came to the synagogue services.

Paul had established a pattern of expository fervor that he would practice in every city he would enter: to present his message to the Jewish community first, then to the Gentiles (Romans 1:16). The usual pattern was Jewish rejection and Gentile acceptance. Since Jewish animosity became organized opposition, we conclude that later Gentile proselyting efforts of Paul and Barnabas were conducted in the homes of private persons and in public places, such as the agora.

The confluence of opposition is noteworthy. First, Jews instruct their wives to incite the Gentile women. Second, Jewish women motivate the Gentile women to use their influence. Third, Gentile women entice their husbands to take action. Then fourth, the chief men (husbands) issue the expulsion order.

They Shake Off the Dust at Antiochia
(Acts 13:51–52 • September AD 45)

The two missionaries were expelled from the town. If the mob had their choice, it would no doubt have been south to the coast and by ship away from their shores. But Paul and Barnabas had no thought of returning or departing to distant shores, for they had a work to perform. Leaving the district of Pisida, they went to the district of Lyconium. The scriptural account says, "But they shook off the dust of their feet against them [see D&C 24:15; 60:15], and came unto Iconium. And the disciples were filled with joy, and with the Holy Ghost" (Acts 13:51–52).

6: The First Mission Tour (II)

The Region of Iconium (Acts 14:16 • Autumn AD 45)

No doubt the time spent in Antiochea aided Paul in his recovery to health. Two middle-aged men were filled with missionary zeal, overflowing with happiness and fearless to the threats on their lives. "Whether we live, we live unto the Lord; and whether we die, we die unto the Lord: whether we live therefore, or die, we are the Lord's" (Romans 14:8).

On the road again, they traveled east over the Roman road from Antiochea to Iconium. "And it came to pass in Iconium, that they went both together into the synagogue of the Jews, and so spake that a great multitude both of the Jews and also of the Greeks [Gentiles] believed. But the unbelieving Jews stirred up the Gentiles, and made their minds evil affected against the brethren" (Acts 14:1–2).

The brethren implies converts or brothers in the gospel. Amid conflict, the gospel takes root and brings forth fruit. "Long time therefore abode they speaking boldly in the Lord, which gave testimony unto the word of his grace, and granted signs and wonders to be done by their hands" (Acts 14:3).

The caliber of the converts can be evaluated as being deep and sincere, for the Lord "granted signs and wonders" at the hands of Paul and Barnabas. "But the multitude of the city was divided: and part held with the Jews, and part with the apostles. And there was an assault made both of the Gentiles, and also of the Jews with their rulers, to use them despitefully, and to stone them" (Acts 14:4–5). On this occasion, our two Apostles "were [made] [a]ware of it, and fled [escaped] unto

Lystra and Derbe, cities of Lycaonia [Lyconium], and unto the region that lieth round about: And there they preached the gospel" (Acts 14:6).

The Towns of Lystra and Derbe
(Acts 14:7; 16:13; 2 Corinthians 11:26;
2 Timothy 1:5 • Autumn AD 45)

The Cilician hinterlands of the Tarsus Mountains held many troublesome tribes that neither Pompey nor the Galatian kings were able to suppress. Upon the death of King Amyntas in 25 BC, Augustus annexed Galatia into the Roman Empire. Sometime in the years 12–1 BC, he appointed Publius Sulpicius Quirinius to remove the troublesome Homonadies tribe from their Tarsus Mountains strongholds. Finally, after much exertion and several campaigns, the robber mountain men were defeated and removed to the plains.

Throughout the region of Lyconium we are told that "there they preached the gospel" (Acts 14:7). As Paul and Barnabas did not preach in the synagogues on the Sabbath day, we must conclude that there were only a few Jews in this remote region. We know of one Jewish family at least, as this was the home of Timotheus (Timothy), his mother, Eunice; and his grandmother Lois. His father was a Gentile (Acts 16:1–3; 2 Timothy 1:5). The next time Paul would come to Galatia, he would select Timothy to be a ministering companion as they journeyed on their way.

The Gods from Mount Olympus (Acts 14:8–18 •
Winter AD 45–46)

"And there sat a certain man at Lystra, impotent [lame] in his feet, being a cripple from his mother's womb [since birth], who never had walked: The same heard Paul speak: who steadfastly beholding him, and perceiving that he had faith to be healed, Said with a loud voice, Stand upright [erect] on the feet. And he leaped and walked" (Acts 14:8–10).

When Paul looked at the cripple, he did so with the perceptive, spiritually discerning eyes (1 Corinthians 12:10). Possessing the spiritual gift of healing (1 Corinthians 12:9), Paul spoke "with a loud voice." This gives us the impression that the cripple was not directly beside him, but sufficiently distant to require him to raise his voice. Attention shifted to the cripple on the ground, the eyes of all watching with eagerness. They have seen him in the agora daily and they know that he does not possess the physical power to use his legs.

Then, before all, he rises to his feet, discarding the implements of his infirmity. An enthusiasm erupts into a frenzied action:

> And when the people saw what Paul had done, they lifted up their voices, saying in the speech [dialect] of Lyconia, The gods are come down to us in the likeness of men.
>
> And they called Barnabas, Jupiter; and Paul, Mercurius, because he was the chief speaker.
>
> Then the priest[s][87] of Jupiter, which was before their city, brought oxen and garlands unto the gates [of the house], and would have done sacrifice with the people. (Acts 14:11–13)

Relief showing a bull with garland from a Lystra temple

These people believed in polytheism, so Paul and Barnabas suddenly became the focus of worship. In a swift excitement, the inhabitants took the two missionaries to be gods come down from their exalted abode upon Mount Olympus, disposed to perform miraculous wonders. Paul, having been the speaker, was thereby considered to be the god called *Mercury* in Latin (*Hermes* in Greek), the messenger of the gods. Barnabas on the other hand, being a tall and imposing individual, was seen to be the god called *Jupiter* in Latin (*Zeus* in Greek).

The Greek word *pulónas*, translated here as "gates," probably does not mean the city gates as it is generally interpreted. In Matthew 26:71, the same word is translated as "porch," meaning the courtyard before a house, inside the gate from the street. Again in Luke 16:20 and Acts 10:17 and 12:13–16, it is translated as "gate," but these obviously mean the gate before the courtyard. We therefore conclude that the gate mentioned in this passage is the gate leading into the courtyard of the house where the two Apostles were staying.

Then the multitude gathered to offer sacrifice to Hermes and Zeus before the gate of the house wherein the Apostles had retired. It took some time for them to grasp just what was happening.

> Which when the apostles, Barnabas and Paul, heard of, they rent [tore] their clothes [in sorrow], and ran [rushed] in among the people, crying out,
>
> And saying, Sirs [Gentlemen], why do ye these things? We also are men of like passions [nature] with you, and preach unto you that ye should turn from these vanities unto the living God, which made heaven, and earth, and the sea, and all things that are therein [quoting Psalm 146:6]:
>
> Who in times past suffered all nations to walk in their own ways.
>
> Nevertheless he left not himself without witness, in that he did good, and gave us rain [Leviticus 26:4] from heaven, and fruitful seasons, filling our hearts with food and gladness. (Acts 14:14–17)

In the Greek culture of that time, various gods held sway over heaven, earth, seas, animals, plant life, time, the harvest, and so on. With just a few words, Paul proclaimed *the Living God* as creator and upholder of all things, independent of any other, least of all idols. "And with these sayings scarce restrained they the people, that they had not done sacrifice unto them" (Acts 14:18).

Antagonists from Antiochia (Acts 14:19–20; Philippians 1:29; 2 Timothy 1:5; 3:10–11 • Winter AD 45–46)

While all this commotion occurred, "there came thither certain Jews from Antioch[ia] and Iconium, who persuaded the people, and, having stoned Paul, drew him out of the city, supposing he had been dead. Howbeit, as the disciples stood round about him, he rose up, and came into the city" (Acts 14:19–20). As to why Jews would have come from Antiochia and Iconium just now, one author suggested that it was the harvest time and it would be normal to expect merchants from the cities and larger towns to travel into the countryside to buy grain. These Jews may have been such merchants.[88]

How could people change from worshipping Paul as a god to stoning him as a criminal in one day? How could the Jewish strangers incite the citizens of Lystra to turn against those whom they had accepted as their gods? They challenged it in the same way that they always did: by saying that it was through the power of Satan (Matthew 9:34; 12:24; Mark 3:22; Luke 11:15). Would they not argue that Paul and Barnabas had said, "We also are men of like nature with you, and preach unto you that ye should turn from these idols." In other words: "These Christians have come here to destroy your gods, and we would advise you to get rid of them immediately!"

They also likely heard that these two missionaries were ordered out of the cities of Antiochia (Acts 13:50) and Iconium. These arrogant visitors easily persuaded the native population that since the two strangers of their own words denied that they were gods, then they assuredly were subtle deceivers of the magic arts. They had apparently healed a cripple, but the next time they might just cast a spell upon the whole village and enslave everyone.

The peasantry was cajoled into action. Paul was singled out since he "was the chief speaker," and it was he who spoke in evil tones of the god Zeus, calling him an idol. So it was that Barnabas was spared the anger of the mob.

As those stones came hurling at Paul, did his mind flash back across the years to that day in Jerusalem when Stephen was martyred, and Paul "was consenting unto his [Stephen's] death" (Acts 8:1)? The stones struck Paul and inflicted bruises and cracked bones until he finally lost consciousness and slumped to the ground lifeless. Paul was dragged by some uncouth hands out of the town gate.

Word soon reached Barnabas and the others. They immediately went after Paul and found him discarded by the wayside. The disciples gathered around him to recover his lifeless tabernacle and a blessing by the power of the priesthood was administered. The breath of life returned and Paul lived again!

Did young Timothy, the future recipient of two Epistles that bear his name, witness this barbaric incident and the miraculous restoration to life?[89] "The natural presumption is that Barnabas raised him from death or near death. However the miracle occurred—stoned, bruised, and deemed dead—Paul would not have been ready to travel the next day without divine intervention."[90]

The congregation of the faithful gathered to the home of Timothy's mother, Eunice, and his grandmother Lois (2 Timothy 1:7), where they washed away the blood and tended to Paul's wounds. Yes, Timothy saw it all that day. Years later, Paul wrote of this event, recollecting the presence of his young companion: "But thou hast fully known my doctrine, manner of life, purpose, faith, longsuffering, charity, patience, persecutions, afflictions, which came unto me at . . . Lystra; what persecutions I endured: but out of them all the Lord delivered me" (2 Timothy 3:10–11).

But in the midst of all this, we read that "the disciples stood around about him" (Acts 14:20). Here, we must be reading the success of their labors, in that certain of the inhabitants—possibly the cripple healed by Paul included—had embraced the gospel and professed discipleship. Undaunted by it all, Paul "rose up" and returned "into the city." It must be concluded, from the absence of further intimidation, that the Lystra people no longer felt animosity toward Paul. Any viewpoint raised by the visiting agitators would not sway the peasantry with the evidence of Paul being raised back to life.

Converts at Derbe (Acts 14:20–22 • Late Winter–Early Spring AD 46)

Some time later, following this event, Paul "departed with Barnabas to Derbe" (Acts 14:20). Since there were several towns and hamlets in the region, we may conclude that the inhabitants of Derbe were not the only people to hear the gospel proclaimed. Their success is expressed in the following words: "And when they had preached the gospel to that city, and had taught many, they returned again to Lystra, and to Iconium, and Antioch[ia], confirming the souls of the disciples [converts], and exhorting them to continue in the faith, and that we must through much tribulation enter in to the kingdom of God" (Acts 14:21–22).

Ordaining Elders in Every Congregation
(Acts 14:23–26 • Spring AD 46)

Upon conversion, the new proselytes to the gospel had become the wheat among the tares. Paul and Barnabas returned to each city to exhort the new converts. Of the new members, leaders had to be chosen to carry on the work of the ministry. Therefore, certain of them were called and ordained with the Melchizedek Priesthood. Ordination to the Aaronic [Levitical] Priesthood must have been done on the previous visits, shortly after the baptisms. "And when they had ordained them elders in every church [congregation], and had prayed with fasting, they commended them to the Lord, on whom they believed" (Acts 14:23).

They preached the gospel throughout the length and breadth of the southern Galatian provincial districts of Lyconium and Pisidia, which in all probability took up the greater part of over a year (autumn AD 45–early AD 47), if not longer.

"And after they had passed throughout Pisidia [Phrygia], they came to Pamphylia" (Acts 14:24). Descending from the Galatian highlands, they reached the coastal plain in Pamphylia. "And when they had preached the word in Perga, they went down into [the port city of] Attalia: and thence [obtaining passage, they] sailed to [Seleucia, and then up to] Antioch, from whence they had been recommended to the grace of God for the work which they fulfilled" (Acts 14:25–26).

Antioch-on-the-Orontes Once Again
(Acts 14:27–28 • Summer AD 46)

With recent thoughts of their labors among the poor and backward provincial Galatians, they entered again the proud and affluent city of Antioch-on-the-Orontes. This missionary tour completed, they made report of their activities covering the time they were away (early AD 45–AD 46). "And when they were come, and had gathered the church together, they rehearsed [reported on] all that God had done with them, and how he had opened the door of faith unto the Gentiles" (Acts 14:27). The finishing touch to this episode is given thus: "And they [Paul and Barnabas] abode [a] long time [AD 48–49] with the disciples [Saints]" (Acts 14:28).

The False Doctrine of Christian Circumcision (Acts 15:1 • circa AD 47)

Time passed and the work progressed in Antioch. "And certain men which came down from Judaea taught the brethren [Saints], and said, Except ye [Gentile converts] be circumcised after the manner of Moses [Jewish converts], ye cannot be saved" (Acts 15:1). These "certain men" were unwittingly endeavoring to tear the Church apart. We observe that the Jews did not question whether Gentiles could inherit salvation—that point was clearly conceded. The question in their minds was, if the Gentiles could be saved without the tenets of the Mosaic law, then clearly without the law a Jew could also be saved.

That precept found no place within their perspective of traditional values. The Judaeo-Christians of Judea were more narrow-minded than any other converts to Christianity. They presumed a superior position in the Church, which they perpetually endeavored to impose upon the Church at large. Had they succeeded in enforcing their doctrine of circumcision as being essential to salvation within the Church, they would have seemed to make Christianity a new appendage to an older Judaism.

And then Paul himself wrote on the subject in a rather clear-cut manner:

> But now in Christ Jesus ye who sometimes were far off [Gentiles] are made nigh by the blood of Christ. For he is our peace, who hath made both one, and hath broken down the middle wall of partition between us; having abolished in his flesh the enmity, even the law of commandments contained in ordinances; for to make in himself of twain one new man, so making peace; and that he might reconcile both unto God in one body by the cross, having slain the enmity thereby: and came and preached peace to you which were afar off, and to them that were nigh. . . . Now therefore ye are no more strangers and foreigners, but fellowcitizens with the saints, and of the household of God. (Ephesians 2:13–17, 19; see also 11–22)

When on the Temple Mount, Gentiles could only go so far as the outer wall of the double Court of the Women and the Court of the Men enclosure. They "were far off." But through the gospel,

Gentiles "are made nigh by the blood of Christ." Through the Atonement, Jesus "hath broken down the middle wall of partition," qualifying the Gentiles with the Jews to come right up to the temple, "having abolished in his flesh the enmity" that separated them. Now the Gentiles "are no more strangers and foreigners, but fellowcitizens."

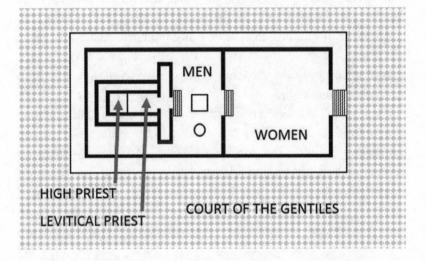

The following is one of the engraved limestone warning notices, discovered in 1871. Translated from Greek, it reads, "Whoever is caught [going beyond the barrier] will have himself to blame that his death ensues." The warning notices were only written in Greek, not Hebrew or Aramaic.

NO MAN OF ANOTHER NATION TO ENTER WITHIN THE FENCE AND ENCLOSURE ROUND THE TEMPLE. AND WHOEVER IS CAUGHT WILL HAVE HIMSELF TO BLAME THAT HIS DEATH ENSUES

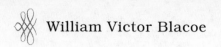

Jerusalem for a Church Council (Acts 11:29–30; 12:24–25; 13:13; 14:14; 15:24; Galatians 2:13 • circa AD 47–48)

From the time of Abraham to Paul, the law of circumcision was a most sacred obligation (see Genesis 17:10–14, 23–27). "When Paul and Barnabas had no small dissension [difference] and disputation with them [from Judea], they [the Saints] determined that Paul and Barnabas, and certain other of them, should go up to Jerusalem unto the [senior] apostles and elders about this question" (Acts 15:2). There are times and questions of such a nature that the decision of the presiding authorities of the Church are needed to clarify and settle a question permanently.

Paul and Barnabas set off for Jerusalem together with "certain other of them." Six years later, in writing to the Galatians, Paul said, "Fourteen years after [his conversion AD 36–49] . . . I went up by revelation, and communicated [reported] unto them [the Apostles]" (Galatians 2:1–2).[91]

Paul, Barnabas, and Titus (Galatians 2:1), "being brought on their way by the church, they passed through Phenice [Phonecia] and Samaria, declaring the conversion of the Gentiles: and they caused great joy unto all the brethren. And when they were come to Jerusalem, they were received of the church, and of the apostles and elders, and they declared all things that God had done with them" (Acts 15:3-4). No doubt they made their report before the Presidency of the Church: Peter, James, and John (AD 50). How they must have rejoiced to hear of the spread of the gospel in Asia by Paul and Barnabas.

Prophets Decide (Acts 13:13; 15:5–23 • AD 47–48)

"But there rose up certain of the sect of the Pharisees which believed [as Christian converts], saying, That it was needful to circumcise them [the Gentiles], and to command them to keep [all] the law of Moses" (Acts 15:5). Before continuing any further, an explanation was needed. "Certain of the sect of the Pharisees which believed," means just what it says.

In the Church of the time, Jewish proselytes of the gospel often remained members of their old denomination. So there were, in effect, Pharisee-Christians who were observing the law of Moses and rabbinical teachings but were baptized and confirmed members of the Church, accepting the authority of Peter, a Pharisaic Christian prophet and chief Apostle. Jewish converts wanted the Gentiles to first embrace Judaism, and then elevate to Christianity with Jesus as the promised Messiah in a higher Jewish sect.

A conference of the Church was convened. "And the apostles and elders came together for to consider of this matter. And when there had been much disputing, Peter rose up, and said unto them, Men and brethren, ye know now that a good while ago [about ten years] God made choice among us, that the Gentiles by my mouth should hear the word of the gospel, and believe. And God, which knoweth the hearts, bare them witness, giving them the Holy Ghost, even as he did unto us; and put no difference between us and them, purifying their hearts by faith" (Acts 15:6–9).

Peter's logic was simple: If God gave unto the Gentiles the Holy Ghost, even though they were not circumcised, who can consider circumcision to be essential to salvation?

"Now therefore why tempt ye God, to put a yoke upon the neck of the disciples, which neither our fathers nor we were able to bear? But we believe that through the grace of the Lord Jesus Christ we shall be saved, even as they" (Acts 15:10–11). Peter had said it with plain clarity: *If our forefathers, who were Jews, could not live the law in earnest, why seek you to impose such upon the Greek? Can you expect them to live what we ourselves do not?* The prophet had spoken, so "the debate [was] over."[92]

Among the Jews themselves, converts existed. "It was difficult to find any justification for making the door of the Church narrower than the door of the synagogue, and there is no record that any one explicitly advocated the view that Christianity should be confined to the chosen people."[93]

"Then all the multitude kept silence, and gave audience to Barnabas and Paul, declaring what miracles and wonders God had wrought among the Gentiles by them" (Acts 15:12). They were, in effect, bearing testimony to the words of Peter by rehearsing the workings of the Holy Ghost among them of the uncircumcised (Gentiles). This may have been the reasoning behind bringing Titus, a Gentile, with them as a living witness of the workings of the Spirit in one who had not submitted to the Mosaic law.

> And after they had held their peace, James answered, saying, Men and brethren, hearken unto me:
>
> Simeon [Peter] hath declared how God at the first did visit the Gentiles, to take out of them a people for his name.
>
> And to this agree the words of the prophets; as it is written,
>
> After this I will return, and build the tabernacle of David, which is fallen down; and I will build again the ruins thereof, and I will set it up:
>
> That the residue of men might seek after the Lord, and all the Gentiles, upon whom my name is called, saith the Lord [quoting Amos 9:11–12], who doeth all these things.
>
> Known only unto God are all his works from the beginning of the world.
>
> Wherefore my sentence is, that we trouble not them, which from among the Gentiles are turned to God:
>
> But that we write unto them, that they [first] abstain from pollutions of idols, and [second] from fornication, and [third] from things strangled, and [fourth] from blood.
>
> For Moses of old time hath in every city them that preach him, being read in the synagogues every sabbath day. (Acts 15:13–21)

The early Brethren apparently set a standard for Gentile converts that had existed prior to Abraham. This is called the "Noahide laws," or the law given to Gentiles, considering that Noah was a Gentile, seeing as there were no Jews then. The seven laws of the Babylonian Talmud are: no idolatry, no murder, no theft, no sexual immorality, no blasphemy, no eating flesh with blood, and maintaining courts for legal recourse. The following letter is based on the first, fourth, and sixth Noahide laws.

In this response, James said that "we trouble not them" and let the circumcision question end with the remarks of Peter. To quell the Pharisees, he added that the Gentiles should be commanded to abstain from eating things offered to idols [false gods], from fornication, and from meat of strangled animals and from blood. The Pharisees wanted some Mosaic restrictions placed upon the Gentiles, but the Church doctrine would not be compromised by factions. The fornication clause was included since the letter is mainly directed to the converts at Syrian-Antioch (Acts 15:23), who were notorious for their heathen temple worship, which was manifest through licentious prostitution. To refrain from immorality, the Gentile converts would be required to terminate their associations with the heathen temples.[94] Keep in mind that the Church authorities did not impose the tenets of Mosaic law upon the Christian Church, but rather decreed—for their day—certain standards of conduct. Simply said: stay away from the appearance of evil (1 Thessalonians 5:22).

Many years later, Paul, in writing to the Galatians, had the following to say in retrospect of this conference:

> And I went up by revelation, and communicated [reported] unto them that the gospel which I preach among the Gentiles, but privately to them which were of reputation, lest by any means I should run, or had run, in vain.
>
> But neither Titus, who was with me, being a Greek, was compelled to be circumcised:
>
> And that because of false brethren unawares brought in, who came in privily to spy out our liberty which we in Christ Jesus, that they might bring us into bondage:
>
> To whom we gave place by subjection, no, not for an hour; that the truth of the gospel might continue with you.
>
> But of these who seemed to be somewhat, (whatsoever they were, it maketh no matter to me: God accepteth no man's person:) for they who seemed to be somewhat in conference added nothing to me:
>
> But contrariwise, when they saw that the gospel of the uncircumcision was committed unto me, as the gospel of the circumcision was unto Peter;
>
> (For he that wrought effectually in Peter to the apostleship of the circumcision, the same was mighty in me toward the Gentiles:)
>
> And when James [Jacob], Cephas [Peter], and John, who seemed to be pillars, perceived the grace that was given unto me, they gave to me and Barnabas the right hands of fellowship; that we should go unto the heathen [Gentiles], and they unto the circumcision [Jews].
>
> Only they would that we should remember the poor; the same which I was forward to do. (Galatians 2:2–10)

From verses 7–9, we read of the decision to divide the missionary work within the orb of ethnic demarcation. Peter presided and ministered to the Jewish Christians, and Paul directed and proselyted among the Gentiles. Within these two main portions of missionary endeavor, there were several missions. We see Paul traveling from one mission to another, instructing and training the presiding leadership of each area. And so it was with these remarks that the doctrinal difficulties were, for the moment, settled. No doubt this solution was accepted by Paul, Barnabas, and Titus.

Letter from the Prophets of the Church (Acts 15:22–29 • circa AD 47–48)

The conference was over. "Then pleased it the apostles and elders, with the whole church, to send chosen men of their own company to Antioch with Paul and Barnabas; namely, Judas surnamed Barsabas [son of Sabas], and Silas, chief men among the brethren [the Apostles]: And they wrote letters by them" (Acts 15:22–23). This was a letter from the three presiding leaders of the Church to the city of Antioch, after this manner:

> The apostles and elders and brethren send greeting unto the brethren which are of the Gentiles in Antioch and Syria and Cilicia:
>
> Forasmuch as we have heard, that certain which went out from us have troubled you with words, subverting your souls, saying, Ye must be circumcised, and keep the [Mosaic] law: to whom we gave no such commandments:
>
> It seemed good unto us, being assembled with one accord, to send chosen men unto you with our beloved Barnabas and Paul,
>
> Men that have hazarded their lives for the name of our Lord Jesus Christ.
>
> We have sent therefore Judas and Silas, who shall also tell you the same thing by mouth.
>
> For it seemeth good to the Holy Ghost, and to us, to lay upon you no greater burden than these necessary things;
>
> That ye abstain from meats offered to idols,[95] and from blood, and from things strangled,[96] and from fornication: from which if ye keep yourselves, ye shall do well. Fare ye well [Peter, James, and John]. (Acts 15:24–29)

From Jerusalem to Antioch-on-the-Orontes (Acts 15:30–35; 16:37; 2 Corinthians 1:19; Galatians 2:1; 1 Thessalonians 1:1; 2 Thessalonians 1:1 • circa AD 47–48)

"So when they were dismissed [given leave of the Brethren], they came to Antioch" (Acts 15:30). Most likely they went that following Sabbath. "When they had gathered the multitude together, they delivered the epistle: Which when they had read, they rejoiced for the consolation [exhortation]" (Acts 15:30–31). Having read the words of the Church authorities to the congregation, the two brethren, sent to give verbal testimony of the epistle, spoke: "And Judas and Silas, being prophets [and apostles] also themselves, exhorted the brethren with many words, and confirmed [verified] them" (Acts 15:32).

These two brethren came from Jerusalem to bear witness of the truthfulness of the letter and testimony of Barnabas, Paul, and Titus. "And after they [the Brethren from Jerusalem] had tarried there a space they were let go in peace from the brethren [of Antioch] unto the apostles [in Jerusalem]. Notwithstanding it pleased Silas to abide there still" (Acts 15:33–34).

Silas, or Silvanus (2 Corinthians 1:19; 1 Thessalonians 1:1; 2 Thessalonians 1:1), was later to be the scribe to Peter in writing what we call his First Epistle General (1 Peter 5:12). Silas was a Roman citizen (Acts 16:37), a position that was to his benefit while in Philippi in the not too distant future.

We are aware that on the journey up to Jerusalem, Titus accompanied Paul and Barnabas (Galatians 2:1), but as to whether he returned with them to Antioch-on-the-Orontes we are not informed.

Another individual who should not be forgotten is John Mark. Recall his sudden departure from the company of Paul and Barnabas on their first missionary tour (Acts 13:13). At that time, he returned to Jerusalem, but we will soon see him again in Antioch. This leads us to believe that, returning from Jerusalem, John Mark accompanied them. I suspect that he did so at the request of Barnabas (his uncle or cousin), and not Paul.

Objection of Paul to the Attitude of Peter (Galatians 2:11–21 • circa AD 48–50)

Sometime after the return of Barnabas and Paul, the prophet Peter decided upon a personal visit to the Saints at Antioch. The account given by Paul in his Galatian Epistle opens: "But when Peter was come to Antioch, I withstood him to the face, because he was to be blamed" (Galatians 2:11).[97] The words of this passage in Greek do not convey an arrogant attitude, but rather simply mean that Paul spoke his mind directly to Peter. From the following verses, it may be inferred that Peter spent much time with members of Gentile origin, visiting and dining among them. It was Peter who previously said, "Truly I perceive that God shows no partiality, but in every nation any one who fears him and does what is right is acceptable to him" (RSV Acts 10:34–35).

Possibly Peter wanted to extend the arm of fellowship from the head of the Church. However, Peter changed his ways, to the disappointment of Paul and others.

> For before that certain came from James, he [Peter] did eat with the Gentiles: but when they [the Jewish brethren] were come, he withdrew and separated himself, fearing them which were come of the circumcision.
>
> And the other Jews dissembled likewise with him; insomuch that Barnabas also was carried away with their dissimulation [hypocrisy].
>
> But when I [Paul] saw that they walked not uprightly according to the truth of the gospel, I said unto Peter before them all, If thou, being a Jew [by birth], livest after the manner of Gentiles, and not as do the Jews, why compellest thou the Gentiles to live as do the Jews?[98]
>
> We who are Jews by nature [birth], and not sinners of the Gentiles,
>
> Knowing that a man is not justified by the works of the law [of Moses], but by the faith of Jesus Christ, even we have believed in Jesus Christ, that we might be justified by the faith of Christ, and not by the works of the law [of Moses]: for by the works of the law [of Moses] shall no flesh be justified.
>
> But if, while we seek to be justified by Christ [see Psalm 143:2], we ourselves also are found sinners, is therefore Christ the minister of sin? God forbid.

> For if I build again the things which I destroyed, I make myself a transgressor.
>
> For I through the law [gospel] am dead to the law [of Moses], that I might live unto God.
>
> I am crucified with Christ: nevertheless I live; yet not I, but Christ liveth in me: and the life which I now live in the flesh I live by the faith of the Son of God, who loved me, and gave himself for me.
>
> I do not frustrate the grace of God: for if righteousness come by the law, then Christ is dead in vain. (Galatians 2:12–21)

As to the reaction of Peter and the others, we can only assume a proper response was forthcoming. No doubt Peter took "the truth to be hard" and it most likely cut him "to the very center" (1 Nephi 16:2). But who can doubt that Paul was "speaking the truth in love" (Ephesians 4:15).

In conclusion of this are the words of Peter, written in later years concerning his love for Paul, calling him "our beloved brother Paul" (2 Peter 3:15). The matter must have come to at least a reasonably successful conclusion because Luke ends the record without further comment.

The John Mark Rejection (Acts 4:36; 14:15; 15:35–41 • Spring AD 51)

However, "Paul also and Barnabas continued in Antioch, teaching and preaching the word of the Lord, with many others also. And some days [actually months] after Paul said unto Barnabas, Let us go again and visit our brethren [the converts] in every city where we have preached the word of the Lord, and see how they do" (Acts 15:35–36).

The area of their concern and focus was the island of Cyprus and the districts of Pamphylia, Pisida and, Lyconia, in Galatia. It had been some years since they preached, baptized, and ordained among these people (AD 45–50). The time had come to return and to strengthen. You will recall that when Paul and Barnabas departed on their previous missionary tour, they had taken John Mark, a nephew (or possibly cousin) of Joseph Barnabas (Acts 13:1–13). However, John Mark terminated his mission after six months and returned home to Jerusalem.

We read in verse 36 that Paul proposed to Barnabas that they should retrace the steps of their previous tour and visit their old proselytes. Barnabas agreed with this proposal, but contrary to the desires of Paul, he had a prerequisite to the journey: "And Barnabas determined [resolved] to take with them John, whose surname was Mark. But Paul thought it not good to take him with them, who departed from them from Pamphylia, and went not with them to the work" (Acts 15:37–38). The resolve of Barnabas may well have been fermenting within him for several months. We read of Paul withstanding Peter (Galatians 2:14), and at the same time Barnabas was "carried away" with this separation from the Gentiles (Galatians 2:13). He may have held a grudge against Paul for that public embarrassment.

Somehow, we feel Luke was being quite diplomatic in the words he used to record this crisis. His commentary on the issue continues thus: "And the contention was so sharp between them, that they departed asunder one from another: and so Barnabas took [his nephew John] Mark, and sailed unto [the island of] Cyprus; and Paul chose Silas, and departed, being recommended by the brethren unto the grace of God. And he went through Syria and Cilicia, confirming the churches [congregations]" (Acts 15:39–41).

As to the resolve of Barnabas and the intransigence of Paul over having Mark to be a companion, it is disheartening to find two Apostles engaged in the work of the ministry, enveloped in sharp contention.

Young John Mark was the innocent in this feud. As Solomon put it, "Only by pride cometh contention" (Proverbs 13:10). Think not that because Paul was somewhat prideful that he was in any way unworthy for the work whereunto he was called. He was still a most admirable Saint, who took the yoke of the gospel upon his shoulders without complaint. Remember what Paul said of Barnabas and himself, "We also are men of like passions with you" (Acts 14:15).

To those who would find the pride of Paul a reason to condemn him, let the words of Christ be a yardstick: "He that is without sin among you, let him [or her] first cast a stone" at Paul (John 8:7; see also Acts 14:15).

Joseph Barnabas, with his nephew (or cousin) John Mark, parted company with Paul and journeyed to Cyprus, the homeland of Barnabas (Acts 14:15). Since we are following the footsteps of Paul, we now drop Barnabas and Mark from our narrative.

7: The Second Mission Tour (I)

Silas and Paul leave Antioch for Galatia (Acts 15:40–41; 16:1 • Spring AD 51)

Silas (Latin *Silvanus*, 1 Thessalonians 1:1; 2 Thessalonians 1:1; 1 Peter 5:12), whom it "pleased to abide" in Antioch (Acts 15:34), now found himself selected to be the companion of the fiery little middle-aged Paul (AD 6–51). "And Paul chose Silas, and departed, being recommended by the brethren unto the grace of God. And he went through Syria and Cilicia, confirming [strengthening] the churches [congregations]" (Acts 15:40–41). They soon ascended the Galatian plateau and eventually reached Derbe in Galatia.

Timothy Joins Paul (Acts 16:15; Galatians 4:13–14; 2 Timothy 1:5 • Summer AD 51)

"Then came he [or rather they, Paul and Silas] to Derbe and Lystra: and, behold, a certain disciple was there, named Timotheus [Timothy; see Acts 20:4], the son of a certain woman [Eunice; see 2 Timothy 1:5)], which was a Jewess, and believed; but his father was a Greek: which was well reported of by the brethren that were at Lystra and Iconium. Him [Timothy] would Paul have to go forth with him; and took and circumcised him because of the Jews which were in those quarters: for they knew all that his father was a Greek [Gentile]" (Acts 16:1–3).

Timothy was of part Jewish parentage. Paul had nothing against a Mosaic custom. But had Timothy been all Gentile, he would in all probability have resisted such pressures. We are aware that Paul suffered the unnecessary punishment of the thirty-nine stripes on three occasions (2 Corinthians 6:5; 11:23–24) to maintain his access to the synagogue. Therefore, we can conjecture that Paul may have considered that Timothy would have greater freedom of synagogue access being a circumcised Jew, rather than an uncircumcised heathen.

"And as they went through the cities, they delivered them the decrees for to keep, that were ordained of the apostles and elders which were at Jerusalem. And so were the churches [congregations] established in the faith, and increased in number daily" (Acts 16:4–5).

Luke used the word *decree*—Greek *dogma*—to describe the pronouncement of the brethren. This same word is used by Luke in the next chapter when he speaks of "the decrees of Caesar" (Acts 17:7).

Lyconia to Alexandria Troas (Acts 16:68; 1 Corinthians 16:1; Galatians 1:2; 1 Timothy 1:18; 2 Timothy 1:5; 3:15 • Summer–Autumn AD 51)

Prior to their departure from the district, Timothy was called to the ministry, being perceived as a man of "unfeigned faith" (2 Timothy 1:5). Indeed more so, for we read that from childhood he had studied and come to know "the holy scriptures" (2 Timothy 3:15). Paul and Silas, who were possibly assisted by certain of the local brethren of Lystra, set Timothy apart to the work.

"Now when they had gone throughout Phrygia [District] and the region [southern districts] of Galatia [Province], and were forbidden of the Holy Ghost to preach the word [gospel] in Asia [Province], after they were come to Mysia [District], they assayed to go into Bythina [Province]: but the Spirit suffered them not. And they passing by Mysia [District] came to [Alexandra] Troas" (Acts 16:6–8).

Having been prompted by the Spirit to alter their course from going to Ephesus, it would appear that "they attempted" (RSV Acts 16:7) to head north to the Black Sea provinces of Bythina and Pontus. Once again, "the Spirit suffered [prompted] them not" to go further in this direction. Having been led of the Spirit, they headed for the Aegean Sea coast at Alexandria-Troas. Traversing the hills, they crossed the historic landscape of Troy. This is the battleground of the Greek epic *The Iliad*, where the mythical Greek gods became a reality in the writings of Homer. Those gods of whom he said were bloodless and were called immortals.[99]

Narrative of Luke (Acts 16:10–13, 16; Colossians 4:14 • Autumn AD 51)

A change now takes place in the narrative of Luke. The amount of detail in many places increases and it becomes easier to follow the progress of the party. The reason for this sudden change is that, during their stay in Troas, Paul, Silas, and Timothy met Luke (Latin *Lucanus*), the author of this record that we are following, and also the author of the Gospel bearing his name. Here begins what are known as the "we" passages, meaning that Luke changes from speaking to readers in the third person to speaking in the first person plural.

Having previously written the Gospel account, Luke wrote the Acts of the Apostles as a continuation. By vocation, he is recorded as a physician (Colossians 4:14) and was an early convert, for he wrote that he "had perfect understanding of all things from the very first" (Luke 1:3). We might assume that Luke had met Paul previously, possibly in Antioch-on-the-Orontes where Luke is traditionally said to have come from.

One more thing needs to be said about Luke before continuing. Though he was trained to be a physician for the body, through his writing the Gospel according to Luke and the Acts of the Apostles, he had since then become a physician of the spirits of mankind; and is yet today dispensing balm of Gilead (see Jeremiah 8:22), which is medicine to the sick in spirit.

Macedonian Vision (Acts 16:9–11; Hebrews 13:2 • Spring AD 52)

Paul retired to his bed for the night, the uncertainty of where the Lord would have him go likely weighing heavily upon his mind. "And a vision appeared unto Paul in the night; There stood a [certain[100]] man of Macedonia [Province], and prayed [pleaded with] him, saying, Come over into Macedonia, and help us" (Acts 16:9).

We observe that this man of Macedonia was the representative for an undefined group of people, since he said help *us*. A nation sat in darkness, seeking the Light and Life in the World. And the messengers of the Holy One awaited their call and, being a visionary man, Paul was "not forgetful to entertain strangers" (Hebrews 13:2).

What was it about the man that made Paul aware that his visitor was from Macedonia? Did Paul actually recognize and know this "certain Macedonian" man? The province of Macedonia covered what today is northern Greece, southern Bulgaria, and part of the Republic of Macedonia. It was ruled by a proconsul of Rome, who resided at Thessalonica.

Motivated by the vision, Paul, Silas, Timothy, and Luke, "after he [Paul] had seen the vision, immediately we endeavored [made preparation] to go into Macedonia, assuredly gathering [concluding] that the Lord had called us for to preach the gospel unto them. Therefore loosing from [Alexandria-]Troas, we came with straight course to Samothracia [Island], and the next day to [the port of] Neapolis" (Acts 16:10–11). Luke records that they made the journey from Alexandria-Troas to Neapolis in two days. On a later trip in the reverse direction, we are told by Luke that it took five days (Acts 20:7).

Neapolis, the Port of Entry to Europe (Spring AD 52)

The next morning, they put out to sea to complete their journey. And so it was that one afternoon, late in the spring of AD 52, Paul, Silas, Timothy, and Luke landed on the continent of Europe. Though we speak of the European and the Asian continents, we should be aware that in the first century, such terminology and divisions did not exist. Paul merely crossed between two Greek-speaking Roman provinces.

Little did Paul know the historical value of that day; how through the corridors of time, Europe would become the home of Christendom. How ordinary it must have appeared to see a party of men disembark at the bustling docks of Neapolis. In a real sense, an invasion had occurred, unbeknownst to the inhabitants of Macedonia.

Philippi (Acts 16:12 • Spring AD 52)

From what we read in the account of Luke, the four brethren did not stay in the port of Neapolis but rather passed through "to Philippi [more correctly, *Colonia Augusta Julia Philippensis*], which is the chief city of that part of Macedonia, and a colony: and we were in that city abiding certain days" (Acts 16:12).

Once again, the teachings of Jesus Christ and their testimonies of the Atonement and Resurrection were about to be declared to new ears. Obedient to the entreaty of the vision, the missionaries went over to Macedonia to seek out the pure and honest in heart. There was no synagogue prominent in this city. But there were some remnants of scattered Israel. The dispersion of the chosen seed had led a handful of Abraham's posterity to this Roman colony. This may be explained by the fact that Philippi was a military city, not mercantile.

The Sabbath Day (Acts 16:13 • Spring AD 52)

Luke writes that "on the sabbath we[101] went out of the city[102] by a [the Gangites] river side, where prayers were wont to be made; and we sat down, and spake unto the women that resorted thither" (Acts 16:13). There exists the possibility that the Jews were forbidden to engage in their religious worship within the city, but were given liberty to do so outside the walls. This substitute for a synagogue was called a *proseuche*.

This was the Sabbath of the Jews, but for the Gentile majority of Philippi there was no Sabbath. The merchants made their trades and sold their wares. Business as usual.

It has been observed by an author that Luke records only women in attendance for prayers. By rabbinical law, there had to be ten men to form a court (*minyan*) or there could be no synagogue. When this was not possible, a place of prayer was then established elsewhere.

Lydia, Paul's First Convert in Europe (Acts 16:14–15 • Spring AD 52)

As had been the practice before in other places, the brethren were invited to address the congregation. As to which of them spoke is not declared, but the following verses reveal the success of the preaching.

"And a certain woman named Lydia, a seller of purple, of the city of Thyatira, which worshipped God, heard us: whose heart the Lord opened, that she attended unto the things which were spoken of Paul. And when she was baptized, and her household, she besought us, saying, If ye have judged me to be faithful to the Lord, come into my house, and abide there. And she constrained[103] [adamantly invited] us" (Acts 16:14–15).

The baptism of Lydia and her household in the River Gangites, of itself, justified the European mission. For here was a household prepared in the Spirit to receive the gospel. There seems to be a time lapse: the baptism apparently did not occur on that first Sabbath, but took place some time later. Lydia must have owned a large house wherein she could accommodate her household and still have room for four male guests. This Lydia was a Greek "which worshipped God," not a Jew but a proselyte. It would appear that the Jews were not to be converted in this city.

Lydia is not a proper name, but rather means the Lydian, or the lady from Lydia. The city of Thyatira in the province of Lydia was famous throughout the Roman world for its purple dye. The *purple* referred to here is cloth that has been dyed with a red-blue dye extract from the purple mussel. Cloth that was dyed so was expensive; we may therefore conclude that Lydia was financially successful.

The Damsel Possessed with a Spirit of Divination (Acts 16:16–18 • Spring AD 52)

"And it came to pass, as we went to prayer, a certain damsel[104] possessed with a spirit of divination[105] met us, which brought her masters much gain by soothsaying:[106] The same followed Paul and us, and cried, saying, These men are servants[107] of the most high God, which shew unto us the way of salvation" (Acts 16:16–17). If it were the girl speaking instead of the evil spirit, she would not have known who the brethren were. There are instances of evil spirits, or devils, recognizing Jesus for whose Son He was (Mark 1:23–24). This slave girl, under the influence of the evil occupant, repeated this procedure many days, for Luke continues the account: "And this did she many days, But Paul, being grieved [troubled or worried], turned and said to the spirit, I command thee in the name of Jesus Christ to come out of her. And he came out the same hour" (Acts 16:18).

There is implication that the departure of the devil was not immediate, for Luke says that the devil "came out the same hour." Possibly, as Paul rebuked the devil and moved on, the devil may not have departed without some show of resistance. On the other hand, the evil spirit may have departed immediately, but the girl was not called upon to exercise her soothsaying capabilities until sometime after Paul had departed.

If this girl was testifying "many days" before the people of the city that Paul and his companions were divinely commissioned, we may conclude that many of the Philippian inhabitants heard this witness. But the servants of the Lord require no testimony from the minions of darkness, and the devils were silenced, no more to speak. The girl was once again the sole possessor of her mortal frame.

Though a slave by status, she had been made free through priesthood ministration. This more than any other reason was what moved Paul to rebuke the demon: "The Spirit of God, which is also the spirit of freedom" (Alma 61:15).

Within that same hour, our four missionaries divided into pairs of two, with Paul and Silas remaining together and Timothy pairing up with Luke. This may be inferred from the events that followed, in which Timothy and Luke are both absent from the narrative until verse 40.

Possibly a paying customer approached the girl's masters, seeking the services of the spirit in the girl. But now that soothsaying spirit was no longer tabernacled within this girl. The source of their income was terminated and exorcized. These masters realized that the exorcism of the slave girl uttered by Paul in their presence had, in reality, taken actual effect.

Philippian Imprisonment (Acts 16:19–29; 2 Corinthians 11:25 • Spring AD 52)

> And when her masters saw that the hope of their gains [occupation] was gone, they caught Paul and Silas, and drew [dragged] them into the market place [agora, or town square] unto the rulers,

> And brought them to the magistrates [praetors], saying, These men, being Jews, do exceedingly trouble our city,
>
> And teach customs, which are not lawful for us to receive, neither to observe, being Romans.
>
> And the multitude rose up together against them: and the magistrates rent off their [Paul's and Silas's] clothes, and commanded [the lictors] to beat them [with sticks].
>
> And when they had laid many stripes [welts] upon them, they cast them into prison, charging the jailor to keep them safely [securely]:
>
> Who, having received such a charge, thrust them into the inner prison, and made their feet fast in the stocks. (Acts 16:19–24)

The populace was in frenzy and the praetors overreacted to stop a riot. They were ushered into the prison and fettered fast. The traditional location of this prison is on the north side of the Via Egnatia, to the west of the agora.

Our missionary companionship was taken for Jews, and under the laws of Rome it was forbidden for Jews to proselyte Roman citizens.[108] This would explain the accusations and sentence: They "[taught] customs, which are not lawful for us to receive, neither to observe, being Romans."

The magistrates (praetors) usually held daily court hearings from a judgment seat built on a platform (*rostra*) in a prominent location (the agora, or market square) in the city. Since Paul and Silas were not of this city, they were not given the opportunity to defend themselves. The accusers could not bring their slave girl as evidence before the praetors, for there was no law condemning exorcism. So the proselyting effort was all that they could condemn. In a Greek city, this law did not exist, but Philippi was a Roman colony with Latin inhabitants, therefore proselyting was unlawful.

Paul and Silas were stripped of their garments by the orders of the praetors[109] and then flogged with the lictors rods[110] in public before a frenzied mob. Afterward, they were taken to the city prison as common criminals.

By this time, news of the expulsion order against Jews, issued by the emperor Claudius (Acts 17:2), must have reached Philippi.

Perhaps this order was the grounds upon which the accusers charged Paul and Silas. The reference to "the inner prison" means the most secure portion of the prison. In addition to the security of the inner chambers, the jailor fastened their legs in stocks. Stocks were made from two thick boards with two holes cut out at their joining, producing two semi-circular cutouts in each board. These stocks were placed across both legs just above the ankles and secured together on both sides.[111]

"And at midnight Paul and Silas prayed, and sang praises unto God: and the prisoners heard them" (Acts 16:25; see also Jeremiah 20:2–3; 29:26; see also Job 13:27; 33:11; Proverbs 7:22). The other prisoners must of a surety have thought Paul and Silas to be strange in every way. One author said the two Apostles "transformed the dungeon into a chapel."[112] Consider the words of King David: "Bring my soul out of prison that I may praise thy name" (Psalms 142:7).

But then the earth begins to groan. "And suddenly there was a great earthquake, so that the foundations of the prison were shaken: and immediately all the doors were opened, and every one's bands were loosed. And the keeper of the prison awakening out of his sleep, and seeing the prison doors open, he drew out his sword, and would have killed himself, supposing that the prisoners had been fled" (Acts 16:26–27).

Why would the jailor intend taking his life if the prisoners escaped? It was common practice to have the jailor committed to the accumulative same punishment of the escaped prisoners (see Acts 12:9; 27:42). So it was that the jailor preferred to take his own life rather than face being beheaded the next day for failing in his duty.

"But Paul cried with a loud voice, saying, Do thyself no harm: for we are all here. Then he called for a light[113] and sprang in [to the cell], and came trembling, and fell down before Paul and Silas" (Acts 16:28–29). Obviously the cell they were in had no light, therefore Paul and Silas could see the jailor drawing his sword. But the jailor saw no one in the darkness within the cell. This accounts for his calling for a light from another jailor or attendant (Latin *diogmitai*) and charging into the cell.

But the boldness of Paul and Silas in remaining within the open cell, unfettered and displaying a confident nature, would account for the trembling actions of the jailor.

Salvation through Belief in Jesus Christ (Acts 16:30–34 • Spring AD 52)

The jailor "brought them out, and said, Sirs, what must I do to be saved? And they said, Believe on the Lord Jesus Christ, and thou shalt be saved, and thy house. And they spake unto him [the jailor] the word of the Lord, and to all that were in his house [family]" (Acts 16:30–32). It was normal procedure to have apartments provided for the chief jailor within the prison complex for his family. This way, the jailor was always on hand for whatever might arise.

We might wonder why the jailor should, without prompting, declare, "What must I do to be saved?" But if we consider that the missionaries were preaching in the city for several days and that the demon that possessed the slave girl bore witness before the population of the city, is it any wonder that he said those exact words?

In the dark hours of the morning, Paul and Silas, still suffering from the beatings of the previous day, took the opportunity to preach the gospel to their jailor. Two manuscripts of later origin record the name of the jailor as Stephanas.[114]

"And he [the jailor] took them the same hour of the night, and washed their stripes [whip welts]; and was baptized, he and all his [family], straightway. And when he had brought them [Paul and Silas, up[115]] into his house [family home], he set meat [on a table] before them, and rejoiced, believing in God with all his house [family]" (Acts 16:33–34).

Luke, being a physician, made mention of the medical assistance ministered to them by the jailor and his family. It would appear that during this time, a certain amount of gospel teaching was delivered by our missionary pair, following the dressing of the wounds.

They departed into the night to perform the baptismal ordinance for this family. "A local tradition identifies a Roman cistern as the place where Saint Paul was imprisoned. The cistern is immediately east of what is known as Basilica A, north of the modern road that cuts through the ruins of Philippi. This 'jail' was divided into two rooms, the outer and the inner prison."[116]

Upon returning to the jailor's home, they partook of some food and most likely slept well into the morning.

Paulus et Silvanus—Civis Romanus Sum! (Acts 16:35–40 • Spring AD 52)

"And when it was day, the magistrates [praetors] sent the serjeants [lictors], saying, Let those men go. And the keeper of the prison told this saying to Paul, The magistrates [praetors] have sent to let you go: now therefore depart, and go in peace. But Paul said unto them, They have beaten us openly [publicly] uncondemned [without trial], being Romans [Roman citizens, literally in Latin *civis romanus sum*], and have cast us into prison; and now they do thrust us out privily [secretly]? nay verily; but let them come themselves and fetch us out" (Acts 16:35–37). Publicly they were condemned and publicly Paul demanded to be exonerated.

To say that the officials were taken aback with shock would be an understatement. To have declared themselves as being in possession of Roman citizenship must have struck the lictors and praetors with terror. Should Paul and Silas bring the circumstances of their imprisonment to the attention of the consul in Thessalonica, the respective officials would have experienced disciplinary measures.

The praetors violated two Roman laws in flogging Paul and Silas, the *Lex Valeria* of 508 BC and the *Lex Porcia* of 300 BC.[117]

Returning to report to the praetors of the city, "the serjeants [lictors] told these words unto the magistrates [praetors]: and they feared, when they heard that they were Romans [Roman citizens]. And they [the praetors] came and besought them, and brought them out, and desired them to depart out of the city" (Acts 16:38–39).

Humiliated by this, the praetors arrived and apologized, while also entreating them to leave. "And they went out of the prison, and entered into the house of Lydia: and when they had seen the brethren [Luke and Timothy], they comforted them, and departed" (Acts 16:40).

It is most likely that Luke and Timothy were residing under the hospitality of Lydia and her household, waiting until they heard word of Paul and Silas. The faith-provoking prayers of Luke and Timothy, combined with Lydia and her family, may have contributed to God intervening with the earthquake and opening of the doors.

Then, as though nothing out of the ordinary had occurred, Paul and Silas turned up, just as Peter had done in arriving under strange circumstances in Jerusalem at the home of Mary, John Mark's mother (see Acts 12:12). Luke the physician surely sought to tend to their wounds from the beatings of the previous day, only to find they had been treated by the jailor's family in the night.

Deciding to leave Luke behind, Paul then set off in company with Silas and Timothy. They travel west along the Via Egnatia to Thessalonica.

Thessalonica (Acts 17:14 • Early Summer AD 52)

"Now when they had passed through Amphipolis and Apollonia, they came to Thessalonica, where was a synagogue of the Jews: And Paul, as his manner was, went in unto them, and three sabbath days [three weeks] reasoned [discussed] with them out of the scriptures, opening and alleging, that [the] Christ must needs have suffered [experienced pain], and risen again from the dead; and that this Jesus, whom I preach unto you, is Christ" (Acts 17:1–3). He *reasoned* from the holy scriptures or, as the Jerusalem Bible translates it, "He developed his arguments from the [holy] scripture."

The "opening and alleging" refers to opening or expounding the scriptures to their understanding. *Alleging*, in this context, means "presenting evidence and facts." "And some of them believed, and consorted [associated] with Paul and Silas; and of the devout [and of the God-fearing] Greeks a great multitude, and of the chief women not a few" (Acts 17:4).

It may have been while among these individuals that Paul related the shameful manner in which they were treated in Philippi (1 Thessalonians 2:2). Of the Gentile proselytes, we are informed that they were a "great multitude." But to Thessalonica goes another status. The gospel attracted a sizeable proportion "of the chief women," or those of the influential and ruling class. But this acceptance of the gospel message in such proportions inevitably brings with it an equally forceful opposition.

8: The Second Mission Tour (II)

Financial Assistance from Philippi (Philippians 4:15–18; 2 Thessalonians 3:7–10 • Summer AD 52)

During the stay of Paul, Silas, and Timothy in Thessalonica, financial aid came to them from Philippi, not just once but twice (Philippians 4:15–18). In addition to this financial assistance, they also labored for their support, as Paul declared later in an Epistle: "For yourselves [the Thessalonians] know how ye ought to follow us: for we behaved not ourselves disorderly among you; neither did we eat any man's bread for naught; but wrought with labor and travail night and day, that we might not be chargeable to any of you: not because we have not power, but to make ourselves an ensample unto you to follow us. For even when we were with you, this we commanded you, that if any would not work, neither should he eat" (2 Thessalonians 3:7–10).

Paul endeavors to consistently practice what he preaches, one being to "work with your own hands" (1 Thessalonians 4:11). The obvious conclusion is that he took to his trade of tentmaking—as he would later in Corinth (Acts 18:1).

Assault on the House of Jason (Acts 17:59 • Summer AD 52)

But the Jews which believed not, moved with envy, took unto them certain lewd [depraved] fellows of the baser sort [rabble], and gathered a company [mob], and set all the city in an uproar, and assaulted the house of Jason, and sought to bring them [Paul and Silas] out to the people [public assembly].

And when they found them not, they drew Jason,[118] and certain brethren unto the rulers [magistrates] of the city, crying, These [are the men] that have turned the world upside down are come hither also;

Whom Jason hath received: and these all do contrary to the decrees of Caesar [that Jews should not proselyte Romans], saying that there is another king [than Caesar], one Jesus.

And they troubled the people and the rulers [authorities, Greek *politarchés*] of the city, when they heard these things.

And when they had taken security [bail] of Jason, and of the other, they let them go. (Acts 17:5–9)

Once again, we hear the rebel Jews declare that they had no king but Caesar (John 19:15). And if they were to let the Christian men go, then they were not Caesar's friends (John 19:12). Jason would answer that the kingdom of which we preach is not of this world (John 18:36). How the city authorities (*politarchés*) responded to the charges suggested when they observed and understood well the trumped-up charges for what they were. The record says that all they did was to release Jason[119] and the others on bail, binding them to keep the peace.

Thessalonica to Berea (Acts 17:10–15 • Summer AD 52)

Upon learning of the measures taken against Jason and the others, "the brethren immediately sent away Paul and Silas by night unto Berea: who coming thither went into the synagogue of the Jews" (Acts 17:10). This journey would have started on the Via Egnatia leaving Thessalonica, but halfway into the journey they would have had to leave the highway and travel south toward their destination.

So it was that they came to Berea and commenced sharing the gospel message, as always starting in the local synagogue. What of the citizens of Berea? "These were [of] more noble [character] than those in Thessalonica, in that they received the word with all readiness of mind, and searched the scriptures daily, whether those things were so" (Acts 17:11).

What was the result of such open-mindedness? "Therefore many of them believed; also of honorable women which were Greeks, and of men, not a few" (Acts 17:12). The Church was organized and a leader was called. "The Greek Orthodox Calendar of Saints, the Synaxar, refers to Karpus, one of the Seventy Disciples, as being the first bishop of this city."[120]

"But when the Jews of Thessalonica had knowledge that the word of God was preached of Paul at Berea, they came thither also, and stirred up the people" (Acts 17:13). While in Berea, Paul came into contact with Sopater, the son of Pyrrhus (Acts 20:4), who was probably instrumental in getting Paul out safely to Athens when circumstances became dangerous for him in Berea.

So it was with persecution following that "then immediately the brethren sent away Paul to go as it were to the sea: but Silas and Timotheus abode there still. And they that conducted Paul brought him unto Athens" (Acts 17:14–15).[121] The text reads that they "sent away Paul to go as it were to the sea." We read from this expression that it was not the intention that Paul should go by sea at all. Once at the coast, the decision was then made to proceed to Athens. Arriving at Athens, they deposited Paul there, "and receiving a commandment [of Paul] unto Silas and Timotheus for to come to him with all speed, they departed" (Acts 17:15) and returned to Berea.

Athens (Acts 17:15 • Early Autumn AD 52)

The Roman Petronius satirically wrote of the Athenians "that it was easier to find a god at Athens than a man" because of the number of altars and temples. "It is more prudent to speak well of all gods, especially at Athens, where altars are erected even to unknown gods. At Athens during a plague Epimendies let loose at the Areopagus black and white sheep, and commanded the Athenians to sacrifice to the proper god, wherever the sheep lay down. Often the proper god could not be clearly ascertained, and so an altar was raised to an 'unknown god.'"[122]

The Greek traveler Pausanias wrote, "Among the things in the market at Athens not well known to everyone is the Alter of Pity. The Athenians are the only Greeks who pay honors to this very important god in human life and human reverses. It is not only that love of the human race is in their institutions, but they worship gods more than other people; they have altars of Shame and Rumor and Impulse."[123]

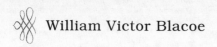

Athenian Philosophers (Acts 17:16–18 • Autumn AD 52)

Paul was alone in Athens without friends. We therefore concluded that the Berean Saints added to his support to enable him to survive in the Athenian metropolis. "Now while Paul waited for them [Silas and Timothy] at Athens, his spirit was stirred in him, when he saw the city wholly given to idolatry. Therefore disputed [reasoned] he in the synagogue with the Jews, and with the devout persons, and in the market [agora] daily with them that met with him" (Acts 17:16–17). Here, we learn that this congregation of Jews also contained "devout persons," or Gentile proselytes. In a city of such pagan idolatry, Paul specifically noted the devotion of the few to God in contrast to the misplaced devotions of the many to paganism.

Athens was unique in that it had two marketplaces instead of one like most cities: the old Greek agora market square, and the new Roman forum market square since the time of Augustus. The two market squares were linked by a wide street with shops on either side.[124]

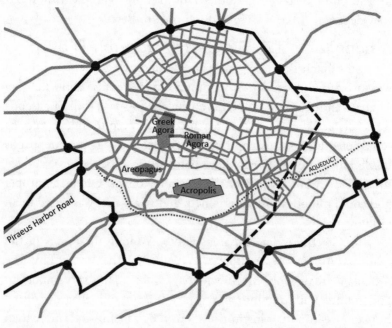

Map of Athens

"Then certain philosophers of the Epicureans, and of the Stoics, encountered him [Paul]" (Acts 17:18). One author noted that Luke mentions in his commentary the philosophical schools of the Epicureans and the Stoics, but made no mention of the Academics or the Peripatetics. Luke "wanted to show that he was fully aware which schools of thought had most influence at this time."[125]

These Epicureans and Stoics encountered Paul, "And some said, what will this babbler say?" (Acts 17:18). While many considered Paul a "babbler," others said, "He seemeth to be a setter forth of strange gods: because he preacheth unto them Jesus, and the resurrection" (Acts 17:18).

The reference to *babbler* has a particular story to its origin. The Greek word *spermológos* is a straightforward insult. The meaning of this insult is particular to Athens. For centuries, the Greek market square attracted the philosophers, teachers, politicians, and gossips of the city and country. The Greek stoa—a shopping mall—was the natural place to congregate for verbal exchange. The Greek agora of Athens had several stoas: on the east side was the main Stoa of Attalus (159–138 BC), on the west the Stoa of Zeus Eleutherios (430 BC), on the north the Stoa Basileios (circa 600–500 BC), and to the south were two stoas, first the Middle Stoa (circa 300 BC) and the second running parallel behind it called the South Stoa (circa 300 BC).

A stoa is a long building (*portico*) with columns supporting a roof; at least the long side facing the agora was open to view with cubicle shops forming the rear wall, as with the Stoa of Attalus. The rear could be a solid wall, like the South Stoa, or open on all sides, like the Middle Stoa. The sale of market produce in ancient times was in an open market with each item weighed and counted out with the customer bartering over quantity, quality, and price.

It was expected that some kernels of grain would fall on the ground, either from the counter of those selling or from the shopping basket of the customer. The birds that gathered to the agora waited for their opportunity from the roof of a stoa to fly down and pick up the seeds that became scattered on the market plaza below, and then return to the roof to digest their good fortune. Such an action is termed in Greek *spermológos*, which means "seed picker" in English.

We need this background to comprehend the following: Apparently it was often the case that someone would learn concepts from the philosophical debate of a teacher under one stoa and later, while engaged in debate with another, pass off such concepts in conversation as being a thought development of their own. The term we use today is *plagiarism*, and the individual is a plagiarist. The Athenians called such an individual a *spermológos*, meaning a "seed picker," implying they picked up these gems of thought from others in the same manner as the birds picked up the seeds that fell on the floor of the agora.

The reference to "strange gods" implies that Jesus Christ was not the only God that was strange to the Athenian philosophers. The "other" god may have come from a misinterpretation of the word *resurrection*. In classic Greek, Paul would have used the word *anastasis* (ἀνάστασις), from which we get the English word *anesthetic*. It may be that the audience just misunderstood and heard the male name *Anastasios* (Αναστασίος) or the female name *Anastasia* (Αναστασία) and took this to be the name for a second god or goddess.

An alteration to the sentence of Luke can highlight the possible misunderstanding: "He seemeth to be a setter forth of strange gods"—the statement, followed by the explanation—"because he preacheth unto them Jesus, and *anastasis*"—with misunderstanding.

Hill of Mars [Ares] (Acts 17:19–21 • Autumn AD 52)

"And they took him, and brought him unto Areopagus [the Hill of Ares, or Mars], saying, May we know what this new doctrine, whereof thou speakest, is? For thou bringest certain strange things to our ears: we would know therefore what these things mean" (Acts 17:19–20).

History says that philosophy was the ultimate pursuit and pastime of the Athenian intelligentsia. Luke wrote, "For all the Athenians and strangers which were there spent their time in nothing else, but either to tell, or to hear some new thing" (Acts 17:21). With the knowledge that Luke had, we might presume that during that summer, Paul wrote to Luke in Philippi with details of what was happening at Athens.

The Hill of Mars at Athens (Coneybeare & Howson, *The Life and Epistles of St. Paul*, v.1. New York: Charles Scribner; Sons, 376.)

> It is clear that Paul appeared to the philosophers as one of the many ambitious teachers who came to Athens hoping to find fame and fortune at the great center of education. Now, certain powers were vested in the Council of Areopagus to appoint or invite lecturers at Athens, and to exercise some general control over the lecturers in the interests of public order and morality. . . . There certainly also existed much freedom for foreigners to become lecturers in Athens, for the great majority of the Athenian professors and lecturers were foreign. The scene described in [Acts 17] verses 18–34 seems to prove that the recognized lecturers could take a strange lecturer before the Areopagus, and require him to give an account of his teaching and pass a test as to its character.[126]

The Athenian Unknown God (Acts 17:22–34; 1 Corinthians 1:20–25 • Autumn AD 52)

"Then Paul stood in the midst of Mars' Hill, and said, Ye men of Athens, I perceive that in all things ye are too superstitious [scrupulous]. For as I passed by, and beheld your devotions [venerated objects], I found an altar with this inscription, *To The Unknown God*.[127] Whom therefore ye ignorantly worship [without knowing], him declare I unto you" (Acts 17:22–23). Paul had changed his name from the Hebrew *Saul* to the Greek *Paul* so his Gentile audience would find him more agreeable. Now, as he arrived at their chambers to engage in a philosophical debate, he put himself on common ground by choosing to consider Jesus Christ and the gospel plan not as being something new or modern, but instead to profess Christ to be the God to whom the altar "to an unknown god" was dedicated. In other words, to forward the notion that what he preached was nothing more or less than the doctrine concerning their own god to whom they had built an altar with a misleading inscription.

Altars to the Unknown Gods
Left: a Greek altar at Pergamum: *To unknown gods, Capito, Torch-bearer.*
Right: a Latin altar at Rome (100 BC): *Sacred to a god or goddess* (*Seo deo sei deivae sac[rum]*).

His discourse before these doctors of philosophy and debate went thus:

> God that made the world and all things therein, seeing that he is Lord of heaven and earth [possibly quoting Isaiah 42:5], dwelleth not in temples made with hands;
>
> Neither is worshiped with men's hands, as though he needed any thing, seeing he giveth to all life, and breath, and all things;

And hath made of one blood[128] all nations of men for to dwell on all the face of all the earth, and hath determined the times before appointed, and the bounds of their habitation;

That they should seek the Lord, if they are willing to find him, for he is not far from every one of us:

For in him we live, and move, and have our being; as certain also of your own [Greek] poets have said, For we are also his offspring.

Forasmuch then as we are the offspring of God, we ought not to think that the [divine nature] Godhead is like unto gold, or silver, or stone, graven by art and man's device [quoting Song of Solomon 13:10].

And the times of this ignorance God[129] winked at [overlooked]; but now commandeth all men every where to repent:

Because he hath appointed a day, in the which he will judge the world in righteousness [possibly quoting Psalm 9:8] by that man [the Son] whom he [the Father] hath ordained [appointed by decree]; whereof he [the Father] hath given assurance [trustworthy witness] unto all men, in that he [the Father] hath raised [restored] him [the Son] from the dead. (Acts 17:24–31; JSIV Acts 17:27)

When Paul said, "For in him we live, and move, and have our being; as certain also of your own poets have said, for we are also God's offspring," he was combining quotations from two Greek poet philosophers. The first part of the verse comes from *The Hymn to Zeus* by his sons Minos and Rhadamanthus, written by Epimenides (circa 7–6 century BC) of Knossos, Crete. The charge that the Cretians were liars was because they lied when asked the whereabouts of the tomb of Zeus. They would show you his tomb in Crete. Alas, Zeus, as a god, was not dead. Therefore, the Cretians would show you an empty grave:

They fashioned a tomb for thee,
O holy and high—
The Cretians, always liars,
Evil beasts, slow bellies!
But thou art not dead;
Thou art risen and alive forever,
For in thee we live and move and have our being.[130]

The latter portion is quoted from the work "Phaenomena 5," a work by Aratus of Soli (315–240 BC), Cilicia. Similar words are in the writings of Cleanthes (330–230 BC) of Assos. These men were noted Stoic philosophers:

> Thou who amid the Immortals
> Art throned the highest in glory,
> Giver and Lord of life,
> Who by law disposest of all things,
> Known by many a name,
> Yet One Almighty for ever,
> Hail, Zeus!
> For to Thee should each mortal voice be uplifted:
> *Offspring are we too of thine,*
> We and all that is mortal around us.[131]

To say that Paul had made a study of Stoic philosophy and the works of Aratus, Epimenides, or Cleanthes is to assume too much. We must not forget that for several years, Paul had been proselyting among the Greeks, of whom, no doubt, there were several well versed in Stoic philosophy. Paul remembered a selection of Stoic maxims in general use, of which his quote on Mars Hill may very likely have been one. Also, during his rabbinical studies while he was in Jerusalem, he would have studied some of the more common passages of the Greek poets. "Paul was influenced not only by the religion of his fathers, but also by the religious movements of the Hellenistic world of his day . . . both Hellenism and Judaism were his tutors unto Christ."[132]

Apart from a few quoted words of Stoic philosophy, let us not overlook the quality and content of the discourse. Just as certain churches of today have the practice of praying before statues of "gold, or silver, or stone, graven by art and man's device," his Greek audience was not much different. "We are the offspring of God," he tells them—and us today.

He then concluded by telling them of the resurrection and of Judgment Day. In some respects, Paul was preaching doctrine over their heads.

"And when they heard of the resurrection of the dead, some mocked: and others said, we will hear thee again of this matter. So Paul departed from among them" (Acts 17:32–33). There was division about his teachings. Luke said some "mocked," and this unique phrase literally meant "to throw out the lip." They were sneering or scoffing[133] in the sense of sarcastic response.[134] The closest word to the Greek *echleuazon* is the Italian *beffa*, from which the French word *befel*, and the English word *baffle* or *bafa* derive. This is an archaic word in English; the more modern word to use in this instance would be *lampoon*. The scoffing, as implied from the Greek word, means "to exhale by vibrating the lips together" in an expression of rejection.

Perhaps Paul was thinking of the Athenians when he later wrote, "Where is the wise? Where is the scribe? Where is the disputer of this world [age]? hath not God made foolish the wisdom of this world [age]? For after that in the wisdom of God the world by wisdom knew not God, it pleased God by the foolishness of preaching to save them that believe" (1 Corinthians 1:20–21).

Paul descended from the Hill of Mars, though not without achieving some success. "Howbeit certain men clave unto him, and believed: among the which [whom] was Dionysus the Areopagite[135] and a woman named Damaris, and others with them" (Acts 17:34). Of those whom Paul had taught, he remembered only two people—or to be more correct, Luke records the names of only these two people.

Arrival of Silas and Timothy (Acts 17:10–12, 15–16; 1 Thessalonians 3:56 • Autumn AD 52)

While in Athens, Paul waited for Silas and Timothy (Acts 17:15–16). This means that Timothy was sent back to Thessalonica to size up the affairs of the Church in that city (1 Thessalonians 3:5–6).

We infer this from a comment that was made by Paul in writing at the time. He deliberately stated that Timothy brought a report to "us" (1 Thessalonians 3:6) and not "me," that is, Paul and Silas. There is also no record of Paul sending for Silas to come from Berea; he is suddenly at Athens with Paul awaiting the arrival of Timothy.

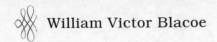

First Epistle to the Thessalonians
(1 Thessalonians • Autumn AD 52)

Timothy returned to Athens and his report prompted Paul to write an epistle of encouragement and direction back to the Thessalonians. This letter was written with greetings from "Paul, and Silvanus, and Timotheus" (1 Thessalonians 1:1). This is the earliest Epistle of Paul that we are aware of.

9: The Second Mission Tour (III)

Second Epistle to the Thessalonians (Autumn AD 52)

One distinctive item is to whom Paul's letters were addressed. The address of this Epistle is "unto the Church of the Thessalonians." While in contrast, the Epistles for the Corinthians were addressed "unto the Church of God which is at Corinth." The emphasis being that Paul began addressing his letters using possessive case—the Thessalonians owned the Church. Then he began addressing his letters, stating that the Church is God's and they belong to it. They were members of their congregation, but they were foremost members of the Church as a whole.

Athens to Corinth (Acts 18:1–6; Romans 16:5; 1 Corinthians 9:24–27; 2 Corinthians 11:7–10 • Winter AD 52–53)

"After these things Paul departed from Athens, and came to Corinth" (Acts 18:1). We must keep in mind that the majority of the inhabitants of the city of Corinth were Roman colonists, not Greeks, though they had adopted many of the Greek customs.

When Paul arrived at Corinth, he "found a certain Jew named Aquila, born in Pontus lately come from Italy, with his wife Priscilla; (because that Claudius had commanded all Jews to depart from Rome) and came unto them" (Acts 18:2). The reported expulsion of Jews from Rome is believed to have occurred in AD 49–50[136] at the decree of the emperor Claudius. The Roman historian Suetonius Tranquilus recorded that Claudius issued this expulsion order because the Jews caused continuous disturbances at the instigation of Chrestus.[137]

"And because he was of the same craft, he abode with them, and wrought: for by their occupation they were tentmakers" (Acts 18:3). We will read of Aquila and Priscilla in several Epistles (Romans 16:3; 1 Corinthians 16:19; 2 Timothy 4:19). Paul now took to his profession for temporal support. Since Aquila had established himself in the business of tentmaking, it would have been easy for Paul to work for him, thereby not having to try and sell the tents that he manufactured. One author considered that Paul took up tentmaking at this time as a therapeutic answer to a nervous problem. As he confessed later in his own writings, he was on the edge of a nervous breakdown: "When we were come into Macedonia, our flesh had no rest . . . without were fightings, within were fears" (2 Corinthians 7:5).

The Gentiles of Corinth, were quite the people. Paul had another new experience before him: the conversion and retention of a most difficult people, not Greek, but Roman in origin. As for culture, a potpourri of Greek philosophy amongst other things graced the Corinthians in all levels of society. Let us say that Achaia was the real Gentile experience for Paul. The Corinthian proselytes would cause more heartache in years to come.

Following his customary pattern, he would first go unto the Jews of this city. How often did Paul attract the displeasure of many a rabbi with his perpetual Christian rendering of the holy writ. Traditions can free or manacle; and the captive is not always ready or willing to be freed. By far the most monumental task in any endeavor is to change entrenched tradition.

"And he reasoned [dialogued] in the synagogue every sabbath, and persuaded the Jews and the Greeks. And when Silas and Timotheus were come from [Thessalonica in] Macedonia, Paul was pressed in the spirit, and testified to the Jews that Jesus was Christ. And when they opposed [systematically resisted][138] themselves, and blasphemed [insulted], he shook his raiment [see Acts 13:51; 1 Nephi 9:44; D&C 24:15; 60:13–15], and said unto them, Your blood be upon your own heads; I am clean: from henceforth I will go unto the Gentiles [in this city]" (Acts 18:4–6).

Paul Departs from the Synagogue
(Acts 18:7–11; 1 Corinthians 1:14, 16, 26–28;
2 Corinthians 12:17 • Early AD 52–53)

Having shaken the dust from the synagogue of the unbelieving, "he departed thence, and entered into a certain man's house, named [Titius] Justus, one that worshiped God [a proselyte], whose house joined hard [was next door] to the synagogue" (Acts 18:7). Some scholars assimilate this Titius Justus with Titus to whom Paul wrote his Epistle of that name. This would go well in explaining why Titus was the bearer of the two surviving Epistles of Paul to the Corinthians (2 Corinthians 12:17), since he was from Corinth.

"And Crispus, the chief ruler [*Archi-synagogos*] of the synagogue, believed on the Lord with all his house[hold]; and many of the Corinthians hearing believed, and were baptized" (Acts 18:8). Not forgetting Aquila, his wife Priscilla, and of course Epaenetus mentioned earlier.

Of this congregation Paul later wrote, in essence, *Brothers, think [recollect] of what you were when you were called. Not many of you were wise by human [worldly] standards; not many were influential; not many were of noble birth. But God chose [what is] the foolish things of [in] the world to shame the wise; God chose [what is] the weak things of [in] the world to shame the strong [powerful]. He [God] chose the lowly things of this [low and despised in the] world and the despised things—and the things that are not [counted as nothing]—[and used them] to nullify the things that are [what the world considers important]* (see 1 Corinthians 1:26–28).

"Then spake the Lord to Paul in the night by a vision, Be not afraid, but speak, and hold not thy peace: For I am with thee, and no man shall set on thee to hurt thee: for I have much people in this city. And he continued there a year and six months, teaching the word of God among them" (Acts 18:9–11; winter AD 51–spring 53). These verses indicate some initial success among the Corinthians. As to the limited success experienced by Paul, he said: "I baptized none of you, but [except] Crispus and Gaius . . . and I baptized also the household of Stephanas: besides, I know not whether I baptized any other" (1 Corinthians 1:14, 16). Perhaps since Paul limited his personal involvement to this selected few, Epaenetus was a member of the household of Stephanas.

Christian Congregation in the House of Justus (Acts 18:8 • Early AD 53)

A Christian congregation was established at the home of Titus Justus next door to the synagogue. Jewish services in the synagogue were on Saturday, and Christian services were next door on Sunday. "Crispus, the chief ruler [rabbi] of the synagogue, believed on the Lord with all his house[hold]; and many of the Corinthians hearing believed, and were baptized" (Acts 18:8). All of this enraged the more violent element of the Jewish community to civil disobedience. We say "more violent element" because we cannot believe that all Corinthian Jews were of the same malignant spirit.

Mural of Paul before Governor Gallio, Greek Orthodox Church, Corinth

Before Governor Gallio of Corinth (Acts 18:12–18; 1 Corinthians 2:15 • Spring AD 53)

"And when [Lucius Junius Annaeus Novatus] Gallio [son of Seneca the Elder] was the deputy [governor] of Achaia, the Jews made insurrection [rose up] with one accord against Paul, and brought him to the judgment seat, Saying, This fellow [person] persuadeth men to worship God contrary to the law" (Acts

18:12–13). The judgment seat as the tribunal, mentioned here is called the *Bema*.

Gallio, being well aware of the Jewish standing in the Empire, considered the whole matter to be too punitive in nature to require his intercession. Gallio would not judge Paul under Jewish law, and under Roman law he had committed no crime. So it was that the Jews declared their charge against Paul: "And when Paul was about to open his mouth, Gallio said unto the Jews, If it were a matter of wrong or wicked lewedness, O ye Jews, reason would that I should bear with you: But if it be a question of words and names, and of your law, look ye to it; for I will be no judge of such matters. And he drave [expelled] them from the judgment seat [tribunal]" (Acts 18:14–16).

The apathy of the deputy ensured the freedom of Paul. The natives reciprocated the action upon Rabbi Sosthenes, the successor to Crispus. "Then all the Greeks took Sosthenes, the chief ruler of the synagogue, and beat him before the judgment seat. And Gallio cared for none of those things" (Acts 18:17).

Writing the Corinthian Epistles later, Paul said of his time among them, "And I brethren, when I came to you, came I not with excellency [eloquence] of speech or of wisdom, declaring unto you the testimony of God. For I determined not to know anything [teach] among you, save Jesus Christ, and him crucified" (1 Corinthians 2:1–2). "And Paul after this tarried there yet a good while, and then took his leave of the brethren, and sailed thence into Syria, and with him Priscilla and Aquila; having shorn his head in Cenchrea, for he had a vow" (Acts 18:18). Aquila made the vow, not Paul.[139]

To Jerusalem via Ephesus (Acts 18:19–22 • Spring AD 54)

We are told that Priscilla and Aquila accompanied Paul on this journey. It would appear that they were moving their home to Ephesus, for when we hear of them again, it is in relation to Ephesus and no longer Corinth (Acts 18:26). We are not informed whether the initial decision to move to Ephesus was instigated by Aquila and Priscilla or by Paul. The most probable reason for Paul to want to reach Jerusalem at the time would be to be at Jerusalem for Passover and give their report to the Brethren.

The sea journey from Corinth to Ephesus meanders from one island to another in the chain of Cyclades (*Kykládes*) Islands across the Aegean Sea. Arriving at the Asian coast, the ship's passengers in all probability disembarked at the port of Panormus[140] and sailed in a small boat up the Cayster (*Kaystros*) River and Canal to the inner harbor of the provincial capital Ephesus.

"And he [Paul] came to Ephesus, and left them [Aquila and Priscilla] there: but he himself entered into the synagogue, and reasoned [dialogued] with the Jews" (Acts 18:19). Once again, following his ever-regular pattern, he preached on the Sabbath day in the synagogue.

But the reception here appears to have been somewhat different than that of other cities, for we read, "When they desired him to tarry longer time with them, he consented not; But bade farewell, saying, I must by all means keep this feast that cometh in Jerusalem: but I will return again unto you, if God will. And he sailed from Ephesus" (Acts 18:20–21). We may presume that the senior Brethren of the Church generally met annually at Jerusalem during the Passover holiday. Therefore, it was not so much the keeping of the Jewish Feast of Passover in Jerusalem that interested Paul, but rather being there for a meeting of the Quorum of the Twelve Apostles gathered together for conference, to report upon their labors and receive new assignments as directed by the President of the Church.

Paul then set sail from Ephesus for Caesarea across the east Mediterranean Sea. "And when he had landed at Caesarea, and gone up, and saluted the Church, he went down to Antioch [in Syria]" (Acts 18:22). Arriving in Jerusalem, he would have made report of his activities and progress in the spread of the gospel message. The annals of time have left us with only a record of the Apostle Luke.

10: The Third Mission Tour (I)

Tour of Galatia, Phrygia, and Asia (Acts 18:23; 2 Timothy 3:10–13 • Summer AD 54)

Following the Passover at Jerusalem, Paul returned once more to Antioch in Syria. "And after he had spent some time there, he departed, and went over all the country of Galatia and Phrygia in order, strengthening all the disciples" (Acts 18:23). The Saints needed much care if they were to survive the gathering opposition of Jewish resentment and Gentile ignorance.

Retracing his footsteps of the previous journey, he once again passed through the cities of Derbe, Lystra, Iconium, and then Antiochia. This was his last Galatian visit as far as we are aware (2 Timothy 3:10–13). He passed into the province of Asia and certainly visited the cities of Colossae, Laodicea, and Hierapolis as he headed west down the valleys to Ephesus. This may have been his first encounter with the household of Philemon, and also Epaphras, who hailed from Colossae.

Ephesus: the Conversion of Apollos (Acts 18:24–28 • Autumn AD 54)

Ephesus was the fifth largest city in the Roman Empire. It had a population of about 250,000 people.[141] The last time that he was in Ephesus, "they desired him to tarry longer time with them," but Luke recorded that "he consented not," but he did promise "I will return again unto you" (Acts 18:20–21).

He was now on the way to Ephesus, but before his arrival, Luke records a certain happening.

And a certain Jew named Apollos [or Apollonius], born at Alexandria, an eloquent man, and mighty in the [holy] scriptures, came to Ephesus.

This man was instructed in the way of the Lord; and being fervent in the spirit, he spake and taught diligently the things of the Lord, knowing only the baptism of John.

And he began to speak boldly in the synagogue: whom when Aquila and Priscilla had heard, they took him unto them, and expounded unto him the way of the Lord more perfectly.

And when he was disposed to pass into Achaia [in southern Greece], the brethren wrote, exhorting the disciples to receive him: who when he was come, helped them much which had believed through grace:

For he mightily convinced the Jews, and that publickly, shewing by the scriptures that Jesus was [is the] Christ. (Acts 18:24–28)

Unto What Were Ye Baptized? (Acts 19:17 • Autumn AD 54)

"And it came to pass, that, while Apollos was at Corinth, Paul having passed through the upper coasts came to Ephesus" (Acts 19:1).

Paul having passed through the upper coasts came to Ephesus: and finding certain disciples,

He said unto them, Have ye received the Holy Ghost since ye believed? And they said unto him, We have not so much as heard whether there be any Holy Ghost.

And he said unto them, Unto what were ye baptized? And they said, Unto John's baptism.

Then said Paul, John verily baptized with the baptism of repentance, saying unto the people, that they should believe on him which should come after him, that is, on Christ Jesus.

When they heard this, they were baptized in the name of the Lord Jesus.

And when Paul had laid his hands upon them, the Holy Ghost came upon them; and they spake with tongues, and prophesied.

And all the men were about twelve [not including women and children]. (Acts 19:1–7)

We are now looking at the Church as a proselyting entity for over twenty years (Acts 19:1–7).[142] The area Paul was covering had been exposed to the gospel influence for the major portion of that time. Therefore, it was by no means strange for Paul to encounter a community of people who were versed to some extent in the gospel doctrines.

The School of Tyrannus (Acts 19:8–10 • Autumn AD 54–Autumn AD 56)

Paul, in keeping with established procedure, "went into the synagogue and spake boldly for the space of three months, disputing [discoursing] and persuading the things concerning the kingdom of God. But when diverse were hardened, and believed not, but spake evil of that way before the multitude, he departed from them, and separated the disciples, disputing daily in the school of one Tyrannus [from the fifth hour to the tenth]" (Acts 19:8–9).[143] "From the Bezan text we know the hours of Paul's lectures. . . . Tyrannus finished his lectures at eleven in the morning, and after a half-hour pause, that is from 11:30 until 4:30, Paul had the use of the auditorium."[144]

This Tyrannus who had a school must have been a local philosopher. It would seem Paul rented these suitable facilities to teach his missionary discussions. "And this continued by the space of two years; so that all they which dwelt in Asia heard the word of the Lord Jesus, both Jews and Greeks" (Acts 19:10).

Was It Two or Three Corinthian Visits? (1 Corinthians 1:11; 2 Corinthians 8:10; 9:2; 12:14, 16–18; 13:12 • AD 55)

Because of another reference made by Paul in his Epistles, we need to interrupt Luke's account. In writing to the Corinthians from Philippi, which would be after his work was completed in Ephesus, he said, "Behold, the third time I am ready to come to you" (2 Corinthians 12:14). And again: "This is the third time I am coming to you. In the mouth of two or three witnesses shall every word [of truth] be established. I told you before, and foretell you, as if I were present, the second time; and being absent now I write to them which heretofore have sinned, and to all other, that, if I come again, I will not spare" (2 Corinthians 13:1–2).

In following the narrative of Luke, we are led to believe that Paul made two visits to Corinth, but here is Paul identifying this second recorded visit by Luke to be his third visit. To solve this difficulty, we must accept that during his two years of sojourn in the region of Ephesus, a flying visit was made to Corinth, in all probability by ship across the Aegean Sea. The necessity of this visit appears to have been brought about because of certain evils being rampant among those professing fellowship with the Saints. This reported state of affairs would appear to have been brought to Paul's attention by Titus and Lucas (Luke), who were the scribes of the second Corinthian Epistle.

For, in the Epistle itself, he reminded them of Titus having been in their presence: "Did I make a gain of you by any of them whom I sent unto you?" said Paul. "I desired Titus, and with him I sent a brother. Did Titus make a gain of you? walked we not in the same spirit? walked we not in the same steps?" (2 Corinthians 12:17–18).

During this visit, he says, "I caught you with guile" (2 Corinthians 12:16). From a small reference in 1 Corinthians, we read, "For it hath been declared unto me of [about] you, my brethren, by them which are of the house of Chloe, that there are contentions among you" (1 Corinthians 1:11).

Two other remarks that point to this visit appear in the third Epistle (2 Corinthians): the Saints—probably according to the testimony of Titus—had waned somewhat in their responsibility toward the poor. Paul, by implication, stated that he knew what they were like "a year ago" when they took better care of the poor (2 Corinthians 8:10).

Then a little later in the same Epistle, another remark indicates likewise: "For I know the forwardness [zeal] of your mind, for which I boast of you to them of Macedonia, that Achaia was ready a year ago; and your zeal hath provoked very many" (2 Corinthians 9:2). Here again reference is made to "a year ago." This Epistle was written from Philippi, and "a year ago" would have placed him in Ephesus; this would therefore seem to corroborate this veiled visit to Corinth from Ephesus.

Such remarks go together to help us comprehend the events and keep us in chronological order. Returning to Ephesus, Paul resumed his labors.

The Spirit of Healing (Acts 19:11–12 • circa AD 55)

Traveling as Paul primarily did on foot would mean that it would have been some time before he could have hoped to return to a certain city. This circumstance led to a spectacular occurrence. Luke records it in these words: "And God wrought special miracles by the hands of Paul: So that from his body were brought unto the sick handkerchiefs [facecloths] or aprons [linens], and the diseases departed from them, and the evil spirits went out of them" (Acts 19:11–12).

The Prophet Joseph Smith performed a similar healing by use of a handkerchief. On 22 July 1839, "a man, not a member of the Church, seeing the mighty miracles which were performed, begged the Prophet to go with him and heal two of his children who were very sick. The Prophet could not go, but said he would send some one to heal them. Taking from his pocket a silk handkerchief he handed it to Elder Wilford Woodruff and requested him to go and heal the children. He told Elder Woodruff to wipe the faces of the children with the handkerchief and they should be healed. This he did and they were healed."[145]

Seven Sons of Sceva (Acts 19:13–17 • circa AD 55)

We now come to a question of priesthood authority in respect to those who are *not* "called of God, as was Aaron" (Hebrews 5:4). The story was recorded by Luke thus:

> Then certain of the vagabond [itinerant] Jews, exorcists, took upon them to call over them which had evil spirits the name of the Lord Jesus, saying, We adjure you by Jesus whom Paul preacheth.
>
> And there were seven sons of one Sceva, a Jew, and chief of the priests [not of the rabbis], which did so.
>
> And the evil spirit answered and said, Jesus I know, and Paul I know; but who are ye?
>
> And the man in whom the evil spirit was leaped on them, and overcame them, and prevailed against them, so that they fled out of that house naked and wounded.
>
> And this was known to all the Jews and Greeks also dwelling at Ephesus; and fear fell on them all, and the name of the Lord Jesus was magnified. (Acts 19:13–17)

Curious Arts (Acts 19:18–20 • AD 56)

Following the incident with the false ministers, another event occurred: "And many that believed came, and confessed, and shewed their deeds" (Acts 19:18). Luke seems to record here that though many of the Ephesians embraced the gospel, they retained a devotion to their old ways. "Many of them also which [had] used curious arts brought their books together, and burned them before all men: and they counted the price of them, and found it fifty thousand pieces of silver [drachma]. So mighty grew the word of God and prevailed" (Acts 19:19–20).

> The worship of Diana and the practice of magic were closely connected together. . . . The mysterious symbols, called "Ephesian Letters," were engraved on the crown, the girdle, and the feet of the goddess. These Ephesian letters or monograms . . . when pronounced, they were regarded as a charm; and were directed to be used, especially by those who were in the power of evil spirits. When written, they were carried about as amulets. . . . The study of these symbols was an elaborate science: and books, both numerous and costly, were compiled by its professors.[146]

This understanding also throws light upon the actions of the sons of Sceva, in that they uttered the name of the Lord Jesus, possibly interpreting the words to be magical. "Many that believed [and were now Christians] came, and confessed, and shewed their deeds. Many of them also which used curious arts brought their books together, and burned them before all men: and they counted the price of them, and found it fifty thousand pieces of silver. So mightily grew the word of God and prevailed" (Acts 19:18–20).

How the minions of Satan must have anguished in heinous adjuration at the spectacle of "the curious arts" ascending in the flames. Their endeavors of many generations of ignoble inspiration consumed. How would they report this conquest of righteousness to their master, the devil? Evil amongst the Ephesians was unshackled by one more chain. This event, and several others, though they do not include Paul, are included here because they are the outcome of having Paul in the community. Others are included since they are recorded in the Acts of the Apostles by Luke, who probably put them in since they were related to him by Paul.

After These Things Were Ended (Acts 19:21–22; 1 Corinthians 16:10–11; 2 Corinthians 1:1 • AD 56)

"After these things were ended, Paul purposed in the spirit, when he had passed through Macedonia and Achaia, to go to Jerusalem, saying, After I have been there, I must also see Rome: So he sent into Macedonia two of them that ministered unto him, Timotheus and Erastus; but he himself stayed in Asia for a season" (Acts 19:21–22).

When last we heard of Timothy, he was with Silas in Corinth when Paul last went to Jerusalem by way of Ephesus. They must have come over to be with Paul during the two years that he was in Asia. In all probability, they came back with him when he made that quick visit to Corinth that we discussed earlier. Or they may have gone to Jerusalem and back with him to Ephesus.

We now have Timothy and Erastus departing for Macedonia and Achaia; and some time later when Paul wrote to the Corinthians, he said, "Now if Timotheus [and Erastus] come, see that he [they] may be with you without fear: for he worketh the work of the Lord, as I also do. Let no man therefore despise him [or Erastus]: but conduct him [them] forth in peace, that he [they] may come unto me: for I look for him [them] with the brethren" (1 Corinthians 16:10–11).

But for the moment, Timothy and Erastus were on their way to Philippi. We know Timothy did not go to Corinth as supposed by Paul, for when Paul arrives in Philippi, he found Timothy there and, of course, Luke. That Timothy was in Philippi we know from the epistle written by Paul while in that city (2 Corinthians 1:1).

Lost Corinthian Epistle (1 Corinthians 4:17; 5:9 • Late AD 56)

Timothy (or possibly another) may have brought word of the current state of affairs in Corinth and troubles such as keeping company with sexually immoral persons. Such information prompted the writing on an epistle of rebuke and chastisement.

The only reference to this epistle is made in 1 Corinthians 5:9. This means that what we designate the first Corinthian Epistle is in fact the second, and what we designate the second is in reality the third. He simply said, "I wrote unto you in an epistle not to company with fornicators: Yet not altogether with the fornicators of this world, or with the covetous, or extortioners, or with idolaters: for them must ye needs go out of this world" (1 Corinthians 5:9–10).

Further exhortation was given in respect to keeping the faith and supporting the leaders of the Church; this was again reiterated in our 1 Corinthians 4:8–16. Most likely, Timothy was sent with this letter to the Corinthians, as Paul says, "For this cause have I sent unto you Timotheus, who is my beloved son, and faithful in the Lord, who shall bring you into remembrance of my ways which be in Christ, as I teach every where in every church" (1 Corinthians 4:17).

> Paul himself had personal knowledge of the temper and feelings of the people. By the whisperings of the Spirit, he knew what should be said to them to reclaim them to the Gospel standard. Hence, he had written them an epistle directing among other things that they refrain from associating with fornicators (1 Corinthians 5:9). What else this epistle commanded, we can only speculate, but undoubtedly it summarized many basic Gospel doctrines and exhorted the Corinthian Saints to serve God and keep his commandments.
>
> Upon receipt of this epistle, the contentious souls in the Corinthian congregation wrote a reply, taking issue with some of the doctrines of the apostles and asking detailed questions about teachings. Thereupon, with vigor and true apostolic zeal, Paul wrote a second epistle, canonized and known as First Corinthians, which answered the points raised by the detractors and further amplified the teachings of the original letter.[147]

Forty years after the writing of this epistle, Saint Clement wrote an epistle to the Corinthians with rebuke:

> But when good repute and rising numbers were granted to you in full measure, the saying of Scripture came to pass: my beloved did eat and drink, he grew and waxed fat and kicked. Envy and jealousy sprang up, strife and dissension, aggression and rioting, scuffles and kidnappings. Men of the baser sort rose up against their betters: the rabble against the respectable, folly against wisdom, youth against its elders. And now all righteousness and peace among you is at an end. Everywhere men are renouncing the fear of God; the eye of faith has grown dim, and instead of

following the commandments, and living as becomes a citizen of Christ, each one walks after the desires of his own wicked heart. All have fallen back into the horrid sin of Envy—the sin that brought death into the World.[148]

11: The Third Mission Tour (II)

First Epistle to the Corinthians (March–April AD 57)

While here in Ephesus, Paul dispatched a second Epistle to the Corinthians, known to us as the First Corinthian Epistle (March–April AD 57[149]). We must remember that the Corinthian Saints were already in the grips of apostasy and strife; Paul had just recently visited them and intended to do so again in a few months. The address of the Epistle was from Paul and Sosthenes. As this was a Corinthian Epistle, we can presume that this Sosthenes was the same one who had been the chief of the synagogue in Corinth and had now become a missionary of the gospel (1 Corinthians 1:1; Acts 18:17).

The state of affairs in Corinth had apparently led certain of the spiritually mature among them to seek the intercession of Paul. These brethren are acknowledged in this return Epistle with the following words: "I am glad of the coming of Stephanas and Fortunatus and Achaicus: for that which was lacking on your part they have supplied. For they have refreshed my spirit and yours: therefore acknowledge ye them that are such" (1 Corinthians 16:17–18).

A Decree of the Ephesians

Before we continue with what happened in Ephesus, let us read a decree that was previously published in the city to the honor of the Jewish inhabitants:

The decree of the Ephesians: When Menophilus was prytanis on the first day of the month Artemisius, this decree was made by the people: Nicanor, the son of Euphemus, pronounced it, upon the pronouncement of the praetors. Since the Jews that dwell in this city have petitioned Marcus Julius Pompeius, the son of Brutus, the proconsul, that they might be allowed to observe their Sabbaths and to act in all things according to the customs of their forefathers, without impediment from anybody, the praetor hath granted their petition. Accordingly, it was decreed by the senate and people, that in this affair that concerned the Romans, no one of them should be hindered from keeping the Sabbath day, nor be fined for so doing; but that they may be allowed to do all things according to their own laws.[150]

By the wording of this edict, we may conclude that the Jewish community was being victimized for its religious observance. The publication of this decree would have removed the outward animosity of the Greeks upon the Jews resident in their community. But, as we shall soon observe, the Greek inhabitants were yet contentious toward their Jewish neighbors.

Artemis (Diana) of the Ephesians (May AD 57)

Now we return to the narrative of events and happenings as Paul remained in Ephesus and continued his proselyting success in the country. Ephesus contained one of the seven wonders of the ancient world: the temple of the goddess Diana. "The Greeks had a saying, 'The Sun sees nothing finer in his course than Diana's temple.'"[151]

> The Ephesians called her Artemis and regarded her as the source of the fruitful and nurturing powers of nature, and so the image in the temple (said to have fallen from heaven) represented her with many breasts. The lower part of the figure was swathed like a mummy. The silversmiths at Ephesus did a large trade in silver "shrines for (or of) Diana." These were probably representations of the goddess seated in a niche or under a canopy. A good many works of art of this kind in marble and terra-cotta have been discovered at Ephesus. They were either placed in the temple or taken home by the worshipers.[152]

The statue itself was made of wood, with a bar of metal inserted into each hand. There were several mysterious signs carved on the figure, which were of priestly interpretation. There was a large contingent of slave priestesses (*melissae*) who, as was usual with heathen temples, were consecrated to the prostitution service of the goddess. The temple of Diana was presided over by a contingent of eunuch priests who were called *megabyzi* (or *megabysos*[153]). Having sex at the Artmesion temple was a form of love worship to the goddess. This should not be confused with the chastity of the Vestal virgins at the temple of Vesta at Rome, where having sex was considered to be a desecration of the temple and the Vestal virgin.

An archeological expedition conducted late in the nineteenth century discovered the temple of Artemis (Diana)[155] by excavating under an average of almost eight meters of soil. Large columns adorned with sculptures and slabs of white marble were all that remained of this wonder of the ancient world.[156] The temple was first designed by Theodorus of Samos. His work was then enlarged upon by Chersiphon of Cnossus and his son Metagnes. The completion of the edifice

An Ephesian "bee" coin that represents the *Megabyzi* priests of the temple of Diana

was done by Demetrius and Paeonius.[157] Alexander the Great had been responsible for completing it in such splendor that, in olden times, the temple was admired and labeled as one of the Seven Wonders of the World.

Enormous cohorts of slaves were needed for the manual labor of cleaning the temple.[158] And to understand how things degraded further, this temple and a wide area precinct around it were given the right of asylum. This asylum (or sanctuary) covered all crimes, so those who could reach this precinct were protected from prosecution. Because of this, a hoard of uncommendable degenerates swarmed around what was supposed to be a sacred edifice but was in fact a concourse of reprehensibility.[159]

Many citizens were critical of the criminals who took refuge in the temple precincts, and in AD 22 they made petition to Emperor Tiberius to have the refuge status of the temple of Artemis rescinded, but their representations were denied.[160]

Temple of Diana at Ephesus
(Johann Bernhard Fischer von Erlach, *Entwurfeiner Historischen Architektur*, 1721).

The structure was originally 129.5 meters in length and 67 meters wide. There were 127 columns 18 meters tall, and 36 of the columns were enriched with ornament and color. The woodwork of the interior was from cypress and cedar trees.[161]

The temple was the central bank of Asia Minor,[162] and the *megabysos* functioned as the directors of the bank, receiving and lending deposits.[163]

At the turn of the last century, a hoard of ivory, gold, silver, and bronze images of the goddess were discovered.[164] The goddess Diana, or Artemis, in Greek mythology was said to be a daughter of Zeus and a sister of Apollo.[165] It might also be of interest to know that the worship of Artemis was one of the oldest cults on the island of Thasos.[166]

But times have changed. "Today it is merely a great rectangular swamp, littered with broken columns,"[167] two-and-a-half kilometers distance from Ephesus.

Demetrius the Silversmith (Acts 19:23–28 • May AD 57)
Every four years, in the month of May, the city celebrated the honor of their goddess. Crowds were attracted from far and wide to the many festivities.

And the same time there arose no small stir about that way.

For a certain man named Demetrius, a silversmith, which made silver shrines [statues] for Diana, brought no small gain unto the craftsmen;

Whom he called together with the workmen of like occupation, and said, Sirs, ye know that by this craft we have our wealth.

Moreover ye see and hear, that not alone at Ephesus, but almost throughout all Asia, this Paul hath persuaded and turned away much people, saying that they be no gods, which are made with hands:

So that not only this our craft is in danger to be set at naught; but also the temple of the great goddess Diana should be despised, and her magnificence should be destroyed, whom all Asia and the world worshippeth.

And when they heard these sayings, they were full of wrath, and cried out, saying, *Great is Diana of the Ephesians.* (Acts 19:23–28; emphasis added)

A Riot Develops (Acts 19:29–20:1a • May AD 57)

During the Diana ceremonial games and religious festivities each May,[168] unusually large crowds flocked to Ephesus. With so many inhabitants of Asia Minor joining the Church, it is obvious they must have been coming from the prevailing religious affiliations. Ephesian merchants had a great business selling trinkets of Diana worship. With many of these worshipers embracing the gospel, the market for Diana statues was shrinking. Is it any wonder that a pretense could be found to enrage the silversmiths?

The silversmith Demetrius incited his guild of silversmiths to take action against the Christians. "And the whole city was filled with confusion; and having caught Gaius and Aristarchus, men of Macedonia, Paul's companions in travel, they rushed with one accord into the theatre. And when Paul would have entered in unto the people, the disciples suffered him not. And certain of the chief of Asia, which were his friends, sent unto him, desiring that he would not adventure himself into the theatre" (Acts 19:29–31). No doubt Paul wished to exchange places with Gaius and Aristarchus, but he was advised by the brethren and his friends in the aristocracy to keep clear of it. So while Paul was a deeply perturbed onlooker, in the city theater trouble was brewing. All were in commotion.

> Some therefore cried one thing, and some another: for the assembly was confused; and the more part knew not wherefore they were come together.
>
> And they drew Alexander out of the multitude, the Jews putting him forward. And Alexander beckoned with his hand, and would have made his defense unto the people.
>
> But when they knew that he was a Jew, all with one voice about the space of two hours cried out, Great is Diana of the Ephesians. (Acts 19:32–34)[169]

For Alexander, Gaius, and Aristarchus, it must have been quite the frightening experience to be in the midst of such a tumultuous gathering, hearing in perpetual chant, "Great Artemis of Ephesians" (*Mégalé é Artemis Éphésiós*). The amphitheater at Ephesus was built into a hillside, with stone terraced benches providing a seating capacity for 25,000 people. It was in the regular Greek pattern, semi-circular in shape with a stage at the fulcrum. As these devotees of Artemis (Diana) exclaimed the glory of their idol, we may presume that the only reason that they were able to maintain such stamina is that such a repetitious outpouring was considered by them to be a form of devotion, a prayer of homage.

Paul and the other brethren no doubt heard the tumultuous noise resounding across the city from the open amphitheater. The city authorities, or supervisors of the games and ceremonies, were sought to intervene.

The town clerk or city magistrate came to the theater to put an end to the disturbance. The town clerk must have been authoritatively charismatic.[170] The town clerk held control over the treasury deposited in the temple of Diana, being the supervisor of anything that would be organized in connection with the festival in honor of the goddess.

Ephesus Amphitheater (*The American Encyclopedia*. New York: D. Appleton Co., New York, 678).

Entering the amphitheater, the town clerk signaled to the mob to be quiet:

> And when the town clerk had appeased the people, he said, Ye men of Ephesus, what man is there that knoweth not how that the city of the Ephesians is a worshipper [custorian] of the great goddess Diana, and of the image which fell down from Jupiter [Zeus]?
>
> Seeing then that these things cannot be spoken against, ye ought to be quiet, and to do nothing rashly.
>
> For ye have brought hither these men, which are neither robbers of churches [temple despoilers], nor yet blasphemers of your goddess.
>
> Wherefore if Demetrius, and the craftsmen which are with him, have a matter against any man, the law is open [court is in session], and there are deputies [magistrates]: let them implead one another [bring charges against].
>
> But if ye inquire anything concerning other matters, it shall be determined in a lawful assembly.
>
> For we are in danger to be called in question for this day's uproar, there being no cause whereby we may give an account of this concourse.
>
> And when he had thus spoken, he dismissed the assembly. (Acts 19:35–41)

There was a challenge given by the town clerk in verse 38: *Go to your homes. Return to your work. Break it up, it's over!* The crowds did depart. Two hours of perpetual chant had worn them down sufficiently, so they became receptive. "And after the uproar was ceased,

Paul called unto him the disciples, and embraced them" (Acts 20:1). The Director of the Ephesus Museum Selahattin Erdemgíl once said, "Actually, the screams of 'Great is Artemis Ephesia' was the last breath of the seven-thousand-year-old mother goddess."[171]

Was Paul Imprisoned at Ephesus? (1 Corinthians 4:9–13)

Many scholars believe that Paul was imprisoned at Ephesus during this visit. He wrote, "I think that God hath set forth us the apostles last, as it were appointed to death: for we are made a spectacle unto the world" (1 Corinthians 4:9).

On his forthcoming journey, he wrote, "We would not, brethren, have you ignorant of our trouble which came to us in Asia, that we were pressed out of measure, above strength, insomuch that we despaired even of life: but we had the sentence of death in ourselves" (2 Corinthians 1:8–9).

And lastly, another statement he wrote reads, "In stripes above measure, in prisons more frequent, in deaths oft" (2 Corinthians 11:23).

Ephesus to Macedonia (Acts 20:1b–4; 1 Corinthians 2:12–13 • Summer AD 57)

Then after all this commotion, Paul felt it best to leave Asia, in particular Ephesus. "And departed for to go into Macedonia. And when he had gone over those parts, and had given them much exhortation, he came into Greece, And there abode three months" (Acts 20:1–3).

"And there accompanied him into Asia Sopater of Berea; and of the Thessalonians, Aristarchus and Secundus; and Gaius of Derbe, and Timotheus; and of Asia, Tychicus and Tromphimus" (Acts 20:4).

On the journey north, they docked at Alexandria-Troas. Paul soon wrote, "When I came to Troas to preach Christ's gospel, and a door was opened unto me of the Lord, I had no rest in my spirit, because I found not Titus my brother: but taking my leave of them, I went from thence into Macedonia" (2 Corinthians 2:12–13). Paul was concerned for Titus, whom he expected to find there waiting for him.

The Second Epistle to the Corinthians (Summer AD 57)

While in Philippi, Paul wrote—as far as we are aware of—the last Corinthian Epistle. It was his intention to be in Corinth before the winter arrived. The next time they heard from him was in person, which would have been a few months from then. The third Epistle to the Corinthian Saints in our New Testament is called Second Corinthians. The Epistle is not in keeping with the usual positive opening chapter; he speaks of "tribulation" (2 Corinthians 1:4), "sufferings" (2 Corinthians 1:5, 6, 7), and that he "despaired even of life" (2 Corinthians 1:8).

We presume that this letter was delivered by Titus, who remained there until the arrival of Paul and Luke after they completed their journey around the Aegean coast. Though he had a different spirit about him following his trial of spirit and body, he was nonetheless the same hard-working Saint he always had been and would always be known for.

12: The Third Mission Tour (III)

Via Egnatia through Illyricum (Acts 18:23; Romans 15:19 • Summer AD 57)

Leaving Philippi, Paul headed along a familiar road (Via Egnatia) passing through Amphipolis and Apollonia, until he arrived in Thessalonica. In this city were many proselytes, among them the chief women of the aristocracy. Others thought Paul to be merely the man who caused trouble before and had stolen away the greater portion of the population.

As to what occurred in Thessalonica, we know not. All the records are silent. We may presume that factions, as in Corinth, had not bedeviled this city as of yet. It is appropriate to insert at this point a comment made by Paul when writing to the Romans from Corinth a few months later (winter AD 57–58). He said that "from Jerusalem, and round about unto Illyricum, I have fully preached the gospel of Christ" (Romans 15:19).[172] Since the previous tour was recorded in sufficient detail so as to be not practical to insert this journey, it must therefore be taken that the reference to Illyricum was related to the present journey.

Illyricum is today, for the most part, Albania and Macedonia. During the second century, it was known to have a Christian community in the regions about the city of Salona, and also in the Macedonian city of Dyrrhachium. We can assume that his journey into Illyricum was made on the Roman highway Via Egnatia from Thessalonica, where instead of turning south to Berea, he carried on farther east, possibly visiting the town of Ottolobus or even going all the way to Dyrrhachium on the Adriatic coast.

Difficulty is experienced by some, in that there was so little said of this portion of the journey. The only reconciliation possible with this event is the description of Paul's journey from Antioch-on-the-Orontes to Ephesus—a much longer journey covering many lands, and passing through several branches of the Church. All that was said of that leg of his travels was he "went over all the country of Galatia and Phrygia in order, strengthening all the disciples" (Acts 18:23).

Illyricum to Corinth (Acts 20:23a; Romans 16:23; 1 Corinthians 16:12; 2 Corinthians 13:2 • Autumn AD 57)

For the place in question, all that the record says is: "And when he had gone over those parts, and had given them much exhortation, he came into Greece" (Acts 20:2). Did he return to Berea, where the people "were more noble than those in Thessalonica" (Acts 17:11)? Did Paul still find them searching "the [holy] scriptures daily" (Acts 17:11)? Would Paul have retraced his steps along the Via Egnatia to the Aegean coast, or did he travel south by the Adriatic coast—on land or on sea—to Nicopolis[173] near the historic site of the battle of Actium, then to Corinth?

There are unknown factors here, primarily to what extent Paul traversed the province of Illyricum. By one side of Greece or the other, he made his way south to the troubled city of Corinth. Once in Corinth, Paul took up residence, as he himself says, under the hospitality of "Gaius mine host" (Romans 16:23). Gaius was one of the few people in Corinth—Crispus being another—whom Paul personally baptized (1 Corinthians 1:14). Paul now paused for awhile "and abode there three months" (Acts 20:3a; winter of AD 57–58).

Winter in Corinth (Winter AD 57–58)

This pause in Corinth was certainly earned, considering the previous six months of intense missionary labor throughout Macedonia, Illyricum, and Achaia, and being sick nigh unto death. In reality, Paul was by no means rested, for there was much unrest and contention among the Saints. Much work was required to put things back in order.

Previously, Paul had requested a gathering of funds for Jerusalem, to be ready at his coming (1 Corinthians 16:1–2). But we are aware that Paul had some cleaning up to do here; the malignant spirit of apostasy needed to be cast out. Once again, Paul was "breathing out threatenings and slaughter" (Acts 9:1). He said when he reached Corinth that he would "not spare" (2 Corinthians 13:2).

While here in Corinth, he should have come into contact with several friends and enemies. What of Justus, whose home "joined hard to the synagogue"? Or Crispus, the "chief ruler of the synagogue" turned Christian? Was he "with all his house[hold]" still firm in the faith (Acts 18:8)? When previously in Corinth, the chief ruler of the synagogue, Crispus, became a proselyte to the Church whom Paul baptized (1 Corinthians 1:14). Sosthenes replaced him in the position (Acts 18:8, 17). It would now appear that in the intervening years, Sosthenes also embraced the gospel, for in writing to the Corinthians from Ephesus, Paul addressed his Epistle thus: "Paul, called to be an apostle of Jesus Christ through the will of God, and Sosthenes our brother, unto the church of God which is at Corinth" (1 Corinthians 1:1).

As to whether Sosthenes was in Corinth this visit, we do not know. But he was with Paul in Ephesus when writing this Epistle the previous year. Let us also consider not only Corinth, but also "all the saints which are in all Achaia" (2 Corinthians 1:1; 2 Corinthians 11:10), to whom Paul addressed the Second Corinthian Epistle. We may therefore assume that if Paul wrote to them, he also visited them during the months in which he used Corinth as a base of operations. Since no places were named, it would be difficult to conjecture.

The Epistle to the Galatians (Winter of AD 57–58)

All indications point to this Galatian Epistle having been written from Corinth, most likely soon after Paul's arrival there. It is assumed that the letter was directed to the branches he had established there with Barnabas on their first missionary tour. These would be: Pisidan-Antiochia, Iconium, Lystra, and Derbe—and possibly others we are not aware of.

The contents of the letter indicate that he received intelligence concerning a wave of apostasy that was then sweeping through the branches of the Church. It may well be that a messenger, possibly a local church leader, had come to Ephesus seeking Paul. But being advised that Paul had departed on a journey around the Aegean Sea with his final destination being Corinth, this bearer of sad tidings took ship directly for Corinth.

Since we believe that Paul had proselyted in Illyricum, his expected arrival in Corinth might have been delayed; such could possibly mean that this messenger was awaiting Paul's arrival, who, when he came soon thereafter, was briefed of the current apostasy at work in the Galatian churches and wrote an epistle with instructions for the restoration of order.

A great gulf had divided the Galatian branches of the Church. The Jewish converts had, through their traditional teaching, per-suaded their Gentile brethren into accepting the Abrahamic token of circumcision as a prerequisite to furtherance in the Church. It would appear that this question had been raised repeatedly in the past and was then once more to the forefront. It should be kept in mind that, relative to circumcision, it matters not with respect to the Church one way or the other. But when one party or other treated the matter as a doctrine essential to the welfare of the eternal soul, then it was in direct conflict with the gospel and was a teaching that led to apostasy.

In this epistle Paul treated this subject strongly, for its perpetrators were advancing the notion that Paul was in opposition to the teachings of the real leadership of the Church in Jerusalem. The focal point of Paul's teaching on the subject was simple: a contrast between faith in circumcision and faith in Christ.

The Epistle to the Romans (Early AD 58)

During this sojourn in Corinth, Paul took to writing another Epistle, this time to the Saints in the metropolis of Rome (possibly in February AD 58). This is the only Epistle, as far as our Bible stands now, that was written by Paul prior to his having visited the city.[174] Such should not be difficult to understand, as the capital could easily have attracted a cross-section of converts from the Pauline branches.

When Paul was first in Corinth, it was following the expulsion order of the Jews from Rome by Emperor Claudius in the year AD 50 (Acts 18:2). Since that time, it would appear the decree was rescinded, causing a return of the Jews, and of course Christians. That Paul knew many Saints in Rome is evidenced by the salutations expressed in the closing remarks of the Roman Epistle itself (Romans 16:1–15).

An Epistle for the Saints

In chapter eleven, verse 13, Paul states, "For I speak unto you Gentiles, inasmuch as I am the apostle of the Gentiles, I magnify mine office." This implies that the Epistle was written to the Gentiles only, but we may assume that one reference to the Gentiles does not exclude the Jews. The following passage is most enlightening relative to this point:

> To whom was the Epistle to the Romans written? To the Gentiles in Rome? To the World in general? To sectarian Christians today? Not by any means. If there is any truth the World can gain from this Epistle, such is all to the good. But Paul wrote to the Saints, to members of the Church, to those who already had the gift of the Holy Ghost, to those who had been born again, to those who held the priesthood and enjoyed the gifts of the Spirit. Hence he was writing to people who already knew the doctrines of salvation, and his teachings can only be understood by people who have the same background, the same knowledge, and the same experience as the original recipients of the message. Romans is a sealed book to the sectarian world; it is an open volume of inspiring Gospel Truth to the Saints of God.[175]

This observation made by Bruce McConkie was also voiced by an author in the last century, and is well declared in the following passage:

> This is Saint Paul's magnum opus. Here we see him at his greatest as a constructive thinker and theologian. The epistle to the Romans is the complete and mature expression of the apostle's main doctrines, which it unfolds in due order and proportion, and combines into an organic whole. No other New Testament writing, except the epistle to the Hebrews, approaches so nearly the character of a doctrinal treatise. For the purpose of systematic theology, it is the most important book in the Bible. More than any other, it has determined the course of Christian thought in its most fruitful epochs; its texts and definitions have been the battleground of momentous conflicts in the history of the Church.[176]

Use of the Greek Septuagint Bible

In writing the Epistle to the Romans, Paul used the Greek Old Testament. Of the scriptural passages quoted from the Old Testament in the Epistle, thirty-nine percent match the Septuagint exactly, four percent have only word-order changes from the Septuagint, thirty percent have slight variation from the Septuagint, and twenty-seven percent have major variation from the Septuagint. Those that have major variation seem to be personal renditions made by Paul because of the Septuagint's weak translation from the original Hebrew.[177]

Since Paul quoted so many verses of scripture in this instance, he must have had access to a set of scriptures to quote from. One author indicates the possibility that Crispus, who had been the chief ruler of the synagogue, may have possessed his own private copy of the Septuagint Old Testament, which Paul may have used.[178]

Context of Old Testament Quotes

Being a graduate of a rabbinical school in Jerusalem, Paul utilized his training in the manipulation of the scriptures to express Christian doctrines. We find him teaching a principle from disjointed and out of context passages. In some instances, some passages were quoted out of context so as to teach the opposite view that they were intended for. This was a common rabbinical practice of the time.

> His Epistles were dictated to a stenographer. Many passages attest that his mind worked faster than his stenographer's pen. His mental agility, indicative of a quick and inventive mind, has its negative side, for all too often Paul gave ingenious clever responses rather than straightforward ones. In using Old Testament passages, he tends to quote out of context, or give them far fetched meanings. When he presents a consecutive argument, he often brilliantly links biblical verses whose connection is not one of pure logic but of associated phrases or words. In such passages, Paul manages to make a telling point not so much through the quotations but in spite of them; such a chain of quotations has a momentum which transmits facets of thought, but not clear and readily communicable ideas.[179]

We might ask, why did Paul write an epistle to the Roman Church in the Greek language rather than in Latin? Greek was the predominant literary language of the eastern portion of the Roman

Empire. We already pointed out that Emperor Claudius wrote "twenty books on Etruscan[180] history and eight on Carthaginian" history, all in Greek.[181] It is also stated that "Greek remained the prevailing language in the Church of Rome for several centuries."[182]

Danger in Corinth (Acts 20:35 • February AD 58)

So it was that in February AD 58 Paul dispatched the Roman Epistle we have just reviewed. But all was not well in Corinth. The evil one had his minions at work. It would appear that those same Jews once more were determined to eliminate Paul: "And when the Jews laid wait for him, as he was about to sail into Syria, he purposed to return through Macedonia" (Acts 20:3). So he intended to set sail for Antioch-on-the-Orontes once more from Cenchrea, the east port.

But it appears that the Jewish rabble found out his intention. This necessitated a change of plan for Paul and his companions. When the rabble last attempted to rid themselves of Paul, they crossed paths with Gallio, the governor of Achaia, and the Corinthian Gentiles. So this time they must have laid wait at the harbor of Cenchrea, away from the possible interference of anyone in Corinth.

From the manner in which the verses covering this incident, it seems most likely that the several brethren mentioned in verse 4 were with Paul in Corinth, and Luke also. This would mean they accompanied him for the whole (or at least part of the) journey from Philippi. Accepting this would explain the wording of Luke when he said, "These going before tarried for us at Troas" (Acts 20:5).

Since it was Paul's intention to be in Jerusalem for Passover (March–April AD 58), he would not have sent these brethren ahead but would have accompanied them, had they left from Philippi. Most probably they set out from Corinth, letting it be known they all would sail from Cenchrea with Paul in their company.

The list of these brethren included one Gaius of Derbe. This could be an error in the rendering of the verse, for in the previous chapter Gaius and Aristarchus were both called Macedonians and were sent by Paul to Macedonia for their safety (Acts 19:29; 20:1).

To our mind, the rendering of the verse should be thus: "And there accompanied him into Asia Sopater of Berea; and of the

Thessalonians, Aristarchus and Secundus; and Gaius of Derbe [Acts 16:1–2], and Timotheus; and of Asia, Tychius and Tromphimus" (Acts 20:4).

Macedonia to Troas (Acts 20:6 • Spring AD 58)

However it may have been, these brethren departed, but Paul, accompanied by Luke, went north over the isthmus. Arriving at the port, these several brethren took passage to Troas—possibly by way of Ephesus—to wait for Paul and Luke to come by land through Macedonia. This change of plan meant that Paul would not get to Jerusalem in the time allotted (from February to the end of March AD 58). So it was that the Passover were spent in Philippi instead.

They had to keep their rendezvous in Troas. "And we sailed away from Philippi[183] after the days of unleavened bread,[184] and came unto them to Troas in five days; where we abode seven days" (Acts 20:6; early April AD 58).

It does not take five days to sail from Neapolis to Troas. It may be that, in making this crossing, they stopped over on the islands of Thasos, Samothrace, and Imbros. Previously, while journeying across these waters, Paul had stopped at Samothrace. Considering that Paul would most likely have been using the available shipping of the day, they would have made passenger callings where feasible, this procedure even allowed the journey to be made in two days. As to what happened to slow the crossing to five days can only mean that there were adverse weather conditions, likely prevailing wind from the east.

Raising Eutychus at Troas that they might be baptized (Acts 20:7–12 • April AD 58)

In Troas, a momentous event took place that does much to portray a portion of Paul's character. Upon the last day of his stay in Troas—it being "the first day of the week [Sunday],[185] when the disciples came together to break bread" (Acts 20:7), or in our language a sacrament meeting—he took to the pulpit to address the congregation, huddled together in a room on the third floor. And, "Paul preached unto them, ready to depart on the morrow; and continued his speech [sermon] until midnight" (Acts 20:7).

Since his sickness that was nigh unto death, Paul was gaining a comprehension of the close of his ministry, which made him avail of every opportunity to the fullest. Here was an audience, eager to hear the word of God, gathered together in this room, "and there were many lights in the upper chamber, where they were gathered together" (Acts 20:8). It was midnight, "the night was dark: three weeks had not elapsed since the Passover, and the Moon only appeared as a faint crescent in the early part of the night."[186] The oil lamps were burning, the room was crowded, the atmosphere was drowsy, and the windows were opened to provide ventilation to the drowsy room. "And there sat in a[n open] window [frame] a certain young man named Eutychus, being fallen into a deep sleep: and as Paul was long preaching, he sunk down with sleep, and fell down from the third loft, and was taken up dead" (Acts 20:9).

No doubt as Eutychus fell, he let out a shout and fright. Such would have brought a halt to Paul's preaching, as attention shifted to the condition of the young man Eutychus.

In a frenzy, the congregation clamored down the stairs[187] to the aid of a now lifeless body and were filled with despair over the sudden demise of a dear fellow Saint. The disembodied spirit of Eutychus stood looking on as others ministered to his lifeless body. He eagerly observed the ministration desiring a reunification of his body and spirit.

With a coolness that came only by great faith and sure testimony in the gospel, Paul descended the stairs to the scene of grief. Luke, in simplistic acceptance, just says, "And Paul went down, and fell upon him, and embracing[188] him said, Trouble not yourselves; for his life is in him" (Acts 20:10). Restoring life to Eutychus through priesthood ministration, they returned. "When he therefore was come up [the stairs] again, and had broken bread, and eaten, and talked a long while, even till break of day, so he departed. And they brought the young man [Eutychus] alive, and were not a little comforted" (Acts 20:11–12).

To Paul, the restoring of life to the young man was in no way a strange or fearful process. Compare the similarity of events with Elijah and Elisha.[189] Somehow, we can see Paul continuing his address after Eutychus's restoration to life, preaching about the reality of the Resurrection, ministration by the priesthood, and faith in Christ.

Troas to Miletus (Acts 20:13–16 • April AD 58)

"And we went before to ship, and sailed unto Assos, there intending to take in Paul: for so had he appointed, minding himself to go afoot" (Acts 20:13). As to why Paul decided to walk across the peninsula instead of going by ship with the others around Cape Lectum[190] is not explained by Luke. It's possible no explanation was offered by Paul. The journey by ship would have been over double the distance by land, add to this the possible cargo exchange at Assos, and we find Paul having more time on his hands to delay his departure from Alexandria-Troas.

Leaving Troas, he passed "through the south gate, past the hot springs, and through the oak woods, then in full foliage, which cover all that shore with greenness and shade, and across the wild water-courses on the western side of Ida."[191] Assos was a large city in the time of Paul, though little of its grandeur remains today. The city of Assos is remembered as the home of the great philosopher Aristotle (384–322 BC), who resided there.

"And when he [Paul] met with us [Luke and the others] at Assos, we took him in, and came to Mitylene" (Acts 20:14). They spent the night[192] on this island. "And we sailed thence, and came the next day over against Chios" (Acts 20:15). "Over against" implies the mainland, suggesting that the present day port of Cesme is in Turkey, which is just fourteen kilometers from the Chios Island. "And the next day we arrived at Samos, and tarried at Trogyllium;[193] and the next day we came to Miletus" (Acts 20:15). It would seem Paul was on a merchant ship that was making the most of paying passengers by calling in at several ports.

The port of Samos today is not the port of the past. Samos is on the northeast side of the island, but the historical Samos was on the southeast side and is the town of *Pythagórion* today. Leaving Samos (*Pythagórion*), the ship traversed the narrow strait to the mainland of Asia Minor again and docked at the port of Trogyllium.

An unusual thing happened next: Paul and his party sailed past Ephesus without making a port of call. Paul may have wanted to avoid any further trouble at Ephesus. The ship sailed on to Miletus further south. Also, since his illness at Philippi the previous year, there was a different spirit about Paul, almost a Stoic outlook and acceptance of the inevitable future—a sense of knowing what lay ahead. "Paul had determined to sail by Ephesus, because he would not spend the time in Asia: for he hastened, if it were possible for him, to be at Jerusalem the day of Pentecost" (Acts 20:16).

Pentecost is fifty days after Passover, or in other words the end of May (see Leviticus 23:16). Since Paul was in Philippi for Passover week (Saturday to Sunday), then it took five days for them to arrive at Troas, where he stayed until the following morning, which would have left a day over four weeks to arrive at Jerusalem (the middle of April AD 58). Commercial shipping of the time—as with us today—did not always go when they were ready to meet each connection, so a generous time frame was necessary.

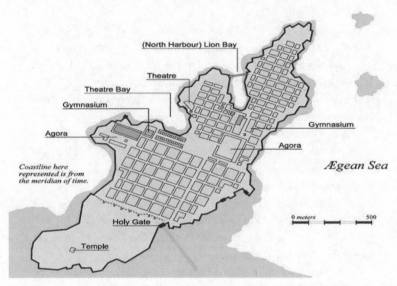

Miletus city and port. Somewhere on this map was the building where the Miletus Conference was held

The Miletus Conference (Acts 20:17–38 • April AD 58)

The ship that brought them to Miletus was not necessarily the same ship that would take them all the way to Caesarea. Therefore, Paul had an enforced interlude at Miletus waiting for a suitable passage further on his intended journey.

While there at Miletus, Paul used the time, "and from Miletus he sent [Tychius and Trophimus][194] to Ephesus, and called the elders of the church" (Acts 20:17). The distance by road from Miletus to

Ephesus would necessitate a one-day journey each way, which would bring the brethren back to Miletus[195] within two days. Paul could not go to Ephesus himself; this may have caused him to miss a suitable connecting passage to Palestine.

And when they were come to him, he said unto them, Ye know . . . after what manner I have been with you at all seasons,

Serving the Lord with all humility of mind, and with many tears, and temptations, which befell me by the lying in wait of the Jews:

And how I kept back nothing that was profitable unto you, but have shewed you, and have taught you publickly, and from house to house,

Testifying both to the Jews, and also to the Greeks [Gentiles], repentance toward God, and faith toward our Lord Jesus Christ.

And now, behold, I go bound in the spirit unto Jerusalem, not knowing the things that shall befall me there:

Save that the Holy Ghost witnesseth in every city, saying that bonds and afflictions abide [with] me.

But none of these things move me, neither count I my life dear unto myself, so that I might finish my course[196] with joy, and the ministry, which I have received of the Lord Jesus, to testify the gospel of the grace of God.

And now, behold, I know that ye all, among whom I have gone preaching the kingdom of God, shall see my face no more.

Wherefore I take you to record this day, that I am pure from the blood [see Acts 18:6] of all men.

For I have not shunned to declare unto you all the counsel of God.

Take heed therefore unto yourselves, and to all the flock, over which the Holy Ghost hath made you overseers, to feed the church of God, which he hath purchased with his own blood.

For I know this, that after my departing shall grievous wolves enter in among you, not sparing the flock.

And of your own selves shall men arise, speaking perverse things, to draw away disciples after them[selves].

Therefore watch, and remember, that by the space of three years [spring AD 54–spring AD 57], I ceased not to warn every one [of you] night and day with tears.

And now, brethren, I commend you to God, and to the word of his grace, which is able to build you up, and to give you an inheritance among all them which are sanctified.

I have coveted no man's silver, or gold, or apparel.

Yea, ye yourselves know, that these hands have ministered unto my necessities, and to them that were with me.

I have shewed you all things, how that so laboring ye ought to support the weak, and to remember the words of the Lord Jesus, how he said, It is more blessed to give than to receive.

And when he had thus spoken, he kneeled down, and prayed with them all.

And they all wept sore, and fell on Paul's neck, and kissed him,

Sorrowing most of all for the words which he spake, that they should see his face no more. (Acts 20:18–38)

Paul gave a touching farewell to the Ephesian brethren. There is a lot of feeling and emotion expressed in those words, a great yearning for the welfare of many, not just those gathered there with him.

But this address holds more than just emotion. There is history and prophesy in it also, as well as a brief overview of his ministry and methods and a justification for honest toil for the welfare of others. Then there is a grim foreboding announcement of impending apostasy. In all ages from Adam to the present day, apostasy has caused many a prophet and apostle to shed tears. Speaking to this group of brethren, he declared, "Of your own selves shall men arise, speaking perverse things, to draw away disciples after them[selves]" (Acts 20:30).

Following the prayer, they bid farewell in the midst of loving tears, as "they accompanied him unto the ship" (Acts 20:38). With the final embraces as he boarded ship, he said, "Finally, brethren, farewell. Be perfect, be of good comfort, be of one mind, live in peace; and the God of love and peace shall be with you" (2 Corinthians 13:11).

Miletus to Caesarea Maritima (Acts 21:1–12 • April AD 58)

"And it came to pass, that after we were gotten [able to withdraw] from them, and had launched, we came with a straight course [due south with a favorable wind] unto Cos, and the day following unto Rhodes, and from thence unto Patara [and Myra]" (Acts 21:1). Luke wrote about "finding disciples," or alternatively, "we sought out the disciples" (Jerusalem Bible, Acts 21:4). This implies that some searching was involved to discover the whereabouts of the small Christian community at Tyre.

Finally, after much questioning, they were directed to a Christian home and abode with the local Saints for the week. Some were prompted through revelation and "said to Paul through the Spirit, that he should not go up to Jerusalem" (Acts 21:4).

We are aware of Paul's intent behind his arriving in Jerusalem for Pentecost: the journey from Miletus was quicker than anticipated, to such an extent that Paul had the possibility of abiding in Tyre for a week while the ship unloaded her cargo. Had time been shorter, he would have sought passage on some other vessel. Following the week spent in Tyre, there should still have remained two full weeks or more to reach Jerusalem. "And when we had accomplished those days [our times was up], we departed and went our way; and they all brought us on our way, with wives and children, till we were out of the city: and we kneeled down on the shore, and prayed" (Acts 21:5).

Paul was fifty-two years old at this time, and he had touched the lives of many over the years since Damascus. But still, what a sight this multitude of men, women, and children in reverential prayer must have presented to passersby.

"And when we had taken our leave one of another, we took ship; and they returned [to their] home[s] again. And when we had finished our course from Tyre, we came to Ptolemais, and saluted the brethren, and abode with them one day" (Acts 21:6–7). They apparently only docked for the night, "and the next day we that were of Paul's company departed, and came unto Caesarea" (Acts 21:8).

While in Caesarea, Luke recorded that "we entered into the house of Philip the evangelist [patriarch], which was one of the seven [Acts 6:5 (1–6)]; and abode with him. And the same man had four daughters, virgins [unmarried daughters (RSV Acts 21:9)], which did prophesy" (Acts 21:8–9).

These daughters followed in the footsteps of their father in spiritual matters. It will be remembered that "the angel of the Lord spake unto Philip" (Acts 8:26), and "the Spirit [also] said unto Philip" (Acts 8:29) and made him instrumental in the conversion and baptism of the Ethiopian eunuch (Acts 8:26–39). Following the baptism of the Ethiopian, "the Spirit of the Lord caught away Philip, that the eunuch saw him no more" (Acts 8:39). These daughters had been well schooled by their parents in the gospel of Jesus Christ.[197]

There seems to have been enough time before the day of Pentecost, as Luke records, "And as we tarried there many days" (Acts 21:10). While they rested, "there came down from Judaea a certain prophet, named Agabus. And when he was come unto us, he took Paul's girdle [belt], and bound his own hands and feet (see Jeremiah 13:18), and said, Thus saith the Holy Ghost, So shall the Jews at Jerusalem bind the man that owneth this girdle, and shall deliver him into the hands of the Gentiles. And when we heard these things, both we [Luke, Aristarchus, and Tromphimus], and they of that place besought him not to go up to Jerusalem" (Acts 21:10b–12). Everyone appeared to be receiving revelations concerning the impending danger to Paul in Jerusalem. Were he to have acted on their forebodings, he would have made void the prophetic utterance.

Caesarea to Jerusalem (Acts 21:13–16 • April AD 58)

Paul knew that it was for a divine purpose that he was going up to Jerusalem. What that purpose was he probably did not fully understand. The perpetual foreboding, from so many for his welfare, was somewhat heavy upon him, and not making the burden of the future any easier to bear. "Then Paul answered, What mean ye to weep and to break mine heart? for I am ready not to be bound only, but also to die at Jerusalem for the name of the Lord Jesus. And when he would not be persuaded, we ceased, saying, The will of the Lord be done" (Acts 21:13–14). This may be paraphrased as: *Brethren, I have faith and courage. Please seek not misleadingly to undermine it by overzealous welfare for my person. Rather, pray unto God that in this hour I will be strengthened.*

About forty days or more had passed since Passover and Pentecost approached, by which time Paul desired to be in Jerusalem. "And after those days we took up [made ready] our carriages, and went up to Jerusalem" (Acts 21:15).

Carriages implies that they loaded their luggage, likely on a cart or mule. "There went with us also certain of the disciples of Caesarea, and brought with them one Mnason of Cyprus, an old [elderly] disciple, with whom we should lodge" (Acts 21:16). The main route to Jerusalem is via Antipatris, Arimathea, and Emmaus.[198] On this road at Emmaus is where the resurrected Jesus walked with two disciples (Luke 24:13–35).

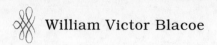

Final Visit to Jerusalem (Acts 21:17–22 • April–May AD 58)

As Paul and his companions approached the city, no doubt a great multitude of feelings swelled up within Paul. "O Jerusalem, Jerusalem, which killest the prophets, and stonest them that are sent unto thee" (Luke 13:34).

As they approached the city, the aqueduct paralleled the right side of the road. Then to the left, Golgotha would have displayed its heinous presence—perhaps another unfortunate person hung in agony to satisfy the demands of misplaced justice. Disparaging as the site of Golgotha may have been, the radiance of the nearby garden tomb still resounded in triumphant exaltation. "O death, where is thy sting? O grave, where is thy victory?" (1 Corinthians 15:55). "He is not here, for he is risen!" (Matthew 28:6; Mark 16:6; Luke 24:6). "And when we were come to Jerusalem, the brethren received us gladly" (Acts 21:17).[199]

"And the day following Paul went in with us unto James; and all the elders were present. And when he had saluted them, he declared particularly [in detail] what things God had wrought among the Gentiles by his ministry. And when they heard it, they glorified the Lord" (Acts 21:18–20). Luke wrote, "Paul went in with us," not *them*, indicating that Luke was also there. Paul related the happenings of the previous four years of labor.

But the fruitful ministry of Paul has stirred up schismal resentment in a number of the brethren. What did Paul say concerning the misguided brethren from Jerusalem who stirred up trouble in Corinth? (1 Corinthians 1:11). Following the report of Paul, one of the brethren "said unto him, Thou seest, brother [Saul], how many thousands of Jews [in Jerusalem] there are which believe; and they are all zealous of the [Mosaic] law:[200] And they are informed of thee,[201] that thou teachest all the Jews [of the dispersion] which are among the Gentiles to forsake Moses, saying that they ought not to circumcise their children, neither to walk after the customs. What is it therefore [then is to be done]? the multitude [crowd] must needs [necessarily] come together: for they will hear that thou art come" (Acts 21:20–22).

13: The First Imprisonment (I)

I Am Become All Things to All Men (May AD 58)

There was a problem in the Judaean Christian community because of Paul's work. During the early days of the Church, Jewish converts to the gospel still practiced being Pharisees or Sadducees. Jewish-Christians considered themselves to be above the Gentile-Christians in status and piety. Reports were circulating in Jerusalem that Paul was telling Jews in the provinces they should be Christians only and forget the Mosaic law. To alleviate this situation, the Brethren instructed Paul to participate in a Jewish temple rite, thereby showing the Jewish-Christians that he had repented and conformed to the traditional order.

This attitude persisted in the early Christian Church until after the destruction of Palestine in AD 70. It was only thereafter that the separation of Christianity from Judaism entrenched itself in the minds of the Church leadership. Properly speaking, the temple was rejected by God with the death of Christ upon the cross (Matthew 27:51; Mark 15:38; Luke 23:45). The God to whom this house was built had been turned away. "The chief priests answered, We have no king but Caesar" (John 19:15). Jehovah did not reject His people, but rather His people rejected Him.

The Temple Purification
(Acts 21:23–26 • May AD 58)

Continuing, the brethren said, "Do therefore this that we say to thee: We have four men which have a vow on them; Them take and purify thyself with them, . . . that they may shave their heads:

and all may know that those things, whereof they were informed concerning thee, are nothing; but that thou thyself also walkest orderly, and keepest the law" (Acts 21:23–24).

The words of Paul echo back from the Corinthian Epistle:

> For though I be free from all men, yet have I made myself servant unto all, that I might gain the more.
>
> And unto the Jews I became as a Jew, that I might gain the Jews; to them that are under the law, as under the law, that I might gain them that are under the law;
>
> To them that are without law, as without the law, (being not without law to God, but under the law to Christ,) that I might gain them that are without law.
>
> To the weak became I as weak, that I might gain the weak: I am made all things to all men, that I might by all means save some.
>
> And this I do for the gospel's sake, that I might be partaker thereof with you. (1 Corinthians 9:19–23; see also Acts 16:13; 18:18).[202]

"Then Paul took the men, and the next day purifying himself with them entered into the temple, to signify the accomplishment of the days of purification,[203] until that an offering should be offered for every one of them" (Acts 21:26; see also Numbers 6:10–15).[204]

Arrest (Acts 21:27–36 • May AD 58)

> And when the seven[205] days were almost ended, the Jews which were of Asia, when they saw him in the temple, stirred up all the people, and laid hands on him,
>
> Crying out, Men of Israel, help: This is the man, that teacheth all men every where against the people, and the [Mosaic] law, and this place: and further brought Greeks [Gentiles] also into the temple, and hath polluted this holy place.
>
> (For they had seen before with him in the city Tromphimus an Ephesian, whom they supposed Paul had brought into the temple.)
>
> And all the city was moved, and the people ran together: and they took Paul, and drew [Acts 16:19] him out of the temple: and forthwith the doors were shut. (Acts 21:27–30)

He was removed from the court of the temple and cast into the court of the Gentiles.[206]

So we have Paul ushered out of the court, and the gates were closed behind him. We conclude that the temple gates mentioned were the gates between these two courts. His accusers claimed he was teaching contrary to the Mosaic law, and "this place," or "this Holy Place," meaning the temple. What we read was the accusation against Stephen all those years ago: "This man ceaseth not to speak blasphemous words against this holy place, and the law" (Acts 6:13).

The mob rushed Paul forth from before the temple doors, which were then forthwith shut. Roman soldiers purveyed the situation from the battlements of the Fortress of Antonia overlooking the temple plaza. "And as they went about to kill him, tidings came unto the chief captain [Tribune Claudius Lysias] of the band [garrison], that all Jerusalem was in an uproar. Who immediately took soldiers and centurions, and ran down unto them: and when they saw the chief captain [tribune] and the soldiers, they left beating of Paul" (Acts 21:31–32).

"Then the chief captain came near, and took him, and commanded him to be bound with two chains" (Acts 21:33), just as Peter had been bound "between two soldiers" (Acts 12:6). "Two chains" are specifically mentioned, which tells us that two soldiers were assigned to guard him.

Then the captain "demanded [to know] who he was, and what he had done. And some cried one thing, and some another, among the multitude: and when he could not know the certainty for the tumult, he commanded him to be carried into the castle [fortress]. And when he came upon the stairs, so it was, that he was borne of the soldiers for the violence of the people. For the multitude of the people followed after, crying, Away with him" (Acts 21:33b–36; see also Luke 23:18; John 19:15). As for Paul, the vulture of Judaism had lost its prey, being borne by the Roman eagle to its fortress lair.

Art Thou That Egyptian?
(Acts 21:37–38 • May AD 58)

"And as Paul was to be led into the castle [fortress], he said unto the chief captain, [Tribune Claudius Lysias,] May I speak unto thee?" (Acts 21:37). Paul, having spoken in Greek, shocked the officer somewhat. "Who said [spoke], Canst thou speak Greek?" (Acts 21:37).

Being able to speak Greek led also to a case of mistaken identity by the tribune. "Art not thou that Egyptian, which before these days madest an uproar, and leddest out into the wilderness four thousand men that were murderers?" (Acts 21:38). An Egyptian Jew had led a revolt with 30,000 men to take Jerusalem and overthrow the Roman garrison. However, Felix thwarted the attempt and the rebels scattered.[207] Since then, the Romans were hunting for that Egyptian leader.

There Was Made a Great Silence (Acts 21:39–40; 22:1–23 • May AD 58)

Possibly the tribune had hopes of the reward for the capture of "that Egyptian." Paul was in no mood to be mistaken for an enemy of the Empire. "But Paul said, I am a man which am a Jew of Tarsus, a city in Cilicia, a citizen of no mean [insignificant] city: and, I beseech thee, suffer me to speak unto the people. And when he had given him license [permission], Paul stood on the stairs, and beckoned with his hand (see Acts 13:16) unto the people" (Acts 21:39–40). Paul said he was "a Jew" instead of a Christian. As far as the tribune was concerned, Christians were a Jewish sect.

> And when there was made a great silence, he spake unto them in the Hebrew [possibly Aramaic] tongue, saying,
>
> Men, [who are my] brethren, and fathers, hear ye my defence which I make now unto you.
>
> (And when they heard that he spake in the Hebrew [Aramaic] tongue to them, they kept the more silence: and he saith,)
>
> I am verily a man which am a Jew, born in Tarsus, a city in Cilicia, yet brought up in this city at the feet of Gamaliel,[208] and taught according to the perfect manner of the law of the fathers, and was zealous toward God, as ye all are this day. (Acts 21:39; 22:1–3)

In opening his address to the mob, Paul uses the same words that Stephen used so many years before: "Men, brethren, and fathers" (Acts 7:2). It is likely that some of those in the mob recognized Paul, and some may have been under the tutelage of Gamaliel concurrent with Paul—or Saul, as he was known back then. Continuing his discourse:

And I persecuted [the followers of] this way unto death, binding and delivering into prisons both men and women.

As also the high priest doth bear me witness, and all the estate [council] of the [Sanhedrin] elders:[209] from whom also I received letters unto the brethren, and went to Damascus, to bring them which were there bound unto Jerusalem, for to be punished.

And it came to pass, that, as I made my journey, and was come nigh unto Damascus, about noon, suddenly there shone from heaven a great light round about me.

And I fell unto the ground, and heard a voice saying unto me, Saul, Saul, why persecutest thou me?

And I answered, Who art thou, Lord? And he said unto me, I am Jesus of Nazareth, whom thou persecutest.

And they that were with me saw indeed the light, and were afraid; but they heard not the voice of him that spake to me.

And I said, What shall I do, Lord? And the Lord said unto me, Arise, and go into Damascus; and there it shall be told thee of all things which are appointed for thee to do.

And when I could not see for the glory of that light, being led by the hand of them that were with me, I came into Damascus.

And one Ananias, a devout man according to the law, having a good report of all the Jews which dwelt there,

Came unto me, and stood, and said unto me, Brother Saul, receive thy sight. And the same hour I looked upon him.

And he said, The God of our fathers hath chosen thee, that thou shouldest know his will, and see that Just One, and shouldest hear the voice of his mouth.

For thou shalt be his witness unto all men of what thou hast seen and heard.

And now why tarriest thou? arise, and be baptized, and wash away thy sins, calling upon the name of the Lord.

And it came to pass, that, when I was come again to Jerusalem, even while I prayed in the temple, I was in a trance [vision];

And saw him saying unto me, Make haste, and get thee quickly out of Jerusalem: for they will not receive thy testimony concerning me.

And I said, Lord, they know that I imprisoned and beat in every synagogue them that believed on thee:

And when the blood of thy martyr Stephen was shed, I also was standing by, and consenting unto his death, and kept the raiment of them that slew him.

> And he said unto me, Depart: for I will send thee far hence unto
> the Gentiles. (Acts 22:4–21)

The Romans were at a loss to know what was being said, as Paul spoke to the crowd in Hebrew (probably Aramaic). The tribune was not of a mind to stop Paul because the mob was quiet, though not for much longer. "And they gave him audience unto this word, and then lifted up their voices, and said, Away with such a fellow from the earth: for it is not fit that he should live. And as they cried out, and cast off their clothes, and threw dust into the air" (Acts 22:22–23).

With the mob once more in an outrage in response to the address of Paul, the tribune was somewhat indignant. Since the tribune did not understand Aramaic, he only knew that the mob was disgusted with Paul, for he saw their dust-throwing gesture.

Civis Romanus Sum!—I Am a Roman Citizen (Acts 22:24–29 • May AD 58)

In his anger, "the chief captain [tribune] commanded him to be brought into the castle [fortress], and bade that he should be examined by scourging; that he might know wherefore they cried so against him" (Acts 22:24). The tribune felt somewhat disgraced by his benevolence toward Paul, having given permission for Paul to speak and ending up a greater tumult than before. So he gives orders to a centurion to have Paul bound and flogged. "And as they bound him with thongs, Paul said unto the centurion that stood by, Is it lawful for you to scourge a man that is a Roman, and uncondemned?[210] When the centurion heard that [Paul was a Roman citizen], he went and told the chief captain [Tribune Lysias], saying, Take heed what thou doest: for this man is a Roman [citizen]" (Acts 22:25–26).

How Tribune Claudius Lysias must have been frightened at the prospect of his having given orders to flog a Roman citizen. Such was a violation of the civil code with the possibility of serious consequences. Stopped in his tracks, he returned to question Paul:

> Then the chief captain [tribune] came, and said unto him, Tell me, art
> thou a Roman [citizen]? He said, Yea. And the chief captain [tribune]
> answered, With a great sum obtained I this freedom. And Paul said, But
> I was born free. Then straightway they departed from him which should

have examined him: and the chief captain [tribune] also was afraid after he knew that he was a Roman, and because he had bound him, and he loosed him from his bonds" (Acts 22:27–28; JSIV Acts 22:29).

Paul was most likely in the Praetorium (Mark 15:16), where Jesus was scourged and mocked of the soldiers. He cast his eyes about, surveying the Praetorium, thinking something like, *I stand today where Jesus stood twenty-five years ago!*

We observe that he was not released from his bands, but rather remained bound for the night.

The Sanhedrin Trial (Acts 22:30 • May AD 58)

"On the morrow, because he would have known the certainty wherefore he was accused of the Jews, he [the tribune] loosed him from his bands, and commanded the chief priests and all their [Sanhedrin] council to appear, and brought Paul down, and set him before them" (JSIV Acts 22:30). The council "was composed of seventy members, Scribes and Priests and Rabbis, Pharisees and Sadducees, and the High Priest presided over its deliberations."[211]

Finally, after a night in bonds, his manacles were removed. The wording of this verse seems to indicate that this inquisition was conducted not in the fortress, but in temple chambers: the word *appear* is better translated as "assemble." The "bringing down" implies from the fortress to the temple grounds, by the same stairs that he spoke from the previous day.

From the wording of the passage, it becomes clear that the tribune did not go down with Paul, but rather sent possibly a centurion with some men to ensure Paul's safety. In such a case, we may rest assured that the proceedings were conducted in Aramaic, not Greek or Latin.

Thou Whited Wall! (Acts 23:15 • May AD 58)

And Paul, earnestly beholding the [Sanhedrin] council said, Men and brethren, I have lived in all good conscience before God until this day.

And the high priest Ananias commanded them that stood by him to smite him on the mouth.

Then said Paul unto him, God shall smite thee, thou whited wall: for sittest thou to judge me after the [Mosaic] law, and commandest me to be smitten contrary to the [Mosaic] law?

And they that stood by said, Revilest thou God's high priest?

Then said Paul, I wist not [could not have guessed], brethren, that he was the high priest: for it is written, Thou shalt not speak evil of the ruler of thy people [quoting Exodus 22:28]. (Acts 23:1–5)

Note that he addressed "men and brethren." He had attended the school of Gamaliel;[212] a great many of those students would have found their way into positions in the Sanhedrin and other positions of prominence in the ecclesiastical hierarchy. Therefore, it is no strange thing to consider that he should recognize many of the council members as being his peers from the past. By using this form of address, he considered himself to be one of the "brethren" and such familiarity would not go over well.[213]

His opening remarks brought the displeasure of the high priest upon him, whereby High Priest Ananias gave direction that Paul should be struck because of his contemptible familiarity. Now, we may rest assured that Paul could identify who was the high priest, not only by his distinctive robes, but also by the prominent seating position he would have taken. His rebuke, "God shall smite thee, thou white[washe]d wall," was a well known one. The term was used by Jesus himself, only he elaborated more on the meaning of such a rebuke (Acts 23:3). This must have been a general form of rebuke, in that no explanation was called for.

It should not be considered that Paul retracted the statement when he discovered that the one whom he rebuked was the high priest. "The Apostle had seen enough to be convinced that there was no prospect before this tribunal of a fair inquiry and a just decision."[214]

I Have Hope in the Resurrection of the Dead (Acts 23:6–10 • May AD 58)

Perceiving the futility of a defense, Paul masterfully used the differences of opinion among the Sanhedrin to his benefit.

But when Paul perceived that the one part were Sadducees, and the other Pharisees, he cried out in the council, Men and brethren, I am a Pharisee, the son of a Pharisee[s]: of the hope [of the] and resurrection of the dead I am called in question.

And when he had so said, there arose a dissension between the Pharisees and the Sadducees: and the multitude was divided.

> For the Sadducees say there is no resurrection, neither angel, nor spirit: but the Pharisees confess both.
>
> And there arose a great cry: and the scribes that were of the Pharisees' part arose, and strove, saying, We find no evil in this man: but if a spirit or an angel hath spoken to him, let us not fight against God.
>
> And when there arose a great dissension,[215] the chief captain [tribune], fearing lest Paul should have been pulled in pieces of them, commanded the soldiers to go down, and to take him by force from among them, and bring him into the castle [fortress]. (Acts 23:6–10)

The centurion must have dispatched intelligence to the tribune up in the fortress that the Jewish court of inquiry had broken into confusion and was now becoming violent. Immediately, he ordered a reinforcement of armed men to go down and to take Paul by force from among the Sanhedrin activists.

The Sanhedrin's bickering and disagreement had only brought shame upon themselves—as the rabble did in the temple court the previous day. Most assuredly as they all brought shame upon the Jewish nation, they shamed the Lord before the Roman Empire by their conduct. Pharisee "hatred against the Sadducees was even greater than their hatred of Christianity."[216]

Comforted of the Lord (Acts 23:11 • May AD 58)

Tribune Claudius Lysias was in a quandary as to how he should handle the situation; for the moment, he detained Paul within the fortress. "And the night following the Lord stood by him and said, Be of good cheer [take courage], Paul: for as thou hast testified of me in Jerusalem, so must thou bear witness also at Rome" (Acts 23:11).

Up to this point, Paul was of the opinion that he would spend the final days of his life on earth and die here at Jerusalem. Now, the Lord told him to "take courage" and that he must "bear witness also at Rome."

It may be that at this time Paul lengthened the perspective of his mortal sojourn by several months. Somehow, we feel he was not aware of the years that lay ahead for him. Whether Paul was in a separate cell or confined in a common chamber with other prisoners matters not. As much as the Spirit strengthened him, it would have also stopped the ears and shrouded the minds of others in a deep sleep, so they being present were not aware to the proceedings of that night (end of May AD 58).

It is notable that the King of the Jews found it more appropriate to come and visit the earth in a prison cell in the Fortress of Antonia than in the adjoining temple. For that night, the Fortress of Antonia became a temple, and the small cell became the Holy of Holies in which the presence of the Lord was manifest.

Assassination Plot (Acts 23:12–15 • May AD 58)

> And when it was day, certain of the Jews banded together, and bound themselves under a curse [an oath], saying that they would neither eat nor drink till they had killed Paul.
>
> And they were more than forty which had made this conspiracy.
>
> And they came to the chief priests and elders, and said, We have bound ourselves under a great curse [oath], that we will eat nothing until we have slain Paul.[217]
>
> Now therefore ye with the council signify to the chief captain [tribune] that he bring him down unto you to morrow, as though ye would inquire something more perfectly concerning him: and we, or ever [before] he come near, are ready to kill him. (Acts 23:12–15)

High Priest Ananias, with the chief priests and elders, in accepting the plot of these oath-bound assassins, had thereby convicted themselves by the laws for which they held office to uphold in righteousness. It may be that the priestly conspirators were of the sect of the Sadducees, seeing as how the Pharisees were more favorable to the testimony of Paul at the previous inquisition (see Jeremiah 22:23, 5).

The request to bring Paul would have required that he be brought down the stairs from the Fortress of Antonia to chambers within the temple complex, where the Sanhedrin would meet in council. The assassins[218] could not get to Paul before he descended the stairs, therefore the proposed assassination would have had to take place on the temple court, thus defiling the House of the Lord. "And when Paul's sisters son heard of their lying in wait, he went and entered into the castle [fortress], and told Paul" (Acts 23:16). Now we wonder, how was it that this nephew of Paul came to know of the assassination plot? From the writings of Luke, we learn that "a great company of the priests were obedient to the faith" (Acts 6:7). This being the case, we conjecture that one of those were amongst the group to whom the assassins revealed their intentions.

Perhaps it went this way: The "chief priests and elders" sent someone to the fortress to convey the wish of the council that Paul be brought down again for further questions. In the meantime, this faithful priest—whomever he may have been—quietly went out to Paul's nephew and told him to get the message to Paul that there was a plot to kill him. So this young man immediately went out through a temple gate and up to the main entrance of the fortress and was granted permission to speak with his uncle. Then an emissary from the Jewish council ascended the stairs from the temple court to a centurion on duty and requested an audience with the tribune. The young man told Paul that there is a request being made to the tribune that he permit Paul to be brought down to the council for further questioning, but that he will be murdered once he reaches the temple court.

"Then Paul called one of the centurions unto him, and said, Bring this young man [my nephew] unto the chief captain [tribune]: for he hath a certain thing to tell him" (Acts 23:17). He must have conveyed the seriousness of the intelligence in that the centurion did not waste any time in bringing the informer to the tribune.

"So he took him, and brought him to the chief captain [tribune], and said, Paul the prisoner called me unto him, and prayed me to bring this young man unto thee, who hath something to say unto thee" (Acts 23:18). It may well be that the deputation from the Jewish council was waiting without for the tribune. Under normal diplomatic protocol, the Roman tribune would not give audience to a Jewish delegation immediately. He would first have put on his armor and kept them waiting an agreeable amount of time to emphasize his commanding position. "Then the chief captain [tribune] took him by the hand,[219] and went with him aside privately, and asked him, What is that thou hast to tell me?" (Acts 23:19).

Paul was born a free citizen in a Greek-speaking country. It is most likely that the sister of Paul was also born there and spoke Greek. This would explain how Tribune Claudius Lysias would take the boy "aside privately," speaking together in Greek.

And Paul's nephew said, "The Jews have agreed to desire thee that thou wouldest bring down Paul [my uncle] to morrow into the council, as though they would inquire somewhat of him more perfectly. But do not thou yield unto them [let them persuade you]: for there lie in wait for him of them more than forty men, which have bound themselves with an oath, that they will neither eat nor drink till they have killed him: and now are they ready, looking for a promise from thee. So the chief captain [tribune] then let the young man depart, and charged him, See thou tell no man that thou hast shewed [told] these things to me" (Acts 23:20–22). The centurion brought the youth back to the front gate and let him depart discreetly.

Now the tribune had a problem to solve. If he refused to bring Paul before the Sanhedrin, it might incite trouble, considering the lengths they were willing to go to for his assassination. Should he bring Paul before them and he be murdered, he would have a greater problem in that he did not take sufficient measures to protect the welfare of a Roman citizen in his custody.

He decided, so long as Paul was in his custody, he had a problem. Therefore, if he removed Paul, he would solve his immediate difficulties and pass the responsibility to the Procurator Felix. In the meantime, the tribune met with the Jewish delegation and heard their judicial request. Without revealing his intention to have Paul removed from Jerusalem, he must have indicated that he considered their request in a favorable manner, but forestalled any conclusive decision until morning, when, unknown to them, Paul would be halfway to Caesarea.

Jerusalem to Caesarea by Night (Acts 23:23–32 • May AD 58)

"And he [the tribune] called unto him two centurions, saying, Make ready two hundred soldiers to go to Caesarea [Maritima], and horsemen threescore and ten, and spearmen two hundred, at the third hour of the night [9:00 p.m.]; and provide them beasts [mounts], that they may set Paul on, and bring him safe unto Felix the governor [procurator]" (Acts 23:23–24).

In council with two of his centurions, the tribune planned the necessary strategy to secure his Roman-Jewish prisoner. The dangers felt by the tribune were expressed in the number of troops he chose to secure Paul's safety. Also, these numbers give us a view of the size of the garrison in the capital in that he could spare four hundred and seventy men to leave the city at a holiday time, and yet maintain the security of Jerusalem.

"And he wrote a letter after this manner" (Acts 23:25). How Luke in his writing the Acts of the Apostles came into possession of certain facts is quite a mystery. We should here observe that a Roman centurion writing a letter to his superior would have certainly written in Latin or Greek.

> [Tribune] Claudius Lysias unto the most excellent governor [procurator of Judea, Samaria, Galilee, and Perea], [Procurator M. Antonius] Felix sendeth greeting.
> This man [Paul] was taken of the Jews, and should [would] have been killed of them: then came I with an army [a detachment], and rescued him, having understood that he was a Roman [citizen].
> And when I would have known the cause wherefore they accused him, I brought him forth into their council:
> Whom I perceived to be accused of questions of their law, but to have nothing laid to his charge worthy of death or of bonds.
> And when it was told me how that the Jews laid wait for the man [*Paulus*], I sent straightway to thee, and gave commandment to his accusers also to say before thee what they had against him. Farewell. (Acts 23:26–30)[220]

The wording of this letter seems designed to represent—in the best interests—the welfare of its author. The character of Tribune Claudius Lysias is well ascertained by the formulation of this document.

Continuing with the narrative: "Then the soldiers, as it was commanded them," under cover of darkness at 9:00 p.m., "took Paul, and brought him by night to Antipatris" (Acts 23:31).[221] Antipatris was a relay station on the road between Jerusalem and Caesarea Maritima. The morning after, "they left the horsemen to go with him" (Paul) to Caesarea Maritima, and the two hundred soldiers and the two hundred spearmen "returned to the castle" Fortress of Antonia in Jerusalem (Acts 23:32).

14: The First Imprisonment (II)

Prison at Caesarea Maritima (Acts 23:23 • June AD 58)

The seventy horsemen "came to Caesarea, and delivered the letter to the governor [procurator], [and] presented Paul also before him" (Acts 23:33). The horsemen would have been quartered in Caesarea Maritima for the night to rest the horses before returning to the Jerusalem garrison. The procurator of Judea was M. Antonius Felix during the years AD 52–60. "He was the first slave and freedman in history ever to become the governor of a Roman province."[222] Tacitus said of him: "Felix exercised the authority of a king, with the disposition of a slave."[223] It was not beneath his dignity to accept bribes to render a favorable judgment.

Caesarea was a new Roman city built in Palestine. The primary reason for its construction was to bypass Jewish resentment to their building of pagan temples of worship in Judea. Therefore, Caesarea was constructed in Samaria outside the pale of orthodox Judaism.

Paul before Felix (Acts 23:34–35; 24:1–9 • AD 58)

The Procurator Felix opened the letter while Paul looked on. It must be assumed that Paul was in his presence to explain how he knew of Felix's reaction. "And when the governor [procurator] had read the letter, he asked of what province he [Paul] was. And when he understood that he was of Cilicia; I will hear thee, said he, when thine accusers are also come. And he commanded him to be kept in Herod's judgement hall [Praetorium]" (Acts 23:34–35).

William Victor Blacoe

And while Paul waited in Caesarea Maritima, back in Jerusalem the minions of apostasy found their plans thwarted. Paul had gone, right out from under their eyes. Judging by Felix's intent to wait for them to come to Caesarea Maritima, it must be concluded that he sent word back all the way to Jerusalem—possibly with

Procurator (Prefect) Felix of Judea

the centurion and his seventy horsemen that Tribune Claudius Lysias sent—for the Sanhedrin to come to him.

> And after five[224] days Ananias the high priest descended with the elders, and with a certain orator named Tertullus, who informed the governor [Felix] against Paul.
>
> And when he was called forth,[225] Tertullus began to accuse him, saying, Seeing that by thee we enjoy great quietness, and that very worthy deeds are done unto this nation by thy providence,
>
> We accept it always, and in all places, most noble Felix, with all thankfulness.
>
> Notwithstanding, that I be not further tedious unto thee, I pray thee that thou wouldest hear us of the clemency a few words.
>
> For we have found this man a pestilent fellow, and a mover of sedition among all the Jews throughout the world, and a ringleader of the sect of the Nazarenes:
>
> Who also hath gone about to profane the temple: whom we took, and would have judged according to our law.
>
> But the chief captain [Tribune Claudius] Lysias came upon us, and with great violence took him away out of our hands,
>
> Commanding his accusers to come unto thee: by examining of whom thyself mayest take knowledge of all these things, whereof we accuse him.
>
> And the Jews also assented, saying that these things were so. (Acts 24:1–9)

As the Roman Empire expanded and new provinces were established, lawyers made a business in and around the procurator's law court.[226] A lucrative business was made in presenting cases for the local population, who now found themselves responsible to a legal code they were not prepared for. These lawyers were always aware of what cases were scheduled before the procurator and solicited their services to the various parties.

Tertullus was one of these lawyers that the Sanhedrin hired to present their case in the Roman fashion. The general idea of Tertullus's argument is found in verse 6. He says Paul was guilty of infringements of Jewish religious laws; he was being tried before a Jewish religious court, the proceedings of which were terminated by Tribune Claudius Lysias forcibly abducting the accused. After this, the Jewish leaders were commanded to take their charges before Governor Felix. This is well presented, for under Roman law Paul had done no wrong. The accusation was intended to provoke Felix to relinquish jurisdiction to the Jewish court, seeing as Paul was a Jew of the Nazarene sect. This approach tactfully overlooked the Roman citizenship of the accused.

Paul Makes His Defense (Acts 24:10–21 • June AD 58)

Then Paul, after that the governor [Felix] had beckoned unto him to speak, answered, Forasmuch as I know that thou hast been of many years a judge unto this[227] nation, I do the more cheerfully answer for myself:

Because that thou mayest understand, that there are yet but twelve days since I went up to Jerusalem for to worship.

And they neither found me in the temple disputing with any man, neither raising up the people, neither in the synagogues, nor in the city:

Neither can they prove the things whereof they now accuse me.

But this I confess unto thee, that after the way which they call heresy [a sect], so worship I the God of my fathers, believing all things which are written in the law and in the prophets:

And have a hope toward God, which they themselves also allow, that there shall be a resurrection of the dead, both of the just and unjust.

And herein do I excuse myself [also], to have always a conscience void of offence toward God, and toward men.

Now after many years I came to bring alms to my nation, and offerings.

Whereupon certain Jews from Asia found me purified in the temple, neither with multitude, nor with tumult.

Who ought to have been here before thee, and object, if they had [have] ought against me.

Or else let these same here say, if they have found any evil doing in me, while I stood before the council,

Except it be for this one voice, that I cried standing among them, Touching the resurrection of the dead I am called in question by you this day. (Acts 24:10–21)

Governor Felix could dismiss the charges. He should have, since there was no evidence. But the High Priest Ananias and the Sanhedrin council were too important to upset at this point, so a stall tactic was instigated to satisfy the moment.

Postponement of the Trial (Acts 24:22–23 • June AD 58)

"And when Felix heard these things, having more perfect [accurate] knowledge of that way, he deferred them, and said, When Lysias the chief captain [tribune] shall come down, I will know the uttermost of your matter [decide your case]. And he commanded a [the] centurion to keep Paul, and let him have liberty, and that he should forbid none of his acquaintance to minister or to come unto him" (Acts 24:22–23).

Just as the high priest had come from Jerusalem to Caesarea to prosecute Paul, no doubt likewise others came to minister to Paul's needs. Since these events were recorded with such insight by Luke, it may be concluded that he was one of those who ministered unto Paul. We are aware that Luke later accompanied Paul on his journey to Rome, as did Aristarchus (Acts 27:2).

Without question, this liberty freely given to Paul was not to the liking of the High Priest Ananias. But we doubt that he in any way protested, so as not to challenge the authority of the procurator.

Caesarea did contain Christians among the Roman military garrison since the conversion of Centurion Cornelius (Acts 10:7–8, 22, 24, 44–48). There is also evidence of Christians among the civilian population of Caesarea (Acts 21:8–10, 16).

Tribune Lysias Gives Evidence (June AD 58)

Tribune Claudius Lysias was sent from Jerusalem. Possibly two days later, the next hearing took place, but we have no record of the proceedings. Considering the shrewdness of Felix and normal Roman military practice, a tribune would not have been called to give evidence before a procurator while Jewish leaders were present to cross-examine or refute an officer's testimonial.

As to what was said, we may safely assume that he did not in any way digress from the written testimonial of his letter. He could not, or his integrity would have been brought into question.[228]

A New Hearing before Felix and Drusilla (Acts 24:24–26 • June AD 58)

"And after certain days, when Felix came with his wife Drusilla, which was a Jewess, he sent for Paul, and heard him concerning the faith of Christ" (Acts 24:24).

Before continuing with the words of Paul, something must be understood concerning Drusilla. She was the daughter of Herod Agrippa I (Acts 12), who was the grandson of Herod the Great. It was Drusilla's father, Herod Agrippa I, who had "stretched forth his hands to vex certain of the church. And he killed James [Jacob] the brother of John with the sword" (Acts 12:1–2). Eventually, Herod Agrippa I was smitten by an "angel of the Lord," with the result that "he was eaten of worms, and gave up the ghost" (Acts 12:23). We may therefore infer that Drusilla knew somewhat of the sect of the Nazarines, as the Jews called the Christian Church.[229]

Felix and Drusilla had Paul arraigned before them. It is doubtful that he was summoned before them in a sincere knowledge of the gospel. Most likely, it was for entertainment. Paul began to speak: "And as he reasoned [exhorted] of righteousness, and temperance [self-control], and judgment to come, Felix trembled, and answered, Go thy way for this time; when I have a convenient season, I will call for thee" (Acts 24:25). As said in the Book of Mormon, "The guilty take the truth to be hard, for it cutteth" (1 Nephi 16:2); here, it cut into the hearts of Felix and Drusilla.

In some respects, there is parallel here with John the Baptist and his condemnation of Herod Antipas and Herodias (Luke 3:19–20).

Possibly even Drusilla recalled hearing of how her uncle was under the condemnation of John and felt a similar sting that her Aunt Herodias did. Feeling uncomfortable as they did, Paul was dismissed from their presence. Drusilla died at Pompeii, or Herculeum, in the volcanic eruption of Mount Vesuvius in AD 79.[230]

Remorse was short-lived in the conscience of Felix, for "he hoped also that money should have been given him of Paul, that he might loose him: wherefore he sent for him the oftener, and communed with him" (Acts 24:26). Justice for sale from Felix, should Paul be willing to pay for it.

"Felix, well knowing how the Christians aided one another in distress, and possibly having some information of the funds with which St. Paul had recently been entrusted, and ignorant of those principles which make it impossible for a true Christian to tamper by bribes with the course of law, might naturally suppose that he had here a good prospect of enriching himself."[231] This escapade continued for two years.

Antonius Felix Is Recalled and Porcius Festus Is Appointed (Acts 24:27; 25:15 • July AD 60)

"But after two years Porcius Festus came into Felix' room: and Felix [at his departing], willing to shew the Jews a pleasure, left Paul bound" (Acts 24:27). It was late summer of AD 60 when Porcius Festus arrived to replace the now recalled M. Antonius Felix. Judea had become infested with bandits and assassination groups, notably the Sicarii,[232] whom Felix had been unable to eliminate. Add to this the flagrant misuse of his authority that raised Jewish resentment to his person, and they were glad to have his "financial corruption" terminated.[233]

It should also be noted that, following his recall to Rome, a Jewish deputation brought charges against Felix before Nero, albeit unsuccessfully. Pallas, his brother, interceded and rescued him.[234]

The "two years" so pointedly recorded by Luke has more a reference to Roman justice than to the coming of Festus (see Acts 28:30). Under Roman law, a citizen could be held in "protective custody" for a maximum period of two years. Therefore, when Felix "left Paul bound," he did in fact contravene Roman judicial law with respect to this detention.[235]

Now when [the new Governor Porcius] Festus was come into the province, after three days he ascended from Caesarea [Maritima] to Jerusalem.

Then the high priest [Ishmael, son of Fabi] and the chief of the Jews informed [presented the charges to] him against Paul, and besought [urged] him,

And desired favour against him, that he would send [summon] for him to Jerusalem, laying wait in the way [planning an ambush] to kill him.

But Festus answered, that Paul should be kept at Caesarea [Maritima], and that he himself would depart shortly thither.

Let them therefore, said he, which among you are able, go down with me, and accuse this man, if there be any wickedness in him. (Acts 25:1–5)

Paul Makes His Appeal to Caesar (Acts 25:6–12 • August AD 60)

"And when he had tarried among them more than ten days, he went down unto Caesarea [Maritima]; and the next day sitting on the judgment seat commanded Paul to be brought. And when he was come, the Jews which came down from Jerusalem stood round about and laid many and grievous complaints[236] against Paul, which they could not prove" (Acts 25:6–7).

This high priest, Ishmael, was a known supporter of much vice within the capital, a fact no doubt communicated to Festus by the tribune of the Jerusalem garrison. But Festus, new in his appointment, did not want to make enemies from the outset, a fact no doubt sensed by Paul as he now stood as a lamb among the wolf pack.

Paul once more took to his personal defense. "While he answered for himself, Neither against the law of the Jews, neither against the temple, nor yet against Caesar, have I offended anything at all" (Acts 25:8). From the brief defense given by Paul can be gathered the nature of the charges and the lack of evidence to support them.

"But Festus, willing to do the Jews a pleasure, answered Paul, and said, Wilt thou go up to Jerusalem, and there be judged of these things before me?" (Acts 25:9). Why not be judged in the city of Caesarea Maritima? Paul must have been aware that should he accept to go up to Jerusalem, in all probability he would never reach the city before the hired assassins fell upon him.

Such a judgment from Festus goes a long way in describing the manner that the province would be governed for the next few years. Coupled together with the level to which the Jewish leadership had descended, is it any wonder the nation was but ten years away from utter destruction?

Having his suspicions of the proposed plot, Paul played his final trump card. "Then said Paul, I stand at Caesar's judgment seat, where I ought to be judged: to the Jews I have done no wrong, as thou very well knowest. For if I be an offender, or have committed any thing worthy of death, I refuse not to die: but if there be none of these things whereof these accuse me, no man may deliver me unto them. I appeal[237] unto Caesar" (Acts 25:10–11).

Let us understand what is being said here. He is before a Roman court and the procurator suggests that Paul should receive judgment before a Jewish court. But Paul declares that "I am standing before Caesar's tribunal, where I ought to be tried" (RSV Acts 25:10).

If Festus as procurator was not willing to administer justice under the auspices of a Roman court, then Paul declared that no course was left open to him but to have his case transferred—not to Jerusalem—but to Rome. As a Roman citizen Paul had the right, if he considered himself falsely accused or tried, to appeal to the higher court. Having not obtained his freedom from Tribune Claudius Lysias, nor from either of two provincial procurators, he therefore claimed the right of citizenship to refer his case to the emperor in Rome, the supreme court in the Empire.

"Then Festus, when he had conferred with the council, answered, Hast thou appealed unto Caesar?" Paul must have said yes, for Festus then said, "unto Caesar shalt thou go" (Acts 25:12).

Refusing to release Paul for fear of Jewish opposition, Festus was left with no choice but to give heed to Paul's plea unto Caesar. In so doing, he has caused a problem for himself. What charges, what crimes could he write of Paul having committed that he was unable to give judgment for as procurator? If he had nothing concrete to claim as charges, he would make a fool of himself before the emperor. This is most likely the reason for the delay in Paul being sent to Rome for his trial.

King Herod Agrippa II Comes to Caesarea Maritima (Acts 25:13–22 • August AD 60)

"And after certain days king Agrippa and Bernice came unto Caesarea [Maritima] to salute Festus" (Acts 25:13). This was King Agrippa II and his sister Bernice. Drusilla, the wife of Felix, was their sister. This King Agrippa attained a much diminished portion of his father's kingdom. As Agrippa was a Jew, he would therefore be more versed in the laws and customs of the Jews that Porcius Festus would be.

> And when they had been there many days, Festus declared Paul's cause unto the king, saying, There is a certain man left in bonds by Felix:
>
> About whom, when I was at Jerusalem, the chief priests and the elders of the Jews informed me, desiring to have judgment against him.
>
> To whom I answered, It is not the manner of the Romans to deliver any man to die, before that he which is accused have the accusers face to face, and have license [opportunity] to answer for himself concerning the crime laid against him.
>
> Therefore, when they were come thither, without any delay on the morrow I sat on the judgment seat, and commanded the man to be brought forth.
>
> Against whom when the accusers stood up, they brought none accusation of such things as I supposed:
>
> But had certain questions against him of their own superstition [religion], and of one Jesus, which was dead, whom Paul affirmed to be alive.
>
> And because I doubted of such manner of questions, I asked him whether he would go up to Jerusalem, and there be judged of these matters.
>
> But when Paul had appealed to be reserved unto the hearing of Augustus [Nero], I commanded him to be kept till I might send him to Caesar.
>
> Then Agrippa said unto Festus, I would also hear the man myself. Tomorrow, said he [Festus], thou shalt hear him. (Acts 25:14–22)

The reference made by Festus about "Augustus" is only titular. Augustus Caesar was emperor from 31 BC until his death in August AD 14. Use of the name Augustus continued for all emperors as a royal title. Technically, Nero could claim use of the name Augustus because he was the last member of the Julio-Claudian dynasty of emperors.

King Herod Agrippa II: Almost a Christian
(Acts 25:23–27; 26:1–32 • August AD 60)

The next day, an official reception was held for King Agrippa and Bernice by Festus with all the influential citizens of Caesarea Maritima. This is how it went: "And on the morrow, when Agrippa was come, and Bernice, with great pomp, and was entered into the place of hearing, with the chief captains, and principal men of the city, at Festus' commandment Paul was brought forth" (Acts 25:23). To warrant the "great pomp," there must have been a substantial audience of those who considered themselves important. Or, to put it into the perspective of our Saint in chains, Paul was the only one not dressed for the occasion.

King Herod Agrippa II
(AD 55–95)—Marcus
Julius Agrippa

"And Festus said, King Agrippa, and all men which are here present with us, ye see this man, about whom all the multitude of the Jews have dealt with me, both at Jerusalem, and also here, crying that he ought not to live any longer" (Acts 25:24). By implication in this statement, none of the Jews at Caesarea were invited to this reception.

> But when I found that he had committed nothing worthy of death, and that he himself hath appealed unto Augustus [Nero], I have determined to send him.
>
> Of whom I have no certain thing to write unto my lord [Nero]. Wherefore I have brought him forth before you, and [e]specially before thee, O king Agrippa, that, after examination had, I might have somewhat to write.
>
> For it seemeth to me unreasonable to send a prisoner, and not withal to signify the crimes laid against him. (Acts 25:25–27)

By the manner in which Festus arranged this trial, Paul was not the one on trial. Rather, the high priest and the Sanhedrin for their unfounded charges against Paul were, and secondly the Jewish nation for their sustaining such leadership. Apart from Agrippa and Bernice (and of course Paul), probably no Jews were present. Festus was, by bringing Paul before a Jewish king while having a Gentile audience, placing Agrippa in a tricky situation. Should Agrippa say Paul was guilty, then Festus had reason to be supportive of Paul in his letter to Nero, thereby finding a charge to save the procurator and satisfy the Jews. If Agrippa found favor in Paul, the Jewish leaders would be made a mock of, as a Jewish king and for Roman justice over Jewish injustice.

In saying such we do not feel that Festus was trying to ridicule or embarrass Agrippa, but rather save his own reputation and credibility, which was at this time questionable in this judicial case.

Let us return to the courtroom:

Then Agrippa said unto Paul, Thou are permitted to speak for thyself. Then Paul stretched forth the hand [and the chains rattled[238]], and answered for himself:

I think myself happy, king Agrippa, because I shall answer for myself this day before thee touching all the things whereof I am accused of the Jews:

Especially because I know thee to be expert in all customs and questions which are among the Jews: wherefore I beseech thee to hear me patiently.

My manner of life from my youth, which was at first among mine own nation at Jerusalem, know all the Jews;

Which knew me from the beginning, if they would testify, that after the most straitest [strictest] sect of our religion I lived a Pharisee.

And now I stand and am judged for the hope of the promise made of God unto our fathers:

Unto which promise our twelve tribes, instantly [earnestly] serving God day and night, hope to come. For which hope's sake, king Agrippa, I am accused of the Jews.

Why should it be thought a thing incredible with you, that God should raise the dead?

I verily thought with myself, that I ought to do many things contrary to the name of Jesus of Nazareth [the Nazarine].

Which thing I also did in Jerusalem: and many of the saints I did shut up in prison, having received authority from the chief priests; and when they were put to death, I gave my voice against them.

And I punished them oft in every synagogue, and compelled them to blaspheme; and being exceedingly mad against them, I persecuted them unto strange [foreign] cities.

Whereupon I went unto Damascus with authority and commission from the chief priests,

At midday, O king, I saw in the way a light from heaven, above the brightness of the sun, shining round about me and them which journeyed with me.

And when we were all fallen to the earth, I heard a voice speaking unto me, and saying in the Hebrew tongue, Saul, Saul, why persecutest thou me? it is hard for thee to kick against the pricks.

And I said, Who art thou, Lord? And he said, I am Jesus whom thou persecutest.

But rise,[239] and stand upon thy feet: for I have appeared unto thee for this purpose, to make thee a minister and a witness both of these things which thou hast seen, and of those things in the which I will appear [show] unto thee;

Delivering thee from the people, and from the Gentiles, unto whom I send thee [see Jeremiah 1:19],

To open their eyes, and to turn them from darkness to light, and from the power of Satan unto God, that they may receive forgiveness of sins, and inheritance among them which are sanctified by faith that is in me.

Whereupon, O King Agrippa, I was not disobedient unto the heavenly vision:

But shewed first unto them of Damascus, and at Jerusalem, and throughout all the coasts of Judaea, and then to the Gentiles, that they should repent and turn to God, and do works meet for repentance.

For these causes the Jews caught me in the temple, and went about to kill me.

Having therefore obtained help of God, I continue unto this day, witnessing both to small and great, saying none other things than those which the prophets and Moses did say should come:

That Christ should suffer, and that he should be the first that should rise from the dead, and should show light unto the people, and to the Gentiles.

And as he thus spake for himself, Festus said with a loud voice, Paul, thou art beside thyself; [so] much learning doth make thee mad [insane]. (Acts 26:1–24)

It must be said that King Agrippa II, before whom Paul stood, was of a much more agreeable kind, than Herod I, before whom Jesus had stood. Since Festus was a Gentile, new to the doctrines and beliefs of the Jews and Christians, most of what Paul was saying went way over his head. His ignorance of the religion did not allow him to pronounce judgment in this case. He needed time to study the people and their culture.

But Agrippa was knowledgeable of the doctrine preached by Paul and the implications of it. Agrippa was interested in the philosophy that Paul preached until the Resurrection was mentioned. It must therefore be concluded that Agrippa espoused the doctrine of the Sadducees, who rejected the notion of a physical resurrection.

This interruption by Festus was curtly and sharply redressed by Paul, who continued, "But he said, I am not mad, most noble Festus; but speak forth the words of truth and soberness. For the king knoweth of these things, before whom also I speak freely: for I am persuaded that none of these things are hidden from him; for this thing was not done in a corner" (Acts 26:25–26).

Concerning Christianity, Agrippa would most certainly have known of its outline and following, for the kingdom over which he ruled included northern Palestine, where there was a large following of Christians.[240] This would account for Paul assuming "that none of these things" were hidden from Agrippa, or strange to his ears.

Paul continued, "King Agrippa, believest thou the prophets? I know that thou believest. Then Agrippa said unto Paul, Almost [momentarily] thou [almost] persuadest me to be a Christian" (Acts 26:27–28). The interpretation of Agrippa's answer is generally one of almost acceptance, but such was not the case. He was being derisive.

Compare the following: "Do you think that in such a short time you can persuade me to be a Christian?" (New International Version). Or, "With trivial proofs [or with little persuasion] like these, you expect me to become a Christian?" (Living Bible).

Lest we forget, the title *Christian* was one of contempt from its inception in Antioch-on-the-Orontes. We know that Agrippa was not inclined to any of the Jewish sects, save possibly the remnants of the Herodians, his family party.

But though we understand that Agrippa spoke in a contemptible manner, Paul used it to make his response. "And Paul said, I would to God, that not only thou, but also all that hear me this day, were both almost, and altogether such as I am, except these bonds" (Acts 26:29). The rather quick-witted reciprocal remark was not taken well by King Agrippa. At this point, he signified that the audience was at an end by arising from his seat, which was the gesture for all others to do likewise. "And when he [Paul] had thus spoken, the king [Agrippa] rose up, and the governor [Festus], and Bernice, and they that sat with them: And when they were gone aside [retired], they talked between themselves, saying, This man doeth nothing worthy of death or of bonds. Then said Agrippa unto Festus, This man might [could] have been set at liberty, if he had not appealed unto Caesar" (Acts 26:30–32).

We must conjecture that there was a friendly servant or soldier in the vicinity of Agrippa, Festus, and Bernice, for how else can we explain that Luke and Paul came to know of these remarks made in private conversation? The position is further understood when we consider that no mention was made concerning the report of the tribune from Jerusalem with Governor Felix, for the two were completely alone. But in the case here with Agrippa, the remarks were spoken in relaxed conversation, where servants or soldiers on guard could hear them.

Paul was returned to his cell. Festus was at loss as to what to write to Nero. Were he to fabricate witnesses, how should he explain the fact that Paul was detained for two years before being tried? Some other pretext had to be forwarded. There was one reason that would suffice, and to which Paul himself could not refute, even before Nero.

The Jewish leaders were in frenzy. They wanted Paul's blood and nothing else would do. Felix and Festus, and with the expert advise of Agrippa, observed that it was in the best interest of peace in the province, and of course for an innocent Roman citizen, not to have any court in the land release him—innocent though he most certainly was. But rather send Paul to Nero who might, at his good pleasure after a suitable time, when the Jews were not so intent upon Paul's life, release him quietly. Thereby the justice of Rome could be done while, at the same time, preserving a tranquil administration in a province where revolt was most obnoxious.

15: The First Imprisonment (III)

Caesarea to Sidon (Acts 27:13 • September AD 60)

The time had now come for Paul to be taken to Rome. He was taken into the custody of Tribune Claudius Lysias in Jerusalem in the middle of AD 58. By this time, it was the end of August or the beginning of September AD 60. This would mean that Paul had spent about twenty-six months in prison in Caesarea.

This is not a lonely journey, as there are several other prisoners in the contingent also going to Rome (Acts 27:1). The prisoners were under the command of Centurion Julius, with a hundred *legionaries* soldiers under his command (Acts 27:1, 42–43). Paul was also not without friends. There were others making the same journeys who were not prisoners. We are told Luke and Aristarchus of Thessalonica accompanied Paul (Acts 27:2). An Imperial prisoner was permitted to be accompanied by two servants or slaves while under arrest.[241] Though Luke is not mentioned by name—neither is he mentioned by name anywhere, for that matter—this record was made by Luke and he included himself by saying "we" throughout the whole journey.

The centurion Julius must have brought with him all documents pertaining to Paul's case for the imperial court. These documents would include "depositions of the witnesses, on both sides, and the record of his (the procurator's) own judgment on the case. This report was called *Apostoli*, or *literae dismissoriae*."[242]

"And when it was determined that we should sail into Italy, they delivered Paul and certain other prisoners unto one named Julius, a centurion of Augustus' band [*Prima Augusta Italica*[243]]. And entering into a ship of Adramyttium, we launched, meaning to sail by the coasts of Asia; one Aristarchus,[244] a Macedonian of Thessalonica, being with us" (Acts 27:1–2). We cannot fail to observe that Luke made the point of saying that the ship was "of Adramyttium," which is located north of Ephesus. He also said they set sail, "meaning [*or* intending] to sail by the coasts of Asia."

Such statements indicate that the original intention of the centurion was to sail up the Aegean coast of west Adria, then cross over to Macedonia and take the highway Via Egnatia to the Adriatic coast. From there, cross over to Brundusium, then follow the Via Appia to Rome.

"And the next day we touched at Sidon. And [Centurion] Julius courteously entreated Paul, and gave him liberty to go unto his friends to refresh himself" (Acts 27:3). No doubt the centurion was given instructions concerning the loose custody with which he was to treat Paul above the other prisoners.

Since Julius would have been carrying the letters from the Procurator Festus to Emperor Nero, he must have been informed concerning the charges against Paul. The liberal manner in which he guarded Paul attests to that. We might also conclude that Julius had knowledge of Paul for some time in Caesarea, as not every prisoner received private audiences before two provincial governors and one king "with great pomp."

Perhaps there were Christians at Sidon who had witnessed the miracles of Jesus Christ. For Luke recorded that on one occasion Jesus "stood in the plain, and the company of his disciples, and a great multitude of people out of all Judea and Jerusalem, and from the sea coast of Tyre and Sidon, which came to hear him, and to be healed of their diseases; and they that were vexed with unclean spirits: and they were healed" (Luke 6:17–18). Jesus had ministered in "the coasts of Tyre and Sidon" (Matthew 15:21). Was that young Greek Syro-Phenician woman (Mark 7:26) whom Jesus had healed, who was "grievously vexed with a devil," to be counted among the Saints in that region (Matthew 15:22 [22–28]; Mark 7:26 [26–31])?

Sidon to the Fair Havens (Acts 27:48 • September AD 60)

"And when we had launched from thence [Sidon], we sailed under Cyprus, because the winds were contrary.[245] And when we had sailed over the sea of Cilicia and Pamphylia, we came to Myra, a city of Lycia. And there the centurion [Julius] found a ship of Alexandria[246] sailing into Italy; and he put us therein" (Acts 27:46). The ship docked at the harbor of Myra for the night, but there was an Egyptian grain ship, bound for Puteoli (or Ostia) in Italy, at anchor in the same harbor. Centurion Julius learned that this ship would set sail on the morrow, just as the ship he came with would, but the prospect of being able to sail into Italy instead of walking a sizeable portion of the journey was enticing enough for him to alter his intended plans.

Therefore, the prisoners were transferred from the medium-sized craft to the larger, more robust Egyptian vessel. Julius must have been grateful to the gods for his good fortune. Paul's hopes of being able to visit with friends in Ephesus, Troas, Neapolis, Philippi, and Thessalonica were lost because of this change of plans.

Centurion Julius would not be required to carry a large purse to pay for all of the passengers—soldiers and prisoners—since he would have the power to requisition whatever means of transport he could procure.

Egypt was the granary of the Empire. It was the one imperial province under direct control of the emperor. It was supervised by a prefect, whose job it was to ensure a bountiful harvest and charter the necessary shipping to get the grain delivered to the capital of Rome. As a further incentive, under the reign of Claudius a new harbor was built at the mouth of the Tiber at Ostia. Also, all grain ships bound for Rome from Egypt were "indemnified" against "loss" while "on the open sea"; and grants were provided for the construction of new grain ships in proportion to their tonnage.[247]

The intended course of this grain ship would have been to sail across the Aegean Sea under Greece, then across the Adriatic Sea and follow the coast all the way to Ostia, outside of Rome. A seemingly straightforward course to follow.

"And when we had sailed slowly many days, and scarce were come over against Cnidus, the wind not suffering us [to sail toward Italy], we sailed [south] under[248] Crete [Island], over against [Cape] Salmone; and, hardly passing it, came unto a place which is called The fair havens; nigh [near where] whereunto was the city of Lasea" (Acts 27:7–8). When Luke said "the wind not suffering us," he meant that there was a strong headwind.

Grain ships were single masted, with just a small foresail only capable of engaging a headwind at about seven points (78.75 degrees off head-on).[249] Therefore, the captain of the merchant ship decided to circumvent the storm by sailing closer to Crete.

This was not successful, so he concluded that they should sail by the south coast of Crete, using the land as a shield against the storm. It is because of these circumstances that the ship came to the Fair Haven port, situated some distance from Lasea, the port serving the city of Gortys.

Paul Advises against Leaving the Fair Havens (Acts 27:9–12)

"Now when much time was spent, and when sailing was now dangerous, because the fast was now already past," or the day of Atonement[250] (Yom Kippur), which coincides with the autumn equinox at the end of September or beginning of October in AD 60. At this time, the trade winds were contrary to westbound shipping.

> Paul admonished them,
> And said unto them, Sirs, I perceive that this voyage will be with hurt and much damage, not only of the lading [cargo] and ship, but also of our lives.
> Nevertheless, the centurion [Julius] believed the master and owner of the ship, more than those things which were spoken by Paul.
> And because the haven [harbor] was not commodious to winter in, the more part advised to depart thence also, if by any means they might attain to Phenice[251] and there to winter; which is a haven of Crete, and lieth toward the south west[252] and north west.[253] (Acts 27:9–12)

Departure from the Fair Havens (Acts 27:13–26)

"And when the south wind blew softly, supposing that they had obtained their purpose, loosing thence, they [the crew] sailed close by Crete. But not long after there arose against it a tempestuous wind, called Euroclydon [a storm from the northeast known today as a levanter]. And when the ship was caught, and could not bear up[254] into the wind, we let her drive"[255] (Acts 27:13–15). The suddenness of this wind was probably caused when the ship rounded the Cape Lithino

(Matala) that forms the south arm of the Bay of Ormos (Messara). It appears that the force of this gale prevented the ship from being maintained on a northwestern course.

"And running under [the lee of] a certain island which is called Clauda [now Gavdos], we had much to come by the [ship's] [life]boat" (Acts 27:16). There was only one oar boat, and it was being towed at the stern of the ship. With such rough seas, there was fear lest this small craft would sink. To this end, it was considered necessary to "hoist it aboard" the ship (New International Version, Acts 27:17).

"Which when they had taken up [the lifeboat], they used helps,[256] undergirding the ship; and, fearing lest they should fall into the quicksands [Syrtis sandbanks], strake [a small] sail, and so we were driven" (Acts 27:17). The force of the storm was enormous, causing a wrenching in the ship's hull, resulting in the planking shearing and opening, allowing the sea into the cargo hold. The captain ordered the use of ropes or chains to undergird the keel to prevent the planks from opening at the seams—"with the help of tackle bound cables round the ship" (Jerusalem Bible).

The sandbanks referred to by Luke are the Syrtis sandbanks in the Bay of Syrtis on the Lybian coast of North Africa. The bay is divided geographically into two portions: Syrtis major (east) and Syrtis minor (west). Without question, Syrtis major is what Luke meant.

Roman Merchant Ships (adapted from Coneybeare and Howson, *The Life and Epistles of St. Paul,* v. 1, 1908, 52; v. 2, 308. New York: Charles Scribner, Sons.)

The storm was relentless, perpetually pounding the hull planking of the ship. "And we being exceedingly tossed with a tempest, the next day they [the crew] lighted the ship" (Acts 27:18).[257] For the most part, the grain probably started shifting in the hold to the port side, causing the ship to lean to the left. The captain would have ordered the passengers from among the two hundred and seventy-six on board to take up position of the starboard side to provide counter balance, while telling the crew to work below in the hold of the ship. Working the hold was dangerous in a storm; if the cargo shifted a seaman could be crushed to death. However, on this occasion, we are informed that all souls were saved.

"And the third day we[258] cast with our own hands the tackling of the ship [see Isaiah 33:23]. And when neither sun nor stars in many days appeared, and no small tempest lay on us, all hope that we should be saved was then taken away" (Acts 27:19–20).

When the sun and stars couldn't be seen by them, there was no possibility for navigation, which naturally led to despair (see Psalm 107:21–29). The anxiety of the moment was expressed in these final words, "We finally gave up all hope of being saved" (New International Version Acts 27:20). The sailors were running to and fro, working to keep the planks of the ship together. Much anxiety was certainly felt by all. The situation was desperate, and no one had any desire to eat.

> But after long abstinence [from food,] Paul stood forth in the midst of them, [calling all the men around him,] and said, Sirs, ye should have hearkened unto me, and not have loosed from Crete, and to have gained this harm and loss.
>
> And now I exhort you to be of good cheer: there shall be no loss of any man's life among you, but of the ship.
>
> For there stood by me this night the angel of the God, whose I am, and whom I serve,
>
> Saying, Fear not, Paul; thou must be brought before Caesar: and, lo, God hath given thee all them that sail with thee.
>
> Wherefore, sirs, be of good cheer: for I believe God, that [which] it shall be even as it was told me.
>
> Howbeit we must be cast upon a certain island. (Acts 27:21–26)

Tossed in a Turbulent Mediterranean Sea (Acts 27:27–29)

"But when the fourteenth night was come, as we were driven up and down in Adria, about midnight the ship men deemed that they drew near to some country; and sounded, and found it twenty fathoms [20 *orguias* or ὀργυιὰς]: and when they had gone a little further, they sounded again, and found it fifteen fathoms. Then fearing lest we should have fallen upon rocks, they cast four anchors out of the stern, and they wished for the day[light]" (Acts 27:27–29).

Luke's phenomenal attention-to-detail is recognized. He said, "About midnight the sailors sensed they were approaching land" (New International Version Acts 27:27). In the darkness of the night and in a raging storm, the sailors discerned that land was near. The waves were coastal breakers and not deep sea waves.

They were "near the low rocky point of Okura," Malta[259] Sounding the sea depth was measured by a rope with fathom knots or markers dropped into the sea with a weight attached. The slack was taken up, and then it was pulled up and the markers counted to establish how much depth there was. Allowance was made for the displacement of the ship itself. In Roman times, a large merchant ship was displaced only about two meters, or six feet.[260]

This large ship required four anchors off the stern to hold it fast. Luke expressed the situation, in that "they wished for the day[light]." There must have been considerable fear and foreboding among the 275 souls on the ship.

The Crew Panic (Acts 27:30–32)

"And as the ship men [sailors] were about to flee out of the ship, when they had let down the boat into the sea, under colour [cover of darkness] as though they would have cast anchors out of the foreship, Paul said to the centurion and to the soldiers, Except these abide in the ship, ye cannot be saved. Then the soldiers cut off the ropes of the boat, and let her fall off" (Acts 27:30–32).

With the crew gone, who would be experienced enough to steer the ship to the shore at daybreak? Without hesitation, Centurion Julius and some of the soldiers "cut the ropes and let the boat fall off" (Living Bible Acts 27:32).

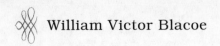

William Victor Blacoe

The Day of Deliverance (Acts 27:33–38 • October AD 60)

> And while the day was coming on, Paul besought them all to take meat, saying, This say is the fourteenth day that ye have tarried and continued fasting, having taken nothing.
>
> Wherefore I pray you to take some meat: for this is for your health: for there shall not a hair fall from the head of any one of you.
>
> And when he had thus spoken, he took bread, and gave thanks to God in presence of them all: and when he had broken it, he began to eat.
>
> Then were they all of good cheer, and they also took some meat.
>
> And we were in all in the ship two hundred three score and sixteen souls.
>
> And when they had eaten enough, they lightened the ship, and cast out the wheat into the sea. (Acts 27:33–38)

It was their intent to beach the ship, so discharging the cargo would mean that the ship would ride higher out of the water and enable it to run to ground closer on the shore. Paul must have possessed a certain degree of charisma, in that he was able to calm the troubled souls in the ship. Luke records that, following Paul's comforting address, "then were they all of good cheer, and they also took some meat" (Acts 27:36).

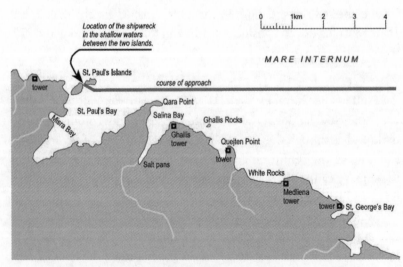

Shipwreck on Malta

Shipwreck on Malta (Acts 27:39–44)

"And when it was day, they knew not the land: but they discovered a certain creek with a shore [beach],[261] into the which they were minded, if it were possible, to thrust in the ship. And when they had taken up the anchors [cut off the anchor lines], they committed themselves into the sea, and loosed the rudder[262] bands, and hoisted up the mainsail to the wind, and made toward shore" (Acts 27:39–40).[263]

Axing the anchor lines, they let the ship run with the wind, and at the same time let the rudders down into the sea and raised the foresail of the ship to catch the wind and drive it with all speed onto the beach before them. They rushed forth upon the waves, passing Qawra Point on the port side, and entered Saint Paul's Bay, heading for the shore ahead. But approaching the bay's shore, they discover that it is not a bay at all, but rather shallow waters between two islands in an open bay, with the mainland in the background beyond.[264]

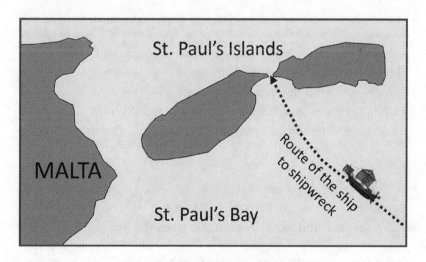

St. Paul's Island, Malta

And falling into a place where two seas meet,[265] they ran the ship aground; and the forepart stuck fast and remained immovable, but the hinder part was broken with the violence of the waves.[266]

And the soldiers' counsel was to kill the prisoners, lest any of them should swim out, and escape.

But the centurion, willing to save Paul, kept them from their purpose; and commanded that they which could swim should cast themselves first into the sea, and get to land:

And the rest, some on boards, and some on broken pieces of the ship. And so it came to pass, that they escaped all safe to land. (Acts 27:41–44)

It was not strange that the soldiers considered executing the prisoners for fear of them escaping, as they, the soldiers, would be held responsible for their delivery to Rome and might be executed for failing in their duties, should they let prisoners escape—just as a jailor would (Acts 12:18–19; 16:27).

Almost one month on a bedeviled sea from Caesarea Maritima; were it not for the fact that they were on an island, many might have vowed to never take to the sea again. Though Paul expressed bold courage while on the ship, no doubt there was a degree of apprehension within him many times during the stormy days.

"Be of good cheer, Paul: for as thou hast testified of me in Jerusalem, so must thou bear witness also at Rome" (Acts 23:11). These words of the Lord Jesus must have, a number of times, come into his mind over the weeks of stormy trial, standing upon a wave-washed deck with a blackened sky full of foreboding gloom, feeling the cold dampness in passing shivers of apprehension. But now drenched from the sea, Paul likely lay himself down upon mother earth and breathed a sigh of deliverance; not only Paul, but all of the others also. The lives of all had been spared.

Since they grounded where "the two seas meet," we may with confidence assume that not all made shore upon the same island, but rather distributed upon both. To reach the mainland, they had to again cross the water, but there is a hundred meters (330 feet) distance between the west end of the larger Selmunett Island and the mainland of Malta. Possibly by use of a rope from the wreck, they drew a line across for all to hold to—their iron rod to safety, as it were.

They must have crossed to the mainland the same day, for Luke recounts the hospitality of the inhabitants, and it is doubtful that anyone lived on either of the two islands where the wreck was.

A Venomous Beast Bites Paul (Acts 28:16)

And when they were escaped, then they knew that the island was called Melita [Malta appendage to the Province of Sicily].

And the barbarous[267] people shewed us no little [unusual] kindness: for they kindled a fire, and received us every one, because of the present rain, and because of the cold.

And when Paul had gathered a bundle of sticks, and laid them on the fire, there came a viper [driven] out of the heat, and fastened on his hand. And when the barbarians saw the venomous beast hang on his hand, they said among themselves, No doubt this man is a murderer, whom, though he hath escaped the sea, yet vengeance [or the goddess *Diké*[268]] suffereth not to [let him] live.

And he shook off the beast into the fire, and felt no harm.

Howbeit they looked when he should have swollen, or fallen down dead suddenly: but after they had looked a great while, and saw no harm come to him, they changed their minds, and said he was a god. (Acts 28:1–6)

From the wording of verse 3, it is possible Paul merely picked up a bundle of faggots already prepared[269] and laid them upon the already burning fire. Since the weather was also inclement on the island, perhaps the snake took refuge amongst the faggots, with Paul being unaware.

When he reached over the fire and dropped the bundle into the flames, the unwelcome smoke and heat disturbed the viper, which made a speedy exit by the only means possible: on Paul's arm. He, like anyone else, was no doubt startled by this viper latching itself onto him. Saying that "he shook off the beast" is likely a somewhat mild description of his shocked response.

But he had a calling to fulfill, therefore "the poison of a serpent shall not have power to harm" him (D&C 84:72). The trials of a Saint are many and varied, as one approaches perfection. The Lord in his unfathomable wisdom has deemed many circumstances and situations beneficial and worthy for man's progression. "For my thoughts are not your thoughts, neither are your ways my ways, saith the Lord. For as the heavens are higher than the earth, so are my ways higher than your ways, and my thoughts than your thoughts" (Isaiah 55:8–9).

The Father of Publius Healed of Dysentery
(Acts 28:16)

While on this island, Paul, Luke, Aristarchus, and possibly also Centurion Julius and others were given shelter by Publius, who was the governor of the island. This may have been in his residence at Mdina—the Roman capital city on the island—which is located about eleven kilometers south from the shipwreck location in the interior of the island.

> The Roman capital, Mdina and a part of Rabat being walled round as one town. The citadel point must, then as now, have been the island's most defendable place, and it contained the governor's palace, the garrison barracks, with perhaps a temple or two. Tradition holds—and there is no reason to doubt it; archeology has vindicated equally old traditions of the sort in Rome and elsewhere—that the house of Publius, "chief man of the islands," stood on the site of the cathedral. The Roman villa and St. Paul's Grotto, however, also have their claim to this dignity.[270]

Returning to Luke's account, we read, "In the same quarters [locality] were possessions of the chief man of the island, whose name was Publius [Popilius]; who received us, and lodged us three days courteously. And it came to pass, that the father of Publius lay sick of a [persistent] fever and of a bloody flux [dysentery]: to whom Paul entered in, and prayed, and laid his hands on him, and healed him" (Acts 28:7–8).

It may have been that Luke offered assistance as a physician to the feverous patient. But be that as it may, Paul exercised his priesthood authority and ministered to him, restoring the man to health. As may be expected, this remarkable recovery was voiced abroad among the inhabitants of Malta. "So when this was done, others also, which had diseases in the island, came, and were healed" (Acts 28:9).

Paul possessed a great and noble spirit. No doubt that among his fellow passengers, Paul had become a highly esteemed companion. He must have found great comfort in his two ministers, namely Luke and Aristarchus. Luke in humble obscurity devoted his narrative to Paul throughout the entire journey, never alluding to himself or to Aristarchus.

The ministrations of Paul among the inhabitants of Malta had placed many in his debt. Luke says they "also honoured [presented] us with many honours [gifts]; and when we departed, they laded us with such things as were necessary. And after three months we departed in a ship of Alexandria, which had wintered in the isle, whose sign was Castor and Pollux"[271] (Acts 28:10–11).

It may be wondered why Luke would remember and record the name of the ship that took them from Malta, but not the name of the ship which brought them there. One author theorized, "The reason lies in the circumstances. He heard the news about the last vessel before he saw it; but he became acquainted with the others by seeing them."[272]

From Malta to Puteoli (Acts 28:12–14 • February AD 61)

They spent three months on Malta Island (November AD 60–February AD 61). Now the worst of the winter was over and it was time to resume the journey to Rome. Passage was obtained on another Egyptian grain ship bound for Italy. "And landing at Syracus[a]e, we tarried there three days" (Acts 28:12). It would be well to assume that Paul was permitted to go ashore at Syracusae like at Sidon. This was the city of Archimedes, the mathematical and engineering genius.

"And from thence we took a compass [took our bearings and tacked the wind], and came to Rhegium: and after one day the south wind blew, and we came to Puteoli: Where we found brethren, and were desired [invited] to tarry with them seven days: and so we went toward Rome" (Acts 28:13–14).

The party moved swiftly from Malta to Sicily, crossing the Mare Siculum, a distance of about 160 kilometers, and from thence to the Italian mainland. Rhegium became the first Italian mainland soil that Paul set foot upon. With a strong wind to speed their journey, they passed through the Straits of Messina (Frentum Siculum) and crossed the Tyrrhenian Sea (Mare Tyrrhenum).

As the ship approached the coast of Campania, the Island of Caprae came into view, where the licentious Emperor Tiberius spent his days. Then, passing Caprae and the Point of Minervae, they sailed into the Bay of Naples (*Sinus Cumanus*). Mount Vesuvius, with its smoking head, would have dominated much of the starboard view. Just twenty-five kilometers from Paul was located Pompeii and Herculaneum, which, like Sodom and Gomorrah of old, waiting for the judgment of God to purge their wickedness in less than a decade.

The final port in this long journey was but twenty-five kilometers away. They passed Portus Misinus on the port side, where a portion of the Roman navy was stationed. Several battle ships with their shackled slaves may have been in port.

The sail was lowered as the ship approached the harbor of Puteoli, and the sea part of the journey to Rome was at an end. "Passengers were landed at Puteoli; but cargo was carried on to Ostia."[273] If the centurion had followed his original plans to come by way of the Via Egnatia across Macedonia, they would have passed by Puteoli several months earlier.

It was observed by one author that this grain ship from Egypt carried, as a cargo, the bread of life for the citizens of Rome—in the temporal sense. But in addition to that cargo of wheat, it carried missionaries of The Church of Jesus Christ, bearing the Bread of Life (John 6:35; Revelation 2:17; Alma 5:34) for the salvation of Rome—in the spiritual sense.[274]

Puteoli to Rome on the Via Appia (Acts 28:15–16)

Following the week they spent as guests in Puteoli, they made out for Rome on the Via Appia.[275] But it somehow appears that word of Paul's coming was sent on ahead of him. "And from thence [Rome], when the brethren heard of us, they came to meet us as far as Appi forum" (Acts 28:15).[276] And traveling a little further, they met more of the Roman Saints at "the three taverns [Tres Tabernae, where the road from Antium joined the Appian Way]: whom when Paul saw, he thanked God, and took courage" (Acts 28:15).

Considering the greetings[277] that Paul sent in his Epistle to the Romans, we can reasonably assume that some, most, or all of them came out to meet him. Seeing so many friends, Luke said, "Paul thanked God and was encouraged" (New International Version Acts 28:15). The highway crosses the Pomptine Marshes (*Palum Pomptinae*), so the prisoners and the brethren of Paul drew nearer to Rome.

Now from the shoulder of the Albian Hills he gets his first view of the Eternal City. He has seen many glorious cities in his time, but nothing like this. Glorious, beautiful Rome, with all her historic associations, the incarnation of earthly power, the mistress of earthly power, the mistress of the World! His friends point out the Capitol and the Imperial Palace, the countless temples and the stately triumphal arches, commemorating the Empire's glories, the vast Circus Maximus on the left, where every year 10,000 victims died, butchered to make a Roman holiday, in that old world without Christ.[278]

"And when we came to Rome [in February AD 61], the centurion [Julius] delivered the prisoners to the captain of the guard: but Paul was suffered [allowed] to dwell by himself with a soldier that kept him" (Acts 28:16). Note that Luke said "captain of the guard" (Greek *stratopedarch*). This is actually the military office (Latin *princeps pergrinorum*).[279]

In turning over his prisoners, Julius would also have handed over any documentation in his possession that he had concerning Paul and the others. Did anything survive the shipwreck? Such documentation would have been written upon parchment, which might have been lost when "the bow of the ship stuck fast and would not move, and the stern was broken to pieces by the pounding of the surf" (New International Version Acts 27:41). If the pouch of documents (*elogium*) were saved by Julius, would they still been readable, or had they become wet by the sea, causing the ink to smudge?

There is a high probability that Julius or another was dispatched to return to Caesarea Maritima for new documents. It was February AD 61, and it would be summer before a courier could be back in Rome with copies of the documents. Therefore, the testimony of Julius and his soldiers would have been all that was readily available concerning the status of the prisoners. Such testimony secured for Paul the privilege of residing "in his own hired house" (Acts 28:30). This delay would mean that preliminary hearings could not convene until later in the year.

His Own Hired House (Acts 28:16)

As for Paul, Burrus had permitted him to be held in custody in private quarters. Centurion Julius would have bid farewell to Paul, who was no doubt the most interesting prisoner he had ever had to deliver to the imperial capital. The centurion would have delivered the surviving letters concerning Paul to the imperial courts.

There is the possibility that Paul was aware of the circumstances under which he was to be retained in Rome. After all, dwelling in his own private quarters was by no means the norm in any time period for a prisoner; house arrest was somewhat selective. But considering the freedom that Paul was given by Centurion Julius—no doubt under the explicit orders of Porcius Festus, the Judean procurator—it is possible, and most likely, that his quarters were arranged by the Roman Saints.

There were three forms of judicial confinement for a Roman prisoner. *Custodia publica* was internment in a jail or dungeon, often accompanied by torture. *Custodia libera* was a free custody under bond of a public official, used for prisoners of high rank. And then *custodia militaris* was military custody under guard by soldiers, either in one of the barracks or a private home.[280]

Since the time of Augustus, judicial cases against Roman citizens were referred to the city praetor. Usually foreigners had their appeal presented before a former consul appointed to look after the affairs of various provinces.[281]

Discourse to the Jews at Rome (Acts 28:17–31)

And it came to pass, that after three days Paul called the chief of the Jews together: and when they were come together, he said unto them, Men and brethren, though I have committed nothing against the people, or customs of our fathers, yet was I delivered prisoner from Jerusalem into the hands of the Romans.

Who, when they had examined me, would have let me go, because there was no cause of death in me.

But when the Jews spake against it, I was constrained to appeal unto Caesar; not that I had ought to accuse my nation of.

For this cause therefore have I called for you, to see you, and to speak with you: because that for the hope of Israel I am bound with this chain.

And they said unto him, We neither received letters out of Judaea concerning thee, neither any of the brethren that came shewed or spake any harm of thee.

But we desire to hear of thee what thou thinkest: for as concerning this sect, we know that every where it is spoken against. (Acts 28:17–22)

These Jewish leaders departed from Paul and spread word among the Jewish community that he desired to preach before them.

> And when they had appointed him a day, there came many to him into his lodging; to whom he expounded and testified the kingdom of God, persuading them concerning Jesus, both out of the law of Moses, and out of the prophets, from morning till evening.
>
> And some believed the things which were spoken, and some believed not.
>
> And when they agreed not among themselves, they departed, after that Paul had spoken one word, Well spake the Holy Ghost by Esias [Isaiah] the prophet unto our fathers,
>
> Saying, Go unto this people, and say, Hearing ye shall hear, and shall not understand; and seeing ye shall see, and not perceive [quoting Isaiah 6:9]:
>
> For the heart of this people is waxed gross, and their ears are dull of hearing, and their eyes they have closed; lest they should see with their eyes, and hear with their ears, and understand with their heart, and should be converted, and I should heal them [quoting Isaiah 6:10].
>
> Be it known therefore unto you, that the salvation of God is sent unto the Gentiles, and that they will hear it [quoting Psalm 67:2].
>
> And when he had said these words, the Jews departed, and had great reasoning among themselves. (Acts 28:23–29)

The Jewish presence at Rome became established following the conquest of Palestine by Pompey. Originally, the Jewish inhabitants were largely slaves and freedmen with a ghetto area in the Trastevere sector to the west of the Tiber River and south of the Vatican Hill. This population was considerable, "that, in AD 19, Tiberius sent four thousand of them to fight in Sardinia."[282]

The likelihood is that Paul rented accommodation for his house arrest in the Jewish quarter. Since house arrest involved the presence an armed military guard, the gospel was being preached in Rome under imperial protection.

"And Paul dwelt two whole years in his own hired house [dwelling], and received all that came in unto him, Preaching the kingdom of God, and teaching those things which concern the

Lord Jesus Christ, with all confidence, no man forbidding him" (Acts 28:30–31).

"Two whole years" passed (February AD 61–February AD 63), during which time the city of Rome had the opportunity to hear and accept the gospel. For those who found the gospel message objectionable, they had the surety that Paul could not preach beyond the confines of "his own hired house."

When writing the Roman Epistle from Corinth, he stated, "Now I beseech you, brethren, for the Lord Jesus Christ's sake, and for the love of the Spirit, that ye strive together with me in your prayers to God for me; That I may be delivered from them that do not believe in Judaea; and that my service which I have for Jerusalem may be accepted of the saints; That I may come unto you with joy by the will of God, and may with you be refreshed" (Romans 15:30–32).

Possibly several, if indeed not all those whom he had addressed in his Epistle to the Romans over two years previously, were yet in residence in the city (Romans 16:3–15). Priscilla and Aquila, with whom Paul found lodging over the winter in Corinth, had returned to Rome following the repeal of the imperial edict banning Jews from the city. The first convert Paul ever managed in the province of Achaia, Epaenetus, had emigrated to Rome. Perhaps he was also there yet. What of Mary, Andronicus and Junia, Amplias, Urbane, Stachys, and Appelles (Romans 16:5–10)? How had the Church of Aristoblus and the Church of Narcissus, two of the Roman city congregations, fared?

There are several others too: Herodian, Tryphena and Tryphosa, Persis, Rufus and his mother (Asyncritus), Phlegon, Hermas, Patrobas, Hermes and the brethren who were with him, Philogus and Julia, Nereus and his sister, and Olympas (JSIV Romans 16:11–15). Paul was not among strangers but friends, and of course, a military guard day and night. Did he take the opportunity to read the Roman daily newspaper *Daily Acts* (*Acta Diurna*),[283] in publication since 131 BC?

Close of the Narrative of Luke

We now come to the end of the narrative provided by Luke in his second book, the Acts of the Apostles. It should be remembered that Luke wrote his Gospel account and the Acts of the Apostles not for us, but for his friend Theophilus (Acts 1:1). Therefore, we now turn to the epistles of Paul to understanding what occurred from this Roman captivity until his execution a few years later. There is sufficient evidence in the writings of Paul and Luke to prove that Paul was not executed at this time.

16: The First Imprisonment (IV)

The Epistle to the Colossians

The Epistle to the Colossians is a letter to dear friends of Paul. The town of Colossae was a short distance across the valley from another Christian congregation of the Church at Laodicea, and also near a third congregation at Hierapolis.

A substantial earthquake occurred at the time Paul was writing this letter to the congregation at Colossae. The earthquake on the Hierapolis fault zone is dated to AD 60, and projected to have been Richter magnitude 6.0, based upon modern geological modeling.[284] All three cities were demolished in the earthquake and subsequently rebuilt.

The Lost Epistle to the Laodiceans (Summer AD 62)

In relation to Colossae, the city of Laodicea was just twelve kilometers to the northwest. Consequently, there would have been much exchange between the brethren in these two communities. There would have been no difficulty in the Colossians bringing their Epistle to the Laodiceans.

As for the Laodicean epistle from Paul, once again, we suffer the loss of yet another missing scripture. From the manner in which Paul relates to it, we may conclude that it was written at a slightly earlier time than the Colossian Epistle. Had it been written at a much earlier date, the Colossians would have no doubt already had opportunity to read, or at least to have heard concerning its contents.

We interpret the words, "Salute the brethren which are in Laodicea" (Colossians 4:15), to mean that the Laodicean epistle was dispatched by another courier or by the same courier carrying both letters.

It would appear that some self-esteeming individual thought it worthwhile to produce a Laodicean epistle, so some centuries later an epistle purporting to be the lost Laodicean epistle was produced from collected fragments of Paul's other letters. No Greek version survives, but a Latin copy exists today. "There is every reason to suppose that this letter (which is almost impossible to date accurately) is a forgery."[285] Several authors consider Ephesians to be the Laodicean epistle, or at least that Ephesians was a circular letter dispatched to several congregations.

The Epistle to Philemon (Summer AD 62)

The short letter from Paul to Philemon is a personal correspondence and not particularly a gospel or Church letter. It concerns the private matter of a runaway slave, Onesimus, who robbed from Philemon prior to his departure. By the strangest coincidence, Onesimus eventually found his way among the throngs of people in the city of Rome. He fortuitously encountered Paul and eventually took on the role of a personal caregiver to Paul. However, Paul recognized the complete necessity of Onesimus returning to his master and owner, Philemon, in the town of Colossae.

There is every reason to believe that Paul's letter to Philemon was sent at the same time as his Epistle to the Colossian congregation. This single sheet letter became an anchor to the souls of millions of Christians in the bondage of slavery for twenty centuries.

The Epistle to the Ephesians (Summer AD 62)

There exists the possibility of Epaphras the Colossian came to Rome via Ephesus. In so doing, he may have had opportunity to meet with certain Saints in Ephesus, thereby bringing news of the conditions among the Saints there. Of course, Paul may have obtained report from others, but Epaphras is a possible candidate.

We also have Tychicus and Onesimus departing with letters to the Laodiceans and to the Colossians (and a private letter for Paul's friend Philemon). They would have most likely taken ship for Ephesus. It would therefore seem a reasonable assumption to believe they brought with them the Epistle to the Ephesians.

Tychius, Epaphras, and Onesimus Depart

Tychicus departed for Asia, in company with Epaphras from Colossae and Onesimus, the runaway slave of Philemon. Together they brought a letter to the Laodicean branch and another for the Colossians nearby. There was also the personal letter to Philemon, who lived in Colossae; this letter was no doubt carried by Onesimus, the returning slave. And of course there was the Ephesian Epistle delivered by Timothy.

Captive, Paul remained behind in Rome with some months to endure before his imprisonment would come to an end. We now have a fifty-six-year-old man awaiting the pleasure of a twenty-four-year-old Emperor Nero, who was eight years upon the Roman throne.

At the time of his writing to Philemon, Paul had expressed an air of eminent release: "But withal prepare me also a lodging: for I trust that through your prayers I shall be given unto you" (Philemon 1:22).

While Paul was detained in Rome, another event was occurring in Jerusalem, the news of which would have reached Paul in Rome. Trouble had broken out in Jerusalem with the High Priest Ananus orchestrating a persecution against the Christians in AD 62. In the ensuing persecutions, "James the brother of the Lord, who was head of the Church in Jerusalem, was martyred."[286]

The Epistle to the Philippians
(Philippians 2:25–30; 4:10–11 • Autumn AD 62)

During the first imprisonment of Paul, the congregation at Philippi decided to send aid to him in Rome. When writing his Epistle to the Philippians, he said, "But I rejoiced in the Lord greatly, that now at the last your care of me hath flourished again; wherein ye were also careful, but ye lacked opportunity. Not that I speak in respect of want: for I have learned, in whatsoever state I am, therewith to be content" (Philippians 4:10–11).

The Philippian financial aid came with one "Epaphroditus, my brother, and companion in labour, and fellowsoldier" (Philippians 2:25). It seems that Epaphroditus was one of the leading brethren in that branch of the Church. No doubt Paul was quite overjoyed to see Epaphroditus; considering the many years he had labored among the Philippian Saints, Paul must have known him well. Perhaps, during the many visits to Philippi, Paul developed a friendship with Epaphroditus. He did know him from the time that he was in Thessalonica, for he brought the financial aid from Philippi to Thessalonica, where Paul, Silas, and Timothy were laboring (Philippians 4:15–18).

Either upon arrival or shortly thereafter, Epaphroditus became "sick nigh unto death." This sickness troubled Paul, especially under the circumstances he then found himself—a prisoner. Epaphroditus made a steady recovery, which certainly relieved the anxiety of Paul. In later writing, he said, concerning his recovery, "but God had mercy on him; . . . lest I should have sorrow upon sorrow" (Philippians 2:27).

Following his recovery, Epaphroditus, as Paul says, "ministered to my wants" (Philippians 2:25). But Epaphroditus yearned in his heart for home, for his friends and family. Paul wrote:

> For he longed after you all, and was full of heaviness, because that ye had heard that he had been sick.
>
> For indeed he was sick nigh unto death: but God had mercy on him; and not on him only, but on me also, lest I should have sorrow upon sorrow.
>
> I sent him therefore the more carefully, that, when ye see him again, ye may rejoice, and that I may be the less sorrowful.
>
> Receive him therefore in the Lord with all gladness; and hold such in reputation [honor]:
>
> Because for the work of Christ he was nigh unto death, not regarding his life, to supply your lack of service toward me. (Philippians 2:26–30)

This yearning pressed Paul to send Epaphroditus home to where his heart was. Such brought about the circumstances for the writing of the Epistle to the Philippians.

From what is written—or omitted—in the Epistle, we may assume that at this writing, Mark and Aristarchus were no longer in Rome with Paul. This is concluded in that they are not mentioned in the greetings from Rome, as they were in the previous Epistles of this period. Had Luke been in Rome with Paul, no doubt there would have been a greeting from him because he had lived for several years among these people (Colossians 4:10, 14; Philemon 24). It may be that they departed since Timothy (Philemon 1) and Epaphroditus were remaining to minister to the aged apostle. So it was now that Paul, though in need of companionship, particularly from friends dear to his heart, was nonetheless willing to release Epaphroditus from his self-imposed commitment to service.

Trial before Nero (Spring AD 63)

And so Paul continued waiting for Emperor Nero to hear his case. Possibly, he was brought to one of the palaces on the Palatine Hill, where the imperial court of justice might have convened. First, his accusers would have been given opportunity to present their case. Perhaps they employed another skillful lawyer like Tertullus at Caersarea Maritima to speak for them (Acts 24:1).

Then Paul would be given his privilege of defending himself. It can be assumed that he related his first vision, subsequent conversion, and his preaching the gospel message to both the Jews and Gentiles throughout Asia Minor, Macedonia, and Achaia. He may also have extolled the virtues of chastity and self-restraint and the reality of the Resurrection of Jesus Christ.

No doubt he also mentioned the need for repentance and godly conduct. As to the imperial reaction, nothing is recorded. The trial before Nero would have been a long one because of the procedure he used.

> When he judged a case he preferred to defer his judgement until the following day, and then gave it after consideration in writing; and ruled that, instead of a case being presented as a whole, every relevant charge should be presented separately by one side and then by the other. On withdrawing to study a problem of law, he never consulted openly with his judicial advisers in a body, but made each of them write out an opinion; then mulled over these documents in private, came to his own conclusion, and passed it off as a majority opinion.[287]

It has been said that Nero was not a tyrant at the beginning of his reign. He was only seventeen years old when he became emperor in AD 54. This is most likely due to the influence of his tutor L. Annaeus Seneca, the most notable Stoic philosopher of the period.

About the time of Paul's trial, Seneca retired and a man named Ofonius Tigellinus, an evil genius, became the devil's advocate in

Nero's ear. This wretched individual became the instigator of much of the evil performed by Nero. As to whether this was true or not depends upon whether his conduct was measured against true principles of justice or against the prevailing standards of the imperial court. What invoked the leniency of the emperor may never be known. Perhaps it was out of a desire to deny the Jewish delegation from Jerusalem their charge against a Roman citizen, which might have been viewed as an attack against the Roman emperor.

The soldiers who had guarded Paul "two whole years in his own hired house" must have been impressed by him. It could be said that he had, for two whole years, a fettered audience of at least one day and night. Most likely among the soldiers, there were several converts. "My bonds [missionary endeavors] in Christ are manifest in all the palace, and in all other places" (Philippians 1:13). This reference probably included not only household staff, but also the imperial guard. One theory behind Nero letting Paul off was, since the Praetorian guards had several Christians among their ranks, Nero was not disposed to upsetting the security of his station by killing the Christian leader Paul. After all, who knows what eye for an eye or head for a head might roll in revenge?

17: The Fourth Mission Tour

Epistle to the Hebrews (Spring AD 63)

Before his departure from Rome, Paul wrote to the Hebrew nation a selective letter for those of the Mosaic background, known to us as the Epistle to the Hebrews. He was no longer a prisoner when he wrote this letter (Hebrews 13:23–24).[288]

But before continuing, we need to clear up the authorship. It has been suggested by many that Paul was not the author of this letter, though others accept Paul as the author.[289] The opposition concludes that it does not bear the mark or style evidenced uniformly throughout his other writings, though it is accepted that the doctrine is of Paul in its concept and presentation.

In this Epistle, Paul did not mention himself as he did in the first verse of every other surviving writing. It cannot be considered to be a change in style—a "new Paul"—for the letters written after this time resemble those written from the first. It reaches out to an audience widely versed in the tenets of the Mosaic law.

This Epistle was written in order to remove the stumbling block of erroneous interpretation in respect to the mind and will of God. Some scholars have concluded that the Hebrews Epistle was a general epistle to the whole Church, but there are several references in the Epistle itself that contradict this, showing that the Epistle was written to one city. The exact truth is unknown.

Not many years from this time (in AD 68), when Peter wrote his second Epistle general to the Hebrew nation, he remarked upon this writing by Paul and the difficulty with which they were receiving this work.

Nevertheless we, according to his promise, look for new heavens and a new earth, wherein dwelleth righteousness.

Wherefore, beloved, seeing that ye look for such things, be diligent that ye may be found of him in peace, without spot, and blameless.

And account that the longsuffering of our Lord is salvation; even as our beloved brother Paul also according to the wisdom given unto him hath written unto you;

As also in all his epistles, speaking in them of these things; in which are some things hard to be understood, which they that are unlearned and unstable wrest, as they do also the other [holy] scriptures, unto their own destruction. (2 Peter 3:13–16)

"Above all, this Epistle—as seems natural when addressed to a people who had looked forward to the delivering might of their Messiah, a people who had great difficulty in accepting Jesus as their promised Redeemer—above all, this Epistle is a witness of the divine Sonship of Him of whom the Jews had said: 'Is not this the carpenter's son?' (Matthew 13:55)."[290] Paul had learned to put Jewish customs in their proper perspective in relation to the Christian Church.

This Epistle was written to those of similar background as Paul, to those who had not yet learned to divorce their devotions from the Jewish religion. The teachings and endless examples from the Jewish scriptures were laid open to the reader. The Gentiles were not mentioned in relation to their salvation or otherwise; this was a purely Jewish audience. This is the only one of Paul's Epistles that contains references to priesthood and priests, which only highlights further the emphasis of the Epistle and its Hebrew audience.

Joseph Smith, while discoursing upon another subject, declared that Paul wrote the "letter to the Hebrew brethren."[291] When one prophet verifies another's writings, we must accept his testimony, or else in denying one we deny the other.

It is believed that Paul wrote this Epistle from Rome because of the salutation at its conclusion. "They of Italy salute you" (Hebrews 13:24). Timothy is considered to have been the scribe, as he is mentioned in the close of the Epistle. "Know ye that our brother Timothy is set at liberty; with whom, if he come shortly, I will see you" (Hebrews 13:23). The reference to Timothy having been "set at liberty" indicates he had been, for his ministerial endeavors, in trouble with the Roman authorities.

This Epistle was written by Paul in Greek, though there is a theory that Paul wrote the Epistle in Hebrew and Luke translated it into Greek for the benefit of the Greek speaking world.

Free to Leave Rome—End of His Imprisonment (Philippians 1:26; 2:24; Philemon 1:22 • AD 63)

Timothy was also freed, and Paul waited for him so that they might journey together. But before departure, there remained the farewells of two years worth of acquaintances. Those to whom Paul had extended salutations, while writing the Roman Epistle from Corinth, may have been there (Romans 16:3–15). No doubt there were personal acquaintances among those who believed and accepted the gospel message. Having Paul as their gospel tutor was likely a spiritual feast. They had everything to gain by his congenial friendship. "Iron sharpeneth iron; so a man sharpeneth the countenance of his friend" (Proverbs 27:17).

We now come to what may be termed the most difficult portion of Paul's life to cover. Leaving Rome in the spring of AD 63 until his return in a few years time (Autumn AD 67), we have only sporadic evidence of his work and travels until execution. We will build a mosaic from the pieces of information we have from his final Epistles, and what he indicated his intentions were. The difficulty is caused by the well of information, until now supplied by Luke, having dried up, so there will be no more flowing narrative to chart our course.

Accepting his most recent intentions to the Philippians: "That your rejoicing may be more abundant in Jesus Christ for me by my coming to you again. . . . But I trust in the Lord that I also myself shall come shortly" (Philippians 1:26; 2:24). To Philemon in Colossae: "But withal prepare me also a lodging: for I trust that through your prayers I shall be given unto you" (Philemon 1:22).

The primary route is the Via Appia to southeast Italy, by ferry to present day Albania, and then following the Via Egnatia to Philippi. There is no indication as to who traveled with him. A new generation of Christians was growing up since the gospel message was first heralded in this European city.

Once again Paul would have counseled the brethren to shed the old mantel of the Mosaic law and clothe themselves in the robes of truth and virtue. Paul and his party had departed from Philippi to Ephesus by the end of the summer AD 63.

There was likely a short stay at Ephesus before heading up the valleys into the interior. It was possibly in autumn of AD 63, and just how long Paul stayed here is unknown, but since we are following his intention of staying with Philemon in Colossae, we may assume he intended on passing winter there. To this end we have Paul departing from Ephesus before the winter of AD 63–64. Eventually Paul arrived at Colossae to stay with Philemon and Apphia. He had earlier requested: "But withal prepare me also a lodging: for I trust that through your prayers I shall be given unto you" (Philemon 1:22). He would likely have been reunited with Onesimus, whom Paul designated "my son . . . begotten in my bonds" (Philemon 1:10).

Where Did Paul Go? (Romans 15:24–28 • Spring AD 64)

In the spring of AD 64, it is traditionally held that Paul went to Spain (actually, the Iberian Penninsula of Spain and Portugal) for two years. Jerome wrote, "It ought to be said that at the first defense, the power of Nero having not yet been confirmed, nor his wickedness broken forth to such a degree as the histories relate concerning him, Paul was dismissed by Nero, that the Gospel of Christ might be preached also in the West."[292]

In the First Epistle of Clement to the Corinthians (AD 97), he mentioned a journey Paul took to Spain: "He preached in the East and in the West, winning a noble reputation for his faith. He taught righteousness to all the World; and after reaching the furthest limits of the West."[293] The usage of the term *west*, for a Roman writer, signified the western portion of the Roman Empire. Depending upon the era of writing, it usually meant the Iberian Peninsula of Spain and Portugal.

When Paul was ordained an Apostle, he received the following words of blessing: "For so hath the Lord commanded us, saying, I have set thee to be a light of the Gentiles, that thou shouldest be for salvation unto the ends of the earth" (Acts 13:47). Back in Paul's time, "the ends of the earth" meant the limits of the Roman Empire. He was in the eastern limit when the words were uttered. The western limit was Lusitania (Portugal), Taraconnesis, and Beatica (Spain).

When he wrote to the Roman Saints from Corinth in the winter of AD 57–58, he said, "Whensoever I take my journey into Spain [Hispania], I will come to you, . . . if first I be somewhat filled with your company. . . . When therefore I have . . . sealed to them [in Jerusalem] this fruit [charity], I will come by you into Spain" (Romans 15:24–28).[294] That intention was not realized within the time frame envisioned by Paul. It may be that the Lord had plans of preparing the way before letting Paul go to Spain. He is considered to have "spent two years" proselyting in Spain.[295]

In the light of these declarations, we conclude that two years, ranging from summer AD 64 to summer AD 66, were spent in Spain. It is considered by some scholars that Paul made a stop over in Marsilia (Marseilles) en route to Spain.[296] "Certain local traditions in Spain point to a visit by the Apostle, as for instances, in Ecija, Lezuza, and especially in Tortosa where Paul is said to have appointed Rufus as bishop."[297]

Trouble at Ephesus (1 Timothy 1:3, 20; 6:10; 2 Timothy 2:16–17 • Winter AD 66–67)

There is every indication that Paul was again at Ephesus in the winter of AD 66–67. We would like to know of epistles he dispatched to branches in Iberia. What words of inspiration flowed freely in sermons unrecorded, in letters lost, in private interviews given? An Apostle of such magnitude, who did more for his country and fellow men that most of his emperors did. He appears to have found abode in "the house of Onesiphorus; for he oft refreshed me," as Paul says (2 Timothy 1:16).

This was the last winter of Paul's freedom. The flames of resentment were ever-growing. When Paul returned to Ephesus, it was a different political climate. The persecutions of Nero were not only experienced in Rome. In addition, a terribly sad event occurred in Ephesus, as the Saints were being taught false doctrine (1 Timothy 1:3) coming from two men, Hymenaeus and Alexander (1 Timothy 1:20). A third man, Philetus, is mentioned in connection with Hymenaeus (2 Timothy 2:17).

This event no doubt tore into Paul's heart and spirit. Developing and progressing, we find Hymenaeus and Alexander in fellowship with the Church. But now, for some unrecorded reason, the blossom of truth had corrupted into petals of apostasy. The Saints of Ephesus found themselves as "children, tossed to and fro, and carried about with every wind of doctrine, by the sleight of men, and cunning craftiness" of Hymenaeus and Alexander (Ephesians 4:14). Paul soon wrote that "they have erred from the faith, and pierced themselves through with many sorrows" (1 Timothy 6:10). Apparently, both Hymenaeus and Alexander, and possibly others, were excommunicated from the Church for apostasy. Even then, they would not leave the Church alone.

Since Paul was then sixty years old, and becoming a target of both Jewish and Gentile resentment, it must be concluded that he had one or more companions to protect him. Onesiphorus, Tychus, Erastus, Timothy, Titus, Damas, Crescens, Luke, and John Mark appear to have served in this capacity (2 Timothy 4:10–12, 20).

Anti-Christian sentiments were on the rise and almost becoming political policy. "It is certain that the laws enacted against the Christians were enacted against the whole body, and not against particular churches, and were consequently in force in the remotest provinces."[298] Tension was on the rise, those with weak testimonies were beginning to fall away, and Diana of the Ephesians regained many departed worshippers. Apostasy through fear arrived. The power of Rome reigned through fear. Depending upon the location and population of a particular branch, and the disposition of the Roman governor and his magistrates, certain areas no doubt suffered more than others.

Fragmenting the Christian Church

Historians say that within a hundred years after Christ, as many as thirty splinter groups and separate denominations of Christianity flourished. Evidence of early apostasy in the Church was forcefully articulated by Paul when he pleaded with the Corinthians: "I beseech you, brethren, . . . that there be no divisions among you; but that ye be perfectly joined together in the same mind and in the same judgement" (1 Corinthians 1:10). Of all the threats to Christianity, the collection of philosophies designated *Gnosticism* were the most threatening. Gnosticism was the doctrine of salvation by knowledge. The Greek word *gnosis* means "knowledge" and the word *gnostikos* means "good at knowing." Judeo-Christian theology declared that the soul (mind, spirit, and body) attain salvation by obedience to the laws and ordinances of God through faith and good works. Gnosticism purported that knowing the secret hidden knowledge of the universe constituted a people who know (*gnosis*) how to be saved.

Macedonia (2 Timothy 4:13 • Spring AD 67)

Events for this year moved rapidly from one place to another. The sequence of events is gleaned from the remaining Epistles: First Timothy, Titus, and Second Timothy. Paul had just spent the winter months in Ephesus with Timothy and with assistance from the house of Onesiphorus. Paul departed from Ephesus in the spring of AD 67 and headed north to Philippi in Macedonia. He apparently made a short stop at Alexandria-Troas, where he deposited some personal possessions with Carpus (2 Timothy 4:13) before continuing on to Philippi.

To make sense of his movements throughout this year, we must conclude that throughout the summer of AD 67, he continued on through Thessalonica, possibly Berea, and proceeded south to Corinth. Without question, Paul proselyted in more places than we can ascertain with the writings we have.

18: I Have Finished My Course

The Three Pastoral Epistles

Four of the surviving Epistles written by Paul were personal letters written to individuals instead of congregations. By name, they are: Philemon, First Timothy, Titus, and Second Timothy. Philemon was written some years earlier concerning a personal matter. The latter three were given the name *pastoral* from the word *pastor*, since they were written to two ministers (pastors) of the Church. They define pastoral duties and qualifications more than the general Epistles, which were, for the most part, written to a whole congregation. The heresies that Timothy and Titus had to encounter are discussed; these in particular are defined as being "the Divine attributes," "the sanctity of nature," "the inspiration of Scripture," and "the ethical qualities of the Christian life and their connection with evangelical doctrine."[299]

First Epistle to Timothy

The years pass and we eventually come to the composition of the First Timothy Epistle, possibly in May AD 67. Traditional indications are that Timothy was enjoying a period of extended residence at Ephesus. This First Epistle includes extensive guidance and counsel to Timothy on the organization of the Church congregations and specific counsel for members, male and female, free and slave, rich and poor, widow and orphan, self-reliant and dependent on Church support.

There is every indication that Paul returned to Ephesus before completing the final journey through Crete. This must have occurred sometime after dispatching the First Epistle to Timothy from Corinth. Though he was going to Ephesus, we conjecture that Timothy was departing on an assignment elsewhere (possibly Galatia) and would not be at Ephesus by the time Paul arrived.

Ephesus to Crete (2 Timothy 1:15; Titus 1 • Summer AD 67)

Paul departed in the company of Erastus, Tromphimus, Titus, and possibly some others, setting sail south. In all probability, Paul landed somewhere on the northeast end of the island and traversed to the west. The two most obvious towns to visit were Cnossus (now Knosos) and the provincial capital Gortys. Cretian tradition holds that Titus was from Gortys and became the first bishop on the island.

We may consider the branches to be quite new at this time and lacking priesthood leadership. This is concluded from the direction given by Paul to Titus: "For this cause left I thee in Crete, that thou shouldest set in order the things that are wanting, and ordain elders in every city, as I had appointed [directed] thee" (Titus 1:5). The converts on Crete struggle to embrace Christian doctrine and values.

> For there are many unruly and vain talkers [idle speakers] and deceivers. . . .
>
> Whose mouths must be stopped, who subvert whole houses, teaching things which they ought not, for filthy lucre's sake.
>
> One of themselves, even a prophet of their own, said, The Cretians are always liars, evil beasts, slow bellies [lazy gluttons].
>
> This witness [observation] is true. Wherefore rebuke them sharply, that they may be sound in the faith;
>
> Not giving heed to Jewish fables, and commandments of men, that turn from the truth. Unto the pure let all things be pure; but unto them that are defiled and unbelieving is nothing pure; but even their mind and conscience is defiled.
>
> They profess that they know God; but in works they deny him, being abominable, and disobedient, and unto every good work reprobate [worthlessness]. (Titus 1:10–16; JSIV Titus 1:15)

The Cretian prophet Paul quoted here was most likely Epimenides (sixth century BC). Cretians acquired the label of being liars and, in all respects, dishonest. At the conclusion of his months on Crete, Paul embarked for the mainland of Greece.

Epistle to Titus

The Epistle to Titus was probably written by Paul from Corinth back to Titus on Cyprus Island. Titus was given authority and commission to organize a new Church leadership among the congregations on the island. This letter was probably written in September or October AD 67.

Because of the authority and power given to Titus, this letter can therefore be termed a *mandatum principiis* or "letter from a ruler or high official to one of his agents, delegates, ambassador, or governors helping him set up shop in his new post and gets things in good order and under control."[300] The letter deals more with specifics and less with generalities. Paul provided instruction and direction for all ages and social groups. Some of the comments made are specific to cultural conditions among the Cretan. This letter is one of those rare occasions when Paul specifically quotes local literature in his letter, utilizing lines to highlight a paradigm shift to Christian doctrinal beliefs.

The Season of Treason (Titus 3:12; 2 Timothy 2:9; 4:14 • Autumn AD 67)

Apathetic reception at Corinth may have instigated the departure to Nicopolis. That Paul had enemies in Corinth is without doubt. His wrath had descended upon many a Corinthian for their wicked behavior. The Second Corinthian Epistle is replete with evidence: "I have told you before, and foretell you, as if I were present, the second time; and being absent now I write to them which heretofore have sinned, and to all other, that, if I come again, I will not spare [anyone]" (2 Corinthians 13:2).

Paul departed from Corinth and possibly sailed west of the Gulf of Corinth to Nicopolis. In writing to Titus before he departed from Corinth, Paul indicated his intentions for the coming winter season: "When I shall send Artemas unto thee [with the letter], or Tychicus, be diligent to come unto me to Nicopolis: for I have determined there to winter" (Titus 3:12).

Why would Paul choose to winter in Nicopolis? He had left his personal items with Carpus at Alexandria-Troas (2 Timothy 4:13), presumably intending to return there before the winter. He settled in Nicopolis and awaited the arrival of Titus. Near Nicopolis (the City of Victory) is the historical site of the Battle of Actium (2 September 31 BC), where Augustus defeated Marcus Antonius and Cleopatra.

In his first-known letter to Timothy, Paul made a small mention of Alexander and Hymenaeus (Acts 20:29–30; 1 Timothy 1:20). But later, in writing the second letter, he wrote, "Alexander the coppersmith did me much evil" (2 Timothy 4:14). We may believe that this "evil" related to his arrest and deportation to Rome. The easiest charges that Paul could be arrested for would be sedition, treason, and being a leader of the now despised Christian denomination.

And so the deed was done. The excommunicated man had completed his vendetta, his evil heart convicting himself, not Paul. As a wayward son, he had removed himself, like Judas Iscariot, from the grace of his God. Paul was taken as the common criminal and passage to the capital was procured; the sail was hoisted and the course was charted.

Paul crossed the Mare Ionicum and the Mare Adriatium to the Italian mainland at Bryndisium. He passed along the Via Appia and Via Latina to Rome. Paul was interred, not "in his own hired house" as before (Acts 28:30), but in the Tullianum Prison, a grim building still existing today. The keys of oppression secured the aged man to his new home with shackles. He sat in "bonds" (2 Timothy 2:9). We learn later, when writing to Timothy in Ephesus, that Onesiphorus ministered unto him in prison: "when he [Onesiphorus] was in Rome, he sought me out very diligently, and found me" (2 Timothy 1:17). As to how Onesiphorus—from Ephesus—came to be in Rome is not elucidated.

At this time in the history of the Roman Empire, the Christian community came under the rod of oppression, being classified as "a sect professing a new and mischievous religious belief."[301]

First Trial before Nero (2 Timothy 4:16–18 • Winter 67–68)

Time passed, and those few Saints who dared entered to minister to Paul's needs. "Eubulus," "Pudens, and Linus, and Claudia," (among others) all took the risk to succor their Apostle (2 Timothy 4:21). But moral support for Paul was lacking.[302] The time had come for his first hearing before the imperial court. Nero was not present at this first trial; he was in Greece.[303] At this time, he had set his Praetorian Guards to the task of excavating a canal across the Corinthian isthmus. This project, however, was eventually abandoned.[304] The judges called for witnesses. Was Alexander there? We may assume that there was some form of prosecution witness, most likely in person, but possibly in written testimonial.

As to the defense, again Paul stood forth to justify his position. His language was the same: "And Paul, earnestly beholding the council, said, Men and brethren [fellow citizens of Rome], I have lived in all good conscience before [my] God until this day" (Acts 23:1). Paul spoke well, but none came forward to speak in his defense. He stood alone. Paul wrote to Timothy:

> At my first answer [defense] no man stood with me, but all men forsook me: I pray God that it may not be laid to their charge.
>
> Notwithstanding the Lord stood by me, and strengthened me; that by me the preaching might be fully known, and that all the Gentiles might hear: and I was delivered out of the mouth of the lion.
>
> And the Lord shall deliver me from every evil work, and will preserve me unto his heavenly kingdom: to whom be glory for ever and ever. Amen. (2 Timothy 4:16–18)

From these words, we may ascertain that the first hearing went well for Paul, raising his expectations and hopes of a favorable outcome. We may understand how Paul came to be "delivered out of the mouth of the lion" (2 Timothy 4:17) when we consider the legal practices of the time. Nero "ruled that, instead of a case being presented as a whole, every relevant charge should be presented separately by one side and then by the other."[305] Therefore, we conclude that at this first hearing he was acquitted of those things for which he had been charged.

A Roman Citizen Identification (2 Timothy 4:13)

Possibly the main defense that Paul had on his side was his Roman citizenship, and he declared that he was free-born (Acts 22:25–29; see also 16:35–38).

The executions of both Peter and Paul occurred at Rome. Peter died by painful crucifixion, not being a Roman citizen. Being a Roman citizen, Paul was beheaded swiftly by the sword, a privilege of his citizenship. But the question to be answered is how was Paul able to prove he was a free-born citizen of the Empire? The answer is those who possessed Roman citizenship also possessed identification parchments, declaring that they were entitled to that honor.[306] In addition to this, there was an official notarized pedigree chart, which detailed how and through whom the citizenship was obtained. These documents (or parchments) were, for all intents and purposes, a

Roman passport. It would be normal for the holder to deposit these valuable documents in a safe place. We therefore conclude that Paul did not carry them about with him, except when they might be needed. As Paul was brought to Rome abruptly, he might not have had such documents in his possession to show. This would explain why, in writing to Timothy, he requested, "The cloke [portfolio] that I left at [Alexandria-]Troas with Carpus, when thou comest, bring with thee, and the books, but especially [above all] the parchments" (2 Timothy 4:13). These may have been his passport parchments of citizenship.

Roman citizenship was a privileged social status with respect to laws, property, and governance. Citizenship was affected by legislation, specifically the *Lex Iulia de Civitate Latinis Danda* (enacted by Lucius Julius Caesar in 90 BC). For a Roman, the documents of citizenship consisted of at least three parchments. The first parchment contained a notarized declaration of entitlement to the honor of Roman citizenship that was issued at the time of his birth in his hometown.[307] A second parchment contained an official notarized pedigree chart called a *stemma*,[308] detailing how and from and through whom the Roman citizenship was first granted. Usually there was a third parchment that included a notarized declaration of political, military, and civil offices, as well as service rendered in the city of Tarsus, province of Cilicia, or the Imperial State.

The content of verse 13 is complicated and somewhat unclear. There are three Greek words of particular interest: first, "cloke" (*phelonen*); second, "but especially" (*malista*); and third, "parchments" (*membranas*). On the first reading, we interpret that Paul entreated Timothy to bring three things: his cloak, books, and parchments. However, the inclusion of "but especially" implies reiterated emphasis for priority of something that was mentioned earlier. The second item on the list, books or scrolls, is clear, yet the third item, parchments, would then be a reemphasis of the first item, the cloak or coat.

The "cloke" (*phelones*) "is a cloak with long sleeves, especially for winter use."[309] We ask ourselves why Paul would request Timothy to collect a winter coat and suffer the inconvenience of carrying it from northwest Turkey, traverse Greece and Italy, and bring it to Rome.[310] If Paul were discomfited in prison, then Luke would have procured a cloak or blanket at Rome, being a generic article. The translation of *cloke* is therefore suspect.

There is the distinct probability that this unique Greek word meant a *portfolio*[311]—"a chest or box for containing books"[312]—or scrolls. In some instances, the papyrus or parchment document rolls were contained in a "vellum wrapper" so that the document "was encased to protect it. This "was called a φαινόλης [*phainoles* in Greek] or *paenula* [in Latin]."[313] This interpretation is substantiated by the literal rendering of the Syriac Peshitta Version of this Epistle. A literal translation from the Syriac Bible of this verse reads, "And when thou comest, bring the bookcase, which I left at Troas with Carpus, and the books, but especially the roll of parchments,"[314] meaning that which is contained in the bookcase.[315] The word *bookcase* in Syriac is *bsheeta*,[316] "a case for writings,"[317] or *book-carrier*.[318] "The parchments were costly, and doubtless were writings of high importance."[319]

In all probability, this contained "the diploma of Paul's Roman citizenship."[320] The idea of a chest or document pouch containing important parchments clarifies why Paul was specific in requesting the portfolio containing the parchments that were not procurable in

Rome.[321] An 1849 translation from Western Peshitta reads, "The case (for) books[322] which I left at Troas with Karpos, when thou comest bring, and the books, and especially the roll of parchments."[323] The roll of parchments was contained in the bookcase, therefore mentioned first and reiterated again at the end.

The "parchments" (Greek *membrana*) means "a written sheepskin." "*Membrana* is a Latin word . . . from *membrum*, 'a limb,' but denoting 'skin, parchment.' The English word 'parchment' is a form of *pergamena* . . . signifying 'of Pergamum,' the city in Asia Minor where 'parchment' was either invented or brought into use."[324] This is the only time this word is found in the New Testament. The books likely referred to documents written on papyrus, while the parchments referred to documents written in animal skin. Only precious and important documents were committed to parchment.[325]

Only Luke Is with Me (2 Timothy 4:11 • Winter AD 67–68)

Back in the Tullianum (*Mamertineum*) Prison, Paul awaited the second trial, following Nero's return from Greece. In words of expressive loneliness, we read, "Only Luke is with me" (2 Timothy 4:11). Luke, who was as old as Paul (or older), had not deserted him.

But we previously read that in his first trial, he stood alone. We cannot believe that Luke was in Rome during that hearing. Had he been, he would have come forth in verbal defense. Therefore, we may conclude that he arrived from some Aegean branch—Philippi—as soon as word reached him of Paul's plight.

Luke's coming was a comfort and a joy to Paul, now that all had forsaken him. But Luke brought sad news, if Paul did not already know; to Timothy, he writes, "For Demas hath forsaken me, having loved this present world, and is departed unto Thessalonica; Crescens to Galatia, Titus unto Dalmatia" (2 Timothy 4:10). Such knowledge did not by any means lighten the miseries of his internment. "Only Luke is with me" (2 Timothy 4:11), "a friend that sticketh closer than a brother" (Proverbs 18:24).

The Second Epistle to Timothy
(2 Timothy 4:9, 11 • Winter AD 67–68)

The Mamertine (Tullianum) Prison was becoming colder. Winter was closing in upon Rome. We will lay hold upon the sincerity of Paul's request to bring Timothy and John Mark to his aid in his prison cell. "Do thy diligence to come shortly unto me. . . . Only Luke is with me. Take Mark, and bring him with thee: for he is profitable to me for the ministry" (2 Timothy 4:9, 11).

If the timing was right, they should have arrived in Rome by the end of October or early November. Let us lay hold upon the hope of Timothy, having procured from Carpus in Troas the parchments and books Paul had requested. There was a happy reunion between Paul, Luke, Timothy, and John Mark in the prison cell. These four seasoned missionaries of the gospel, bound together in a union of hope. Tears of joy likely fell freely, a bond of love that the shackles of bondage could not bind. They no doubt made as many visits as they possibly could.

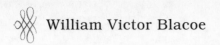

William Victor Blacoe

The Master Comforts Paul (2 Timothy 4:17)

In addition to these visits of comfort and joy, let us not forget his closest friend, one who needs no permission and certainly no key to visit: the Lord Jesus Christ. "Notwithstanding the Lord stood with me" (2 Timothy 4:17). Many times it could have been said, for the "night following the Lord stood by him and said, Be of good cheer, Paul" (Acts 23:11).

There had, since that wondrous day on the Damascus Road, been a developing friendship between Paul and the Savior, association that had come to pass through the efforts of a labor of love. Paul, through his efforts and energy for the welfare of his fellow men, had earned the privilege of personal communion with the Master. We too may stand in the presence of the Redeemer of mankind, just as Paul did—and yet does—if we, like Paul, are willing to pay the price and become as He would have us become: a Saint.

President Kimball said, "I love Paul for he spoke the truth. He leveled with people. He was interested in them. I love Paul for his steadfastness, even unto death and martyrdom. I am always fascinated with his recounting of the perils through which he passed to teach the gospel to member and non-member."[326]

Second Trial (Early AD 68)

Nero had returned from Greece to Rome, and Paul was then arraigned before him. This venomous tyrant held a cold heart for his fellow men. Paul would be given little opportunity to make any sort of defense before Nero. Sentence was heralded forth: guilty of crimes against the empire.

Once again, the prison doors closed upon a man of the Lord. Temporarily, Paul was returned to the Mamertine Prison, pending execution. The Saints of Rome withdrew in horror. Prayers ascended unto the heaven in behalf of the condemned Apostle. The Senate had passed a law to the effect that a period of ten days must elapse between sentence and execution, so that if the emperor felt so disposed, he might have opportunity to grant a royal pardon of clemency. Saint Jerome reported that Paul suffered martyrdom "in the fourteenth year of Nero's reign; that is, sometime between 13 October AD 67 and 9 June AD 68."[327]

The Last Day of Mortality (Spring AD 68)

A morning in the early spring of the year AD 68, Paul stepped forth from the Mamertine Prison into the cool air, the crispness of the air causing him to hold his cloak, along with Timothy, Luke, John Mark, and others—possibly Eubulus, Prudens, Linus, Claudia, and all the brethren (2 Timothy 4:21). They formed his associates on this last day of Paul's mortality.

The Praetorian soldiers and lictors marched the condemned to execution. The tears likely flowed freely from those Saints who had ventured forth that morning to bid farewell. Marching forth through "the Porta Trigemina past the Pyramid of Cestius,"[328] they departed and went beyond the city on the Via Ostiensa. It was the rule in Rome that if the execution of an individual might provoke unrest, then the condemned should be conducted beyond the walls of the city for execution, thereby limiting the threat of reprisal.

Leaving the Via Ostiensa, they "turned off on the Via Laurentiana and, after about half an hour, they came to the Salvian Marsh (*Aquae Salviae*)."[329] Here the execution took place.

Since prior to 507 BC, the Roman constitution had lain down the form of execution for the criminals who were Roman citizens. "The condemned criminals were bound to the stake." Then "the consuls took their seats on the tribunal; the lictors were ordered to carry out the sentence. The prisoners were stripped, flogged, and beheaded."[330] The executioner awaited, axe in hand, the approaching warmth of the new day dispelling the chill of the morn. Paul bid farewell to those Roman Saints, and his closest companions: Luke, Timothy, and John Mark, among others.

Conclusion

We now speak of body and spirit, as the soul of Paul was divided. The spirit finds a time of peace and freedom from mortal cares, the earthly tabernacle is laid down to rest in the earth. It is asserted that one called "Prudens, after retrieving the body of Paul, interred it on their estate on the Via Ostiensa."[331] Later, Emperor Constantine had the bones from the traditional site reinterred, and a new Basilica of St. Paul's Outside-the-Walls (*Basilica di San Paolo fuori le Mura*) was constructed over the sarcophagus. The basilica was destroyed by fire on 15 July 1823 and the current enlarged basilica was thereafter constructed and completed in 1840. The tomb is inscribed with the epitaph: "For me to live is Christ and to die is gain" (*Mihi vivere Christus est et mori lucrum*).

> Follow the labors of this Apostle [Paul] from the time of his conversion to the time of his death, and you will have a fair sample of industry and patience in promulgating the Gospel of Christ. Derided, whipped, and stoned, the moment he escaped the hands of his persecutors he as zealously as ever proclaimed the doctrine of the Savior. And all may know that he did not embrace the faith for honor in this life, not for the gain of earthly goods. What, then, could have induced him to undergo all this toil? It was, and he said, that he might obtain the crown of righteousness from the hand of God. No one, we presume, will doubt the faithfulness of Paul to the end. None will say that he did not fight the good fight that he did not preach and persuade to the last. And what was he to receive? A crown of Righteousness.[332]

Let us here say that Paul is not dead. He lives on! To Timothy, he wrote, "For I am now ready to be offered, and the time of my

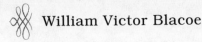

departure is at hand. I have fought a good fight, I have finished my course, I have kept the faith: Henceforth there is laid up for me a crown of righteousness, which the Lord, the righteous judge, shall give me at that day: and not to me only, but unto all them that love his appearing [manifestation]" (2 Timothy 4:6–8).

We may, without reservation, declare the fact that the endeavors of Paul have abounded since his temporal demise. The written word that he bequeathed to mankind and the contributions of Luke the physician and fellow Apostle with Paul have been and are fountains for the posterity of Adam to quench their ever-present spiritual thirst. Paul led a life of service, worthy of emulation by any people, in any age—especially the present.

Endnotes

1. Findlay, *The Epistles of Paul the Apostle*, preface.
2. Ramsay, *Saint Paul the Traveler and the Roman Citizen*, 93.
3. Smyth, *The Story of Saint Paul's Life and Letters*, 3.
4. Cary, *A History of Rome*, 338.
5. Graves, *Suetonius: the Twelve Caesars*, 157.
6. Cary, *A History of Rome*, 355.
7. Graves, *Suetonius: the Twelve Caesars*, 158.
8. Graves, *Suetonius: the Twelve Caesars*, 217.
9. Conybeare, *The Life and Epistles of Saint Paul*, 2.
10. Léon-Dufour, *Dictionary of Biblical Theology*, 428; Barclay, *Ambassador for Christ*, 20; Edersheim, *Jesus the Messiah*, 56.
11. Firmage, *Paul and the Expansion of the Church Today*, 27.
12. Edersheim, *Jesus the Messiah*, 61.
13. Stacey, *The Pauline View of Man*, 22.
14. Stacey, 1956, *The Pauline View of Man*, 22; quoting Gilbert Murray, 'Hellenistic Philosophy,' *Hibbert Journal*, October 1910, 20; F. J. Foakes-Jackson, 1926, *The Life of Saint Paul: the Man and the Apostle*, 47.
15. Hayward, *The Concise English Dictionary*, 382, "Epicure."
16. Barclay, *Ambassador for Christ*, 109.
17. Hayward, *Concise English Dictionary*, 1117, "Stoic."
18. Barclay, *Ambassador for Christ*, 108.
19. Stacey, *The Pauline View of Man*, 62.
20. Drane, *Paul*, 22.
21. Drane, *The Early Life of the Church*, 4647.
22. Pollock, *The Apostle*, 5.

23. This term conveys the message that his ancestors were of uncontaminated Hebrew lineage and not converts from Gentile origins among any of his paternal or maternal ancestors.

24. Greenough, *The Roman Constitution*, Introduction: VI.

25. Smith, *Teachings of the Prophet Joseph Smith*, 180.

26. Of the names mentioned, Junia and Lucius are Latin, while Andronicus, Herodian, Jason, and Sosipater are Greek.

27. Smyth, *The Story of Saint Paul's Life and Letters*, 21–22.

28. Montague, *The Living Thought of St. Paul*, 2.

29. Farrar, *The Life of Christ*, 77.

30. Wallace, *The Early Life and Background of Paul the Apostle*.

31. Farrar, *The Life of Christ*, 158.

32. Perhaps one of his known cousins: Junia, Lucius, Andronicus, Herodian, Jason, or Sosipater.

33. Jeremias, *Jerusalem in the Time of Jesus*, 83, quoted in Kim, *The Origin of Paul's Gospel*, 33.

34. Davies, *Paul and Rabbinic Judaism*, 5–6.

35. Gamaliel (died circa AD 50) was the son of Simeon ben Hillel, and grandson of Hillel the Elder (110 BC–AD 10).

36. Drane, *Paul*, 16.

37. Free men who were descendants of former prisoners of war taken to Rome by General Pompey and later given their liberty (Holzner, *Paul of Tarsus*, 24).

38. On the North African coast.

39. "A legend says that there were more than 400 synagogues in Jerusalem" (Barclay, *Ambassador for Christ*, 45). "The city was filled with national synagogues; some scholars enumerate about 480 alien synagogues" (Holzner, *Paul of Tarsus*, 24, quoting Mackey, *The Adventures of Paul of Tarsus*).

40. The word is a vivid term, "it is the word used for the damage that a wild boar did when he got into a vineyard" (Barclay, *Ambassador for Christ*, 39).

41. The reference to chief priests could mean the Sanhedrin or the presidents of the twenty-four courses of the priests, also known as the chief priests. The Gospels are replete with references to the chief priests (1 Chronicles 24:6–19; Matthew 2:4; Luke 1:5). There are over sixty references alone in the New Testament.

42. Barclay, *Ambassador for Christ*, 51.

43. Conybeare, *The Life and Epistles of Saint Paul*, 59, fn. 6.

44. Eusebius, *Historia Ecclesiae*, bk. 3, 30:2, 93; quoting Clement, *Miscellenies*, bk. 3.6:52.

45. The word *arose* implies he raised himself; however, it should read *was raised* (Marshall, *Interlinear Greek: English New Testament*).

46. The term seems to imply that he did not open his eyes immediately, but after a time.

47. Barclay, *Ambassador for Christ*, 56.

48. Holzner, *Paul of Tarsus*, 48; also called the River Abana.

49. The AKJV translates *Christ*, but the Greek manuscripts read *Jesus*. Greek *Christos* is not in the best manuscripts.

50. "The word used for an army sacking a city" (Barclay, *Ambassador for Christ*, 39).

51. The Greek text does not mention a window, but it is implied: "by night through the wall let down him lowering in a basket" (Marshall, *Interlinear Greek: English New Testament*).

52. Acta Pauli et Thecalae circa AD 160; quoted in Drane, *Paul*, 14; see also Barclay, *Ambassador for Christ*, 12.

53. Renan, *Life of the Apostles*, 165; quoted in Roberts, *Outlines of Ecclesiastical History*, 86.

54. Conybeare, *The Life and Epistles of Saint Paul*, 178, fn. 4.

55. Ibid., 178–79.

56. Smith, *Teachings of the Prophet Joseph Smith*, 180.

57. McConkie, *Doctrinal New Testament Commentary*, 2:92.

58. Josephus, *Wars of the Jews*, bk. 3, 2:4.

59. Downey, *A History of Antioch in Syria*, 582–83 for details of sources. Others suggest that the population was 800,000 (Laymon, *Acts & Paul's Letters*, 43; Anderson, *Understanding Paul*, 12, 34.). Another estimate that has been proposed is 250,000 for the total population (Barclay, *Ambassador for Christ*, 63).

60. Downey, *A History of Antioch in Syria*, 188.

61. Ibid., 193.

62. Ibid., 197.

63. Ibid., 197.

64. Malalas, *Chronographia*, 242:16–17; Dindorfii, *Ioannis Malalae Chronographia*, 494.

65. Downey, *A History of Antioch in Syria*, 275.

66. Ibid., 277; Gibbon, *The Decline and Fall of the Roman Empire*, 281.

67. Eusebius, *Historia Ecclesiastae*, 3:22.

68. Eusebius, *Historia Ecclesiastae*, 3:36.

69. Conybeare, *The Life and Epistles of Saint Paul*, 99; Ramsay, *Saint Paul the Traveller and the Roman Citizen*, 47–48.

70. Smyth, *The Story of Saint Paul's Life and Letters*, 53–54; Holzner, *Paul of Tarsus*, 98.

71. "They passed the first and second guards and came to the iron gate leading to the city. It opened for them by itself, and they went through it. When they had walked the length of one street, suddenly the angel left him" (New International Version, Acts 12:10).

72. Josephus, *Antiquities of the Jews*, bk. 19, 8:2; see also 2 Maccabees 9:89.

73. Strong, *Greek Dictionary*, #630.

74. Burton, *Discourses of the Prophet Joseph Smith*, 80.

75. Holzner, *Paul of Tarsus*, 103.

76. Findlay, *The Epistles of Paul the Apostle*, 289.

77. Sperry, *Paul's Life and Letters*, 41–42.

78. Ramsay, *Saint Paul the Traveler and the Roman Citizen*, 94; see also Barton, *He Upset the World*, 48.

79. Ramsay, *Saint Paul the Traveler and the Roman Citizen*, 95–96.

80. Holzner, *Paul of Tarsus*, 123; see also Minn, *The Thorn That Remained*, 29–30.

81. Holzner, *Paul of Tarsus*, 112.

82. Greek *archisunagogoi* translates directors of the synagogue services.

83. Davies, *Paul and Rabbinic Judaism*, 7.

84. Farrar, *The Life of Christ*, 184.

85. Joshua died in 1429 BC, and in 1095 BC Saul was anointed king; therefore the period of the Judges is reckoned to have been 1429–1095 BC which is 334 years (LDS Bible Dictionary, 1979).

86. Ramsay, *Saint Paul the Traveler and the Roman Citizen*, 100.

87. The Bezan Text reads priests. "Since the sacrificial slaughter of an animal was generally attended to by several priests, we concur with the plural form" (Ramsay, *Saint Paul the Traveler and the Roman Citizen*, 118).

88. Barclay, *Ambassador for Christ*, 89.

89. "Some manuscripts add that the companions of Paul stayed by him until evening, when he was revived" (Laymon, *Acts & Paul's Letters*, 54).

90. McConkie, *Doctrinal New Testament Commentary*, 2:133.

91. See Skousen, *The First 2000 Years*, 308–9.

92. Elaine Cannon, "If We Want to Go Up, We Have to Get On," *Ensign*, November 1978, 108.

93. Ramsay, *Saint Paul the Traveler and the Roman Citizen*, 42.

94. "Profligate sanctuaries" (Conybeare, *The Life and Epistles of Saint Paul*, 173).

95. *Idol-sacrifices*: the word *meats* is interpolated in AKJV. The RSV has more correct translation: "That you abstain from what has been sacrificed to idols" (Marshall, *Interlinear Greek: English New Testament*).

96. Some manuscripts omit and from what is strangled (Marshall, *Interlinear Greek: English New Testament*, 536, fn. j).

97. The harshness is mellowed in the following: "I opposed him to his face, because he was in the wrong" (New International Version).

98. The following interpretation may be of interest: "If thou, being a Jew by birth, yet hast [spiritual] life on the same terms as the Gentiles, and not by virtue of thy being a Jew, why dost thou urge the Gentiles to Judaise?" (Whately, *Lectures on the Characters of Our Lord's Apostles*, 193; quoted in Conybeare & Howson, *The Life and Epistles of Saint Paul*, 179, fn. 6).

99. "Out came the goddess' immortal blood, the ichor that runs in the veins of the happy gods, who eat no bread nor drink our sparkling wine and so are bloodless and are called immortals" (Homer, *The Iliad*, bk. 5 [line ~330], 101).

100. "To Paul appeared, a man Macedonian certain was standing and beseeching him" (Marshall, *Interlinear Greek: English New Testament*; see also Ramsay, *Saint Paul the Traveler and the Roman Citizen*, 202).

101. That is Peter, Silas, Luke, Timothy.

102. Many Bible translations say gate instead of city. The Greek word *pólis* commonly translated as city really means a city "with walls, of greater or less size" (Strong, *Greek Dictionary*, #4172). We therefore conclude that they went outside the city wall.

103. "She would take no refusal" (Jerusalem Bible).

104. Greek *paidské* denotes a young female slave.

105. Greek *puthón* this is the only occasion of this word in the Greek scriptures. The word comes from *Puthó*, the name of the region Delphi is located, the seat of the famous Greek oracle. This type of oracle was called a *Python* (Strong, *Greek Dictionary*, #4436.) "Python is the name of Apollo in his oracular character" (Conybeare, *The Life and Epistles of Saint Paul*, 231, fn. 2).

106. Greek *mantéuómal* this is the only occasion of this word in the Greek scriptures. One who "raves through inspiration," "to rave as a maniac" (Strong, *Greek Dictionary*, #3132, #3105).

107. Greek means "slaves" or "bondsmen."

108. Jones, *Jerusalem Bible*, 291, fn. b.

109. "The magistrates rent off their clothes," does not mean that the praetors tore their own clothes, rather "the magistrates ordered them to be stripped and beaten" (New International Version).

110. "Thrice was I beaten with [lictor] rods" (2 Corinthians 11:25). These beatings must have occurred in Roman settlements where the Roman judicial system was enforced.

111. Use of stocks and pollory was abolished by France in 1832, and the United Kingdom and the United States in 1837. However, the State of Delaware only abolished use of the pillory in 1905.

112. Meinardus, *St. Paul in Greece*, 17.

113. The Greek *phós* means "illumination" (Strong, 1890, Greek Dictionary, #5457). Most translations read plural lights, not singular light (AKJV). "Trembling with fear, the jailer called for lights and ran to the dungeon and fell down" (Living Bible). "So he asked for lights and leaped in and, siezed with trembling, he fell down" (New World Translation). "The jailer called for lights, rushed in and fell trembling" (New International Version).

114. Laymon, *Acts & Paul's Letters*, 64.

115. RSV translates more correctly, inserting up. The meaning being rendered that the home of the jailor was higher than the prison cell, which most likely was below ground.

116. Meinardus, *St. Paul in Greece*, 18.

117. Conybeare, *The Life and Epistles of Saint Paul*, 239, fn. 3.

118. *Jason* is Greek name, as a Hellenistic Jew it may actually be *Joshua*, like *Paul* had from *Saul*.

119. Is it possible that this is the Jason mentioned in Romans 16:21 as a kinsman of Paul?

120. Meinardus, *St. Paul in Greece*, 38.

121. There is an interesting addition that is made to the Bezan text of verse 15: "And they which conducted Paul brought him as far as Athens; and he neglected Thessalia, for he was prevented from preaching the Word unto them" (Ramsay, *Saint Paul the Traveler and the Roman Citizen*, 234–35).

122. McConkie, *Doctrinal New Testament Commentary*, 2:155.

123. Levi, *Pausanias: Guide to Greece*, 1:47.

124. Ministry of Culture, *Historical Map of Athens: Akropolis & Plaka*, Athens.

125. Gärtner, *The Aeropagus Speech and Natural Revelation*, 47.

126. Ramsay, *Saint Paul the Traveler and the Roman Citizen*, 246–47.

127. Greek *Agnostô Theô* correctly translates an "Unknown God" (RSV). Oecumenius stated the full inscription was: "to the gods of Asia and Europe and Libya, to the Unknown and Strange Gods;" Tertullian retains the plural, "to Unknown Gods" (Meinardus, *St. Paul in Greece*, 46).

128. One blood may not refer, to Jewish, but Greek exclusiveness; for they considered themselves to be on a higher plateau than their barbarian neighbors.

129. By implication, both the Father and the Son.

130. Stacey, *The Pauline View of Man*, 37; quoting Bruce, *The Acts of the Apostles*, 338.

131. Conybeare, *The Life and Epistles of Saint Paul*, 292, fn. 3. Paul may have known this poem by Cleanthes instead of the earlier work by Aratus.

132. Stacey, *The Pauline View of Man*, 38; quoting Davies, *Paul and Rabbinic Judaism*, I.

133. Marshall, *Interlinear Greek: English New Testament*.

134. Betteridge, *Cassell's German English Dictionary*; Die Heilige Schrift: Einheitsubersetzung.

135. Member of the high court, Dionysus was "the first convert after Paul's address to the Athenians in the Areopagus. He became the first bishop of Athens" (Eusebius, *Historia Ecclesiae*, bk. 3, 4:10). "Dionysus the Areopagite . . . was the first to be appointed Bishop of Athens" (bk. 4, 23:3).

136. 25 January AD 49–24 January AD 50 (Meinardus, *St. Paul in Greece*, 66).

137. Graves, *Suetonius: the Twelve Caesars*, 202; Conybeare, *The Life and Epistles of Saint Paul*, 233, fn. 5.

138. Greek *antitassomai* is a military term which implies a professional and strategically planned opposition.

139. A literal translation of the Greek word *order*: "And with him Priscilla and Aquila having shorn in Cenchrea the head for he had a vow" (Marshall, *Interlinear Greek: English New Testament*).

140. Holzner, *Paul of Tarsus*, 271.

141. Keskin, *Ephesus*, 3. During the April Artemis festivities, the population increased to a million.

142. While Paul is at Ephesus, the emperor Claudius died, and Nero became emperor in AD 54.

143. The additional words "from the fifth hour to the tenth" are in the 5th century Codex Bezae Cantabrigensis (see Rius-Camps, *The Message of Acts in Codex Bezae: Acts 18:24–28:31 Rome*, 4:101; Marshall, *Interlinear Greek: English New Testament*, 553, fn. m; RSV: Catholic Edition, 128, fn. r).

144. Holzner, *Paul of Tarsus*, 283.

145. Smith, *Essentials in Church History*, 224.

146. Conybeare, *The Life and Epistles of Saint Paul*, 371.

147. McConkie, *Doctrinal New Testament Commentary*, 2:309–10.

148. The First Epistle of Clement to the Corinthians 3; Stainforth, *Early Christian Writings*, 24.

149. The time of year that this letter was written is ascertained from what is said in the epistle: "Purge out the old leaven that ye may be a new lump, as ye are unleavened. For even Christ our Passover is sacrificed for us: Therefore let us keep the feast, not with old leaven, neither with the leaven of malice and wickedness; but with the unleavened bread of sincerity and truth" (1 Corinthians 5:7). The wording of this passage would seem to indicate that it was Passover time, which would be March or April. Compare also: "I will tarry at Ephesus until Pentecost" (1 Corinthians 16:8). Pentecost is fifty days after Passover.

150. Josephus, *Antiquities of the Jews*, bk. 14, 10:25.

151. Barclay, *Ambassador for Christ*, 119.

152. LDS Bible Dictionary, 657.

153. Erdemgíl, *Ephesus*, 28.

154. "The bee was the symbol of Ephesus, and it is often seen on coins and statues in Ephesus" (Erdemgíl, *Ephesus*, 28).

155. Though we call this goddess Diana, this goddess is more generally known as Artemis. About 2000 BC it is recorded that it was called Déesse-Mére Cybéle (Keskin, *Ephesus*, 6).

156. Keller, *The Bible as History*, 400–1.

157. Conybeare, *The Life and Epistles of Saint Paul*, 422, fn. 2.

158. Barclay, *Ambassador for Christ*, 120.

159. Barclay, *Ambassador for Christ*, 121.

160. Erdemgíl, *Ephesus*, 2829.

161. Conybeare, *The Life and Epistles of Saint Paul*, 423.

162. "Aristida a writer who lived in Ephesus during the Roman period, is recorded as having said that 'Ephesus is the bank of Asia Minor'" (Keskin, *Ephesus*, 7).

163. Erdemgíl, *Ephesus*, 28.

164. Keller, *The Bible as History*, 400–1.

165. Wynne-Thomas, *Legacy of Thasos*, 78.

166. Wynne-Thomas, *Legacy of Thasos*, 79.

167. Drane, *Paul*, 79.

168. Smyth, *The Story of Saint Paul's Life and Letters*, 132.

169. "A crowd began to gather and soon the city was filled with confusion. Everyone rushed to the amphitheater, dragging along Gaius and Aristarchus, Paul's traveling companions, for trial. Paul wanted to go in, but the disciples wouldn't let him. Some of the Roman officers of the province, friends of Paul, also sent a message to him, begging him not to risk his life by entering. Inside, the people were all shouting, some one thing and some another–everything was in confusion. In fact, most of them didn't even know why they were there. Alexander was spotted among the crowd by some of the Jews, and dragged forward. He motioned for silence and tried to speak. But when the crowd realized he was a Jew, they started shouting again and kept it up for two hours: Great is Diana of the Ephesians!" (Living Bible).

170. "Ephesus had a board of principle magistrates called the Strategoi. It had an elected senate called the Boulé. And it had an assembly of all her citizens called the Demos or the Ecclesia." [The town clerk in question] "was the keeper of the archives and public records; in the senate he read and introduced the principle business; and it was he to whom all letters and communications to Ephesus were addressed" (Barclay, *Ambassador for Christ*, 118).

171. Erdemgíl, *Ephesus*, 6.

172. Eusebius, *Historiae Ecclesiae*, bk. 4.1; bk. 6, 25:7.

173. We know that he did visit Nicopolis some years later when he was arrested (Titus 3:12).

174. For evidence that Paul did not previously preach in Rome, consider his own words (Romans 1:11, 13, 15).

175. McConkie, *Doctrinal New Testament Commentary*, 2:216.

176. Findlay, *The Epistles of Paul the Apostle*, 145.

177. Martin, *Thesis*, 12.

178. Martin, *Thesis*, 4.

179. Sandmel, *The Genius of Paul*, 7.

180. The Etruscans were the founding tribe of Rome.

181. Cary, *A History of Rome*, 356.

182. Conybeare, *The Life and Epistles of Saint Paul*, 498, fn. 1.

183. More correctly "the port of Neapolis."

184. "They did not leave Philippi till the seventh day after the fourteenth of Nisan was past" (Conybeare, *The Life and Epistles of Saint Paul*, 543).

185. In the previous verse, we were informed that it took five days from Philippi to Troas. By this we might presume that they were traveling from Tuesday to Saturday, and then preaching on Sunday. "And upon the first day of the week" does not indicate the time lapse between their arrival in Troas and the Sabbath.

186. Conybeare, *The Life and Epistles of Saint Paul*, 545.

187. Stairs were normally on the outside of buildings, not inside as we are accustomed to.

188. See Elisha in 1 Kings 17:21.

189. For Elijah, see 1 Kings 17:17–23; for Elisha, see 2 Kings 4:18–37.

190. Laymon, *Acts & Paul's Letters*, 77.

191. Conybeare, *The Life and Epistles of Saint Paul*, 547.

192. "Counting the time from Pentecost, we realize that it was necessary to be in port by night since it was the time of the dark moon, and would require daylight to proceed further on their way through these island strewn waters" (Conybeare, *The Life and Epistles of Saint Paul*, 549).

193. "And tarried at Trogyllium" are omitted by several translations.

194. Holzner, *Paul of Tarsus*, 361.

195. One author described Miletus as "the Venice of antiquity." Holzner, *Paul of Tarsus*, 286.

196. "Run his course" or "run his race," fig. "complete his career" (see Acts 13:25; 2 Timothy 4:7).

197. "Though men are appointed to hold rule in the home and in the Church, women are not one whit behind them in spiritual endowments. They prophesy, receive visions, entertain angels (Alma 32:33), enjoy the gifts

of the Spirit and qualify with their husbands for full exaltation in the highest Heaven" (McConkie, *Doctrinal New Testament Commentary*, 2:81).

198. Josephus, *Antiquities of the Jews*, bk. 13, 11:2; and *Wars of the Jews*, bk. 1, 3:5. 600 furlongs = 75 milliliters = 120 kilometers.

199. "Gave us a warm welcome" (Jerusalem Bible).

200. Still observing the Mosaic law (in other words, still Pharisees and Sadducees, Zealotes, and so on).

201. The Jews who live in Greece and Turkey where Paul preached.

202. "To humor Jewish-Christians—particularly converted Church members who still practice false rites and cling to false ordinances; who are giving lip service to Christ while following the Mosaic performances which Christ abolished; who are Christians in name, but largely Jewish in act; who have had the laying on of hands for the gift of the Holy Ghost, but have never attained the spiritual maturity to gain the full companionship of that member of the Godhead—to humor these weak members of the Church, Paul is asked, officially, as a matter of Church discipline to pretend that he is a Jew who keeps the Law of Moses. . . . As with all men, the Lord was giving Gospel Truths to them line upon line, precept upon precept. It was better to have them in the Church, seeking the Spirit, striving to keep the commandments, and trying to work out their salvation, than to leave them without the fold until they gained a full knowledge of all things. Even Peter was not converted to the full until long after he was ordained an Apostle." (McConkie, *Doctrinal New Testament Commentary*, 183–84).

203. The Nazarite vow is given in Number 6:221.

204. "Take these men, join in their purification rites and pay their expenses" (New International Version).

205. The mention here of seven days is verified in Acts 24:1 wherein it is recorded that "after five days Ananias the high priest descended with the elders." Then in 24:11 Paul says "there are yet twelve days since I went up to Jerusalem for to worship."

206. Josephus, *Wars of the Jews*, bk. 5, 5:2; bk. 6, 2:4.

207. Josephus, *Wars of the Jews*, bk. 2, 13:5; *Antiquities of the Jews*, bk. 20, 8:6.

208. Gamaliel was still alive at this time.

209. Greek *presbuterion* from which comes the English word *presbytery*. In the context used by Paul the word means *Sanhedrin* (Strong, *Greek Dictionary*, #4244; see also Luke 22:66).

210. The word *uncondemned* is correctly translated from Greek, but conveys the wrong impression. On a matter of declaring *civis Romanus sum*, it would be expected that such would be spoken in Latin: therefore, with respect to being *uncondemned*, Paul used the Latin term *re incognita*.

211. Barclay, *Ambassador for Christ*, 132.

212. Rabbi Gamaliel was still alive at this time.

213. "The normal beginning was, 'Rulers of the people and elders of Israel.' Paul pointedly ignored the address of humble inferiority and bluntly addressed the court as an equal" (Barclay, *Ambassador for Christ*, 133).

214. "The words themselves mean that Ananias had the semblance of the high priest's office without the reality" (Conybeare, *The Life and Epistles of Saint Paul*, 590, fn. 6).

215. "And when the dissension became violent" (RSV Acts 23:10).

216. Conybeare, *The Life and Epistles of Saint Paul*, 591.

217. "Jewish law laid down that under certain circumstances murder was justified. If a man was a public danger to life and morals, it was right to remove him. . . . Such a vow was called cherem" (Barclay, *Ambassador for Christ*, 134).

218. They may have been members of the Scarii bandits who were known for their activities during this period (Josephus, *Antiquities of the Jews*, bk. 20, 8:10).

219. That the tribune took the nephew "by the hand," indicates that this "young man" was a minor.

220. "[Tribune] Claudius Lysias to his Excellency the Governor [Procurator (of Judea, Samaria, Galilee, and Perea)], [Procurator M. Antonius] Felix, greetings. This man had been seized by the Jews and would have been murdered by them but I came on the scene with my troops and got him away, having discovered that he was a Roman citizen. Wanting to find out what charge they ware making against him, I brought him before their Sanhedrin. I found that the accusation concerned disputed points of their Law, but that there was no charge deserving death or imprisonment. My information is that there is a conspiracy against the man, so I hasten to send him to you, and have notified his accusers that they must state their case against him in your presence" (Jerusalem Bible).

221. Josephus describes the route from Jerusalem to Caesarea (see Josephus, *Wars of the Jews*, bk. 2, 19:1).

222. Barclay, *Ambassador for Christ*, 137.

223. Dean Aldrich quoted in Josephus, *Wars of the Jews*, 2:12, 482, fn.

224. "Any Roman citizen who was arrested must be brought to trial within three days. There was no regulation as to when the trial should end but it must begin in three days" (Barclay, *Ambassador for Christ*, 138).

225. "The notice that Paul is called suggests that he has received a legal summons" (Laymon, *Acts & Paul's Letters*, 89).

226. Conybeare, *The Life and Epistles of Saint Paul*, 607.

227. Note that Paul said "this," not "our" nation. By this remark, he places distance between the accusers and himself.

228. For his epistle to Felix, see Acts 23:26–30.

229. Smyth, *The Story of Saint Paul's Life and Letters*, 190, 195. As a point of interest historian and military general Flavius Josephus was living at Caesarea during this time.

230. Smyth, *The Story of Saint Paul's Life and Letters*, 192.

231. Conybeare, *The Life and Epistles of Saint Paul*, 611.

232. Called after the sickle shaped daggers that they used.

233. Cary, *A History of Rome*, 367.

234. Josephus, *Antiquities of the Jews*, 20:8:57; *Wars of the Jews*, 2:13:18.

235. Jerusalem Bible, Acts 24:27, 309, fn. c.

236. "Heavy charges" (Marshall, *Interlinear Greek: English New Testament*).

237. "The expression here used (equivalent to the Latin *appellare*) was the regular technical phrase for lodging an appeal. The Roman law did not require any written appeal to be lodged in the hands of the Court; pronunciation of the single word *appello* was sufficient to suspend all further proceedings" (Conybeare, *The Life and Epistles of Saint Paul*, 616, fn. 2). "It was Roman law that any citizen, if he felt that he was not getting justice in the provincial courts, might appeal direct to the Emperor. If the man was a murderer or a pirate or a bandit caught in the act, that appeal was disallowed; but otherwise the appeal was valid and at once it stopped all local proceedings" (Barclay, *Ambassador for Christ*, 140).

238. Without question, Paul was manacled by his right hand to the left hand of his guard by a long chain.

239. See Ezekiel 2:1. The resurrected Jesus was using the same words that he said to Ezekiel when issuing his prophetic call.

240. Josephus, *Antiquities of the Jews*, 20:7:1.

241. Barclay, *Ambassador for Christ*, 144; Holzner, *Paul of Tarsus*, 403.

242. Conybeare, *The Life and Epistles of Saint Paul*, 617 & fn. 3). Alternatively another author called them "elogium, or commitment papers" (Holzner, *Paul of Tarsus*, 419).

243. "The Imperial Police Commissariat" (Holzner, *Paul of Tarsus*, 403).

244. Aristarchus was an old friend of Paul's in missionary service. He was among the group that were with him in Corinth, and which "accompanied him into Asia," and remained with him all the way to Jerusalem, where this trouble he was now in began (Acts 20:45).

245. "We are apt to consider the ancients as timid and unskillful sailors, afraid to venture out of sight of land, or to make long voyages in the winter. I can see no evidence that this was the case. The cause of their not making voyages after the end of the summer arose, in great measure, from the comparative obscurity of the sky during the winter, and not from the gales which prevail at that season. With no means of directing their course, except by observing the heavenly bodies, they were necessarily prevented from putting to sea when they could not depend on their being visible" (Conybeare, *The Life and Epistles of Saint Paul*, 624, fn. 4).

246. "The ship belonged to the Alexandrian fleet in the Imperial service" (Ramsay, *Saint Paul the Traveller and the Roman Citizen*, 324).

247. Graves, *Suetonius: the Twelve Caesars*, 197–98; Cary, *A History of Rome*, 297, 326–27, 364–65.

248. "For some days we made little headway, and we had difficulty in making Cnidus. The wind would not allow us to touch there, so we sailed under the lee of Crete off Cape Salmone and struggled along the coast until we came to a place called Fair Havens, near the town of Lasea" (Jerusalem Bible).

249. Conybeare, *The Life and Epistles of Saint Paul*, 628.

250. The tenth day of the month Tisri. Mediterranean Sea voyages were not made between 11 November and 10 March, a voyage after 14 September was considered dangerous (Laymon, *Acts & Paul's Letters*, 99).

251. Also called Phoenix; Porto Loutro; Plakias.

252. "East" (RSV)—manuscripts differ here.

253. "East" (RSV)—manuscripts differ here.

254. "Drive into the wind." The term implies that the intended course was too acute so as to prevent such close tacking of this forceful wind.

255. Greek *epididómi* means "to give over (by hand or surrender): deliver unto" (Strong, *Greek Dictionary*, #1929). We take this to mean that the sail was taken down and the ship was let run with the wind. This would explain why, in verse 17, Luke said they "strake sail," which meant that the sail had to be up in order to let it down.

256. Using chain lashing under the hull and across the deck to keep the planking together.

257. "We took such a violent battering from the storm that the next day they began to throw the cargo overboard" (New International Version); "As we were making very heavy weather of it, the next day they began to jettison the cargo" (Jerusalem Bible).

258. Take note that Luke recorded "we cast out with our own hands." This means that circumstances were sufficiently desperate that the passengers were enlisted into the task in hand; therefore, this included Paul and Luke.

259. Ramsay, *Saint Paul the Traveller and the Roman Citizen*, 335.

260. Hohlfelder, "Caesarea Maritima," *National Geographic*, 265.

261. Greek *aigialos* means "a beach on which the waves dash" (Strong, *Greek Dictionary*, #123).

262. "Untied the ropes that held the rudders" (New International Version). Greco-Roman ships had a pair of paddles instead of a rudder, one on each side of the after part of the ship.

263. These verses are not a good translation. Compare, "Now when it was day, they [the sailors] did not recognize the land, but they noticed a bay with a beach, on which they planned if possible to bring the ship ashore. So they cast off the anchors and left them in the sea, at the same time loosening the ropes that tied the rudders; then hoisting the foresail to the wind they made for the beach" (RSV).

264. Both of these islands are known today as St. Paul's Islands. Atop the larger sandstone island called Selmunett, is erected a white marble statue to Saint Paul (Bradford, *The Great Siege*, 220; see also Kininmonth, *The Traveler's Guide to Malta and Gozo*, 200–1.) Much of the coastline around this bay and these two islands are rocky and precipice like, except for the facing shores of these two islands; which were deceivingly mistaken for a mainland cove.

265. "But the cross-currents carried them into a shoal" (Jerusalem Bible); "a sand-bar" (New International Version).

266. The force of the sea would be pounding the ship broadside starboard.

267. Neither Jew nor Greek (Romans 1:14; Colossians 3:11). The ancestry of the Maltese is attributed to Phoenician.

268. The Greek word *diké* could also be translated as "justice" (Strong, *Greek Dictionary*, #1349). Specifically, *Diké* was also the namde of the goddess of vengeance and justice. The inhabitants of Malta Island can therefore be understood to have said, "yet the goddess *Diké* suffereth not to live" (Laymon, *Acts & Paul's Letters*, 102).

269. Since it is specifically recorded that it was raining, it cannot be said that Paul gathered up sticks into a bundle, for ground wood would be too wet for the fire; so there must have been some bundles already bound and dry, this explains how the snake got into the bundle unawares to Paul.

270. Kininmonth, *The Traveller's Guide to Malta and Gozo*, 166; see also Bradford, *The Great Siege*, 204.

271. Castor and Pollux were twin Roman deities, sons of the god Zeus, on the altar of their temple in Rome was offered twin animal offerings.

272. Ramsay, *Saint Paul the Traveller and the Roman Citizen*, 346.

273. Ramsay, *Saint Paul the Traveller and the Roman Citizen*, 324, see also 345–46.

274. Smyth, *The Story of Saint Paul's Life and Letters*, 210.

275. It should be pointed out that Puteoli was not on the Via Appia, therefore they travelled by minor road to reach the highway. There were two principal routes, inland to Capua or by the coast to Sinuessa. The major of the two is the inland route to Capua.

276. The Forum of Appius was sixty-nine kilometers south of Rome. This "was a place where horses were changed and was a rough and disorderly town" (Barclay, *Ambassador for Christ*, 153).

277. Priscilla and Aquila, Epaenetus, Mary, Andronicus and Junia, Amplias, Urbane, Stachys, Apelles, Aristobulus and his branch, Herodian, Narcissus and his branch, Tryphena, Tryphosa, Persis, Rufus and his mother, Asyncritus, Phlegon, Hermas, Patrobas, Hermes, and the brethren which are with them, Philologus, Julia, Nereus and his sister (see Romans 16:3–15).

278. Smyth, *The Story of Saint Paul's Life and Letters*, 212.

279. Ramsay, *Saint Paul the Traveller and the Roman Citizen*, 347–48.

280. Conybeare, *The Life and Epistles of Saint Paul*, 612–13.

281. Graves, *Suetonius: the Twelve Caesars*, 73.

282. Carter, *The Religious Life of Ancient Rome*, 105.

283. Abbot, *The Common People of Ancient Rome*, 212.

284. Piccardi, *Myth and Geology*, 97.

285. Drane, *Paul*, 107.

286. Downey, *A History of Antioch in Syria*, 286; quoting Eusebius, *Historae Ecclesiastae* 2.23, 64 fn.

287. Graves, *Suetonius: the Twelve Caesars*, 220.

288. "I want you to know that our brother Timothy has been released. If he arrives soon, I will come with him to see you. Greet all your leaders and all God's people. Those from Italy send you their greetings" (New International Version Hebrews 13:23–24).

289. Augustine, *City of God*, 16:22:7, 680.

290. McConkie, *Doctrinal New Testament Commentary*, 133–34.

291. Smith, *Teachings of the Prophet Joseph Smith*, 59.

292. McBirnie, *The Search for the Twelve Apostles*, 283, quoting Jerome, *1886/1900, The Nicene and Post-Nicene Fathers*, 63.

293. Stainforth, *Early Christian Writings*, 25; *The First Epistle of Clement to the Corinthians*, 5.

294. The Textus Receptus reads *Spania* in Greek (Strong, *Greek Dictionary*, #4681).

295. Sperry, *Paul's Life and Letters*, 285.

296. Holzner, *Paul of Tarsus*, 471.

297. Holzner, *Paul of Tarsus*, 471.

298. Mosheim, *Historiae Ecclesicae*, Century 1, Part 1, 5:14; quoted in Talmage, *The Great Apostasy*, 78.

299. Findlay, *The Epistles of Paul the Apostle*, 201–2.

300. Witherington, *Letters and Homilies for Hellenized Christians*, 90.

301. Graves, *Suetonius: the Twelve Caesars*, 221.

302. Being aware that Nero was not present, we must therefore conclude that Paul was arraigned before the city prefect: Prefectus Urbi (Conybeare, *The Life and Epistles of Saint Paul*, 767).

303. Sperry, *Paul's Life and Letters*, 303.

304. Graves, *Suetonius: the Twelve Caesars*, 222.

305. Graves, *Suetonius: the Twelve Caesars*, 220.

306. The Old Testament records the earliest mention of identification of diplomatic documents as a passport. These documents were issued

to Nehemiah in 445–444 BC by King Artaxerxes I (Artaxerxes Longimanus) at Shushan in Persia: "Moreover I [Nehemiah] said unto the King [Artaxerxes], If it please the king, let letters be given me to the governors beyond the River [Euphrates], that they may convey me over till I come into Judah" (Nehemiah 2:7). Nehemiah needed documents of safe passage to all the pashas or provincial governors all the way through to Judea. This verse is expressed with greater clarity in a paraphrased version: "If it please the king, give me letters to the governors west of the Euphrates River instructing them to let me travel through their countries on my way to Judah" (Living Bible).

307. Paul was born free and inherited the Roman citizenship. There are four primary candidates who were associated with the city of Tarsus and the province of Cilicia, who could have granted citizenship to either his father or grandfather. They are: General Mark Anthony, General Pompey the Great, General Octivanus (Augustus), or General Publius Sulpicius Quirinius. An immediate ancestor of Paul must have accomplished some great service to the Roman state, or directly to one of the above military commanders. Each of these generals was stationed at Tarsus in previous decades during the Roman Republic.

308. Stemma: "A pedigree, genealogical table, genealogical tree" (White, *Latin-English Dictionary*, 581, "Stemma").

309. Wordsworth, *The NT of Our Lord and Saviour Jesus Christ*, 3:467.

310. "The word φαιλενην [*failonen*] signifies either a cloak or a bag—if the apostle meant a cloak, he is sending for it at so great a distance" (MacKnight, *Apostolical Epistles*, 3:267). "We cannot see what use Paul would have for the mantle when he was expecting death so soon" (Huther, *Critical and Exegitical Handbook to the Epistles of Saint Paul to Timothy and Titus*, 325). Why should "Paul give orders to have either a garment or a chest brought to him from a place so distant, as if there were no workmen, or as if there were not abundance both of cloak and timber? If it be said, that there was a chest filled with books, or manuscripts, or epistles, the difficulty will be solved; for such materials could not have been procured at any price" (Calvin, *Commentaries on the Epistles to Timothy, Titus, and Philemon*, 265).

311. "'Others translate the rare Greek word as *book-holder*, and think of a case or bag in which Paul kept his precious rolls. That he had left such a piece of baggage behind him would be more easily understood that

than he should after so long a time ask for his cloak.' The books and parchments would then be the contents of the portfolio" (Köhler, as quoted in Strachan, *The Captivity and the Pastoral Epistles*, 255).

312. Calvin, *Commentaries on the Epistles to Timothy, Titus, and Philemon*, 265. "A bag in which the books were contained" (Brown, *The Pastoral Epistles*, 86).

313. Bernard, *The Pastoral Epistles*, 146. In other instances, this word may also refer to "a woollen wrap for carrying books safely," as opposed to a box, chest, folder, or vellum wrap (Lock, *The Pastoral Epistles*, 118). The type of portfolio depends upon the importance of the documents, and the inclination of the owner.

314. Murdock, *The New Testament: Translated from the Syriac Peshito Version*, 390.

315. "There is some foundation for the interpretation 'a book-case' or 'portfolio,' which the Syriac versions support" (Humphreys, *The Epistles to Timothy and Titus*, 199).

316. Brockelmann, *Lexicon Syriacum*, 37.

317. Ellicott, *The Pastoral Epistles*, 159.

318. Magiera, *Aramaic Peshitta New Testament*, 3:138.

319. Harvey, *Commentary on the Pastoral Epistles*, 118.

320. Bernard, *The Pastoral Epistles*, 147.

321. Calvin, *Commentaries on the Epistles to Timothy, Titus, and Philemon*, 265–66.

322. "The book-carrier {fn. A bag made of leather or woolen cloth} which I left at Troas with Carpus, bring it with you when you come, and the books, especially the parchment scroll" (Lamsa, *Holy Bible: from the Ancient Eastern Text*, 1192).

323. Etheridge, *The Apostolic Acts and Epistles from the Peschoto, or Ancient Syriac*, 369.

324. Strong, *Greek Dictionary*, #3200.

325. "The vellum rolls, what were these? Perhaps among them was the diploma of his Roman franchise" (Livermore, *The Epistles of Paul*, 290).

326. Kimball, *Teachings of Spencer W. Kimball*, 483.

327. Sperry, *Paul's Life and Letters*, 303.

328. Holzner, *Paul of Tarsus*, 485.

329. Holzner, *Paul of Tarsus*, 485.

330. Titus Livius 2:6.

William Victor Blacoe

331. Jowett, *The Drama of the Lost Disciples*, 130; quoted in McBirnie, *The Search for the Twelve Apostles*, 285.

332. Joseph Smith Jr., quoted in *Doctrinal History of the Church*, 2:19–20.

References

Abbot, F., *The Common People of Ancient Rome*. New York: Charles Scribner & Sons, 1911.

Anderson, R., *Understanding Paul*. Salt Lake City: Deseret Book, 1983.

Angus, S., *Religious Quests of the Greco-Roman World: A Study in the Historical Background of Early Christianity*. New York: Charles Scribner & Sons, 1930.

Augustine of Hippo [Bettenson, H. translator], *City of God*. London: Penguin Books, 1984.

Barclay, W., *Ambassador for Christ*. Edinburgh: Saint Andrew Press, 1980.

Barton, B., *He Upset the World*. London: Oxford University Press, 1932.

Bernard, J., *The Pastoral Epistles*. Cambridge: Cambridge University Press, 1899.

Betteridge, Harold T., *Cassell's German—English / English—German Dictionary*. New York: Cassell & Company, 1987.

Black, D. A., Paul, *Apostle of Weakness*. New York: Peter Lang Publishing, 1984.

Bradford, E., *The Great Siege (Malta 1565)*. London: Hodder & Stoughton, 1961.

Brenton, L., *The Septuagint with Apocrypha: Greek and English*. Peabody: Hendrickson Publishers, 2009.

British Government [publisher], *The Apocrypha of The Old Testament: The King James Authorized Version*. London: Oxford University Press, 1611.

Brockelmann, C., *Lexicon Syriacum*. Edinburgh: T & T Clark, 1895.

Bruce, F. F., *The Acts of the Apostles*. Grand Rapids: W. B. Erdman, 1951.

Burton, A. P. [compiler], *Discourses of the Prophet Joseph Smith*. Salt Lake City: Deseret Book, 1974.

Calvin, J., *Commentaries on the Epistles to Timothy, Titus, and Philemon*. Edinburgh: Calvin Translation Society, 1856.

Cannon, Elaine, *The Ensign*, Salt Lake City: The Church of Jesus Christ of Latter-day Saints, November 1978.

Carter, J., *The Religious Life of Ancient Rome*. Boston: Riverside Press, 1911.

Cary, M. & Scullard, H. H., *A History of Rome Down to the Reign of Constantine*. London: Macmillan Press, 1984.

Catholic Biblical Association of Great Britain, *Revised Standard Version of the Holy Bible: Catholic Edition*, London: Oxford University Press, 1966.

The Church of Jesus Christ of Latter-day Saints, Bible Dictionary. Salt Lake City: The Church of Jesus Christ of Latter-day Saints, 1979.

Cole, S., *Theoi Megaloi: The Cult of the Great Gods at Samothrace*. Leiden: E. J. Brill, 1984.

Conybeare, W. J. & Howson, J. S., *The Life and Epistles of Saint Paul*. Grand Rapids: William B. Eerdmans Publishing, 1984.

Davies, W. D., *Paul and Rabbinic Judaism*. Guilford: Biddles Ltd, 1979.

Det Danske Bibelselskab, *Den Hellige Skrifts Kanoniske Bøger*. Copenhagen: Det Danske Bibelselskab, 1931.

Dindorfii, L., *Ioannis Malalae Chronographia* (Corpus Scriptorum Historiae Byzantintinae). Bonn: Impensis Ed. Weberi, 1831.

Division of Christian Education, *Holy Bible: New Revised Standard Version with Apocrypha*. New York: Oxford University Press, 1980.

Downey, G., *A History of Antioch in Syria*, New Jersey: Princeton University Press, 1961.

Drane, J., *The Life of the Early Church*. Tring: Lion Publishing, 1982.

Edersheim, A., *Jesus the Messiah*. Grand Rapids: William B. Eerdmans Publishing. 1985.

Ellicott, C., *The Pastoral Epistles*. London. John W. Parker, 1856.

Erdemgil, S., *Ephesus*. Istanbul: NET Turistik Yayinlar Sanayi ve Ticaret AS, 1986.

Etheridge, J., *The Apostolic Acts and Epistles from the Peschoto*, or *Ancient Syriac*. London: Brown, Green, & Longman, 1849.

Eusebius Pamphilus [Williams, G. A. translator], *Historiae Ecclesiastae* or *The History of the Church: from Christ to Constantine*. London: Penguin Books, 1985.

Farrar, F., *The Life of Christ*. Salt Lake City: Bookcraft Publishing, 1998.

Findlay, G., *The Epistles of Paul the Apostle*. London: C.H. Kelly, 1895.

Finley, M. I., *The Ancient Greeks*. London: Penguin Books, 1984.

Firmage, E. B., *Paul and the Expansion of the Church Today*. Salt Lake City: Deseret Book, 1979.

Foakes-Jackson, F. J., *The Life of Saint Paul: The Man and the Apostle*, New York: Boni & Liveright Publishing, 1926.

Furnish, V. P., *Biblical Archeological Review: Corinth in Paul's Time*. Vol. 15, nr. 3, Washington DC: May/June 1988.

Gibbon, E., *The Decline and Fall of the Roman Empire: Abridged Version*. London: Penguin Books, 1985.

Graves, Robert [translator], *Suetonius: the Twelve Caesars*. London: Penguin Books, 1979.

Greenough, J. B. & Kittredge, G. L. [editors], *The Roman Constitution: Introduction: VI. The Roman Constitution, Select Orations and Letters of Cicero*. Boston: The Society for Ancient Languages, 1902.

Gärtner, Bertil [King, C. H., translator], *The Areopagus Speech and Natural Revelation: Acta Seminarii Neotestamentici Upsaliensis XXI*. Uppsala: Almqvist & Wiksells, 1955.

Harvey, H., *Commentary on the Pastoral Epistles*. Philadelphia: American Baptist Publication Society, 1890.

Hayward, A. & Sparkes, J., *The Concise English Dictionary*. London: Cassell, 1987.

Hohlfelder, R., "Caesarea Maritima," *National Geographic Magazine*, Vol. 171, nr. 2, Washington DC: National Geographic Society, February 1987.

Holzner, J. [Eckhoff, F. C., translator], *Paul of Tarsus*. Missouri: B. Herder Book, 1955.

Homer, Rieu, E. [translator], *The Iliad*. London: Penguin Books, 1986.

Humphreys, A., *The Epistles to Timothy and Titus*. Cambridge: Cambridge University Press, 1895.

International Bible Society, *Holy Bible: New International Version*. New York: International Bible Society, 1978.

Jeremias, J. [Cave, C. H., translator] (1969–1975), *Jerusalem in the Time of Jesus*. Minneapolis: Fortress Press, 1975.

Jerome [Eusebius Sophronius Hieronymous], *Biblia Sacra juxta Vulgatam Clementinam*, edition electronic. London: Council of Bishop's Conference of England & Wales, 2005.

Jones, Alexander [editor], *The Jerusalem Bible*. New York: Doubleday, 1969.

Josephus, Flavius [William W. translator], *Complete Works of Flavius Josephus: Antiquities of the Jews; Wars of the Jews; Flavius Josephus against Apion; Disertations*. London: Pickering and Inglis, 1960.

Jowett, G. F., *The Drama of the Lost Disciples*, Heber Springs: Covenant Publishing Company, 1961.

Katolisches Bibelwerk [publisher], *Die Heilige Schrift: Einheitsübersetzung*. Stuttgart: Verlag Katolisches Bibelwerk, 1981.

Keller, W. [William N. translator], *The Bible as History*. New York: Hodder and Stoughton, 1982.

Kelly, W., *The Pastoral Epistles of Paul*. London: Thomas Weston, 1901.

Keskin, N., *Ephesus*. Istanbul: Keskin Color, 1987.

Kim, S., *The Origin of Paul's Gospel*. Tübingen: J. C. B. Mohr (Paul Siebeck), 1981.

Kimball, S. W. [Kimball, E. L. editor], *The Teachings of Spencer W. Kimball*. Salt Lake City: Bookcraft Publishing, 1982.

Kininmonth, C. (1967), *The Travellers Guide to Malta and Gozo*. London: Jonathan Cape, 1967.

Lamsa, G., *Holy Bible: From the Ancient Eastern Text*. Philadelphia: A. J. Holman, 1933.

Laymon, C. M. [editor], *Acts, & Paul's Letters: Interpreter's Concise Commentary*, vol. VII. Nashville: Abingdon Press, 1983.

Léon-Dufour, X. [Cahill, P. & Stewart, E. translators], *Dictionary of Biblical Theology*. New York: Seabury Press, 1973.

Levi, P. [translator], *Pausanias: Guide to Greece*, volume 1 Central Greece. London: Penguin Books, 1985.

Livermore, A., *The Epistles of Paul*. Boston: Lockwood & Brooks, 1881.

Livius, Titus [de Sélincourt, A. translator], *Rome and the Mediterranean: Books 31–45: The History of Rome from its Foundation*. London: Penguin Books, 1983.

Livius, Titus [Bettenson H. translator], *The Ward with Hanibal: Books 21–30: The History of Rome from its Foundation*. London: Penguin Books, 1965.

Livius, Titus [de Sélincourt, A. translator], *The Early History of Rome: Books 1–5: The History of Rome From Its Foundation*. London: Penguin Books, 1987.

Livius, Titus [Radice, R. translator], *Rome and Italy: Books 6–10: The History of Rome From Its Foundation*. London: Penguin Books, 1987.

Lock, W., *The Pastoral Epistles*. Edinburgh: T & T Clark, 1924.

Lundwall, N. B. [compiler], *The Vision: The Degrees of Glory*. Salt Lake City: Bookcraft, 1948.

MacGregor, G. & Purdy, A., *Jew and Greek: Tutors unto Christ*. London: Ivor Nicholson & Watson, 1936.

Mackey, H. F. B., *The Adventures of Paul of Tarsus*, London: Phillip Allan, 1931.

Magiera, J., *Aramaic Peshitta New Testament*, 3 vols. Erwin: Light of the World Ministry, 2009.

Marshal, A. [translator] (1958–1985), *Interlinear Greek: English New Testament with the Revised Standard Version*. Basingstoke: Marshall Morgan and Scott Publications, 1985.

Marshall, A. [compiler], *The Revised Standard Version Interlinear Greek–English New Testament: The Nestle Greek Text*, 3rd ed. Basingstoke: Marshall Morgan & Scott Publications, 1985.

Martin, R., Thesis. Fort Worth: Southwestern Baptist Theological Seminary, 1985.

McBirnie, William, *The Search for The Twelve Apostles*. Illinois: Living Books Publishers, 1982.

McConkie, Bruce R., *Doctrinal New Testament Commentary*, 3 volumes. Salt Lake City: Deseret Book, 1970.

Meinardus, O. A., *Saint Paul in Greece*. Athens: Lycabettus Press, 1984.

Ministry of Culture, Greece, *Historical Map of Athens*: Akropolis & Plaka, Athens, 1989.

Minn, H. R., *The Thorn That Remained*. Auckland: Institute Press, 1972.

Montague, G., *The Living Thought of St. Paul*, Milwaukee: Bruce Publishing, 1966.

Murdock, J., *The New Testament: Translated from the Syriac Peshito Version*. New York: Stanford & Sword, 1852.

Papahatzis, N., *Ancient Corinth*. Athens: Ekdotike Athenon S.A. 1985.

Parry, J. H. [translator], *The Book of Jasher*. Salt Lake City: J. H. Parry, 1973.

Piccardi, L., *Myth and Geology*. Florence: Instetudo de Geoscienze e Georisorce, 2007.

Picirilli, R., *Paul the Apostle*. Chicago: Moody Press, 1986.

Pollock, J., *The Apostle: a Life of Paul*. Colorado Springs: David C. Cook, 1972

Ramsay, W., *St. Paul the Traveller and Roman Citizen*, London: Hodder & Stoughton, 1903.

Renan, E., *Life of the Apostles*. New York: Carleton Publishing, 1866.

Ridolfini, C., *Saint Paul's Outside the Walls of Rome*. Rome: Officine grafiche, Poligrafici il Resto del Carlino, 1967.

Rius-Camps, J. & Read-Heimerdinger, J., T*he Message of Acts in Codex Bezae: Acts 18:24–28:31*, V. 4. London: T & T Clark, 2009.

Roberts, B. H., *Outlines of Ecclesiastical History*. Salt Lake City: Deseret Book, 1979.

Sandmel, S., *The Genius of Paul*. New York: Farrar, Straus & Cudahy, 1958.

ScottKilvert, I. [translator], *Plutarch: Makers of Rome*. London: Penguin Books, 1984.

Skousen, W. C., *The First 2000 Years*. Salt Lake City: Bookcraft, 1979.

Smith, J. F. [compiler], *Teachings of the Prophet Joseph Smith*. Salt Lake City: Deseret Book, 1977.

Smith, J. F., *Essentials in Church History*. Salt Lake City: Deseret Book, 1979.

Smith, J., *Inspired Version of The Holy Bible*. Nauvoo: Joseph Smith, 1844.

Smith, W., *Dictionary of Greek and Roman Antiquities*. London: John Murray, 1890.

Smyth, J. P., *The Story of Saint Paul's Life and Letters*. London: Sampson Low, Marston & Co. 1939.

Sperry, S., *Paul's Life and Letters*. Salt Lake City: Bookcraft, 1955.

Stacey, W., *The Pauline View of Man*. New York: Macmillan, 1956.

Stainforth, M. [translator], *Early Christian Writings: the Apostolic Fathers*. London: Penguin Books, 1988.

Strachan, J., *The Westminister New Testament: Captivity and the Pastoral Epistles*. London: Fleming H. Revell, 1883.

Strong, J., *The Exhaustive Concordance of the Bible including New Testament Greek–English Dictionary*. Nashville: Abingdon Press, 1890.

Tacitus, P. Cornelius, [Church, A. & Jackson-Brodribb, W., translators], *Tacitus: the Annals*.

Tacitus, P. [Church, A. & Jackson-Brodribb, W., translators], *Tacitus: the Histories*.

Talmage, J. E., *The Great Apostasy*. London: Deseret Enterprises, 1909.

Tvveedale, M. [general editor] (Jerome / Eusebius Sophronius Hieronymous], *Biblia Sacra juxta Vulgatam Clementinam* edition electronic. London: Council of Bishop's Conference of England and Wales, 2005.

Tyndale House, *The Living Bible*. Carol Stream: Tyndale House Publishers, 1971.

Wallace, Q., *The Early Life and Background of Paul the Apostle*. The American Journal of Biblical Theology, 2002. Retrieved at http://www.biblicaltheology.com/Research/WallaceQ01.html.

Wallace-Hadrill, D. S., *Christian Antioch: A Study in Early Christian Thought in the East*. London: Cambridge University Press, 1982.

Watch Tower, *New World Translation of the Holy Scriptures*. New York: Watch Tower Bible and Tract Society of Pennsylvania, 1961.

Wynne-Thomas, R., *Legacy of Thasos*. Springwood, Australia: Springwood Books, 1978.

Whately, R., *Lectures on the Characters of Our Lord's Apostles*. London: John W. Parker & Sons, 1859.

White, J., *Latin-English Dictionary*. Boston: Ginn, 1904.

Witherington, B., *Letters and Homilies for Hellenized Christians*. Downers Grove: InterVarsity Press, 2006.

Wordsworth, C., *The New Testament of Our Lord and Saviour Jesus Christ*. London: Gilbert & Rivington, 1859.

Xenophon, *Conversations of Socrates: Memoirs*. London: Penguin Books, 1970.

Vickers, M., *The Roman World*. Oxford: Phaidon Press, 1977.

von Mosheim, J. [Archibald Maclaine translator], *Ecclesiastical History*, 6 vols. London: T. Cadell, 1774.

About the Author

William Victor Blacoe hails from Ireland, where he became a member of the LDS Church in 1978. His early career was in mechanical engineering design and thereafter as a cartographer with Irish offshore exploration. He earned a degree in business management from the University of Phoenix. For the past few decades, he worked as manager of several Church operations in Europe. Currently, he is the manager of LDS Family Services in Europe.

Living in Germany since 1982, William has served in several capacities in US military wards, including twice as bishop and three times as counselor in bishoprics. He is married with three children. William and his wife, Reingard, live near Frankfurt, Germany.

For over twenty-five years, William has had a passionate interest in the New Testament and has conducted extensive research into the life and Epistles of the Apostle Paul. This compact work is a condensed rendition of that research.